The Protection of Ambient Air in International and European Law

Bologna, den 18.Oktober [1786], nachts.

Der Mann ließ mich auch die gesunde Lage und Luft der Stadt daran bemerken, daß ihre Dächer wie neu aussähen und kein Ziegel durch Feuchtigkeit und Moos angegriffen sei.

Johann Wolfgang Goethe

(from: Italienische Reise, Hamburger Ausgabe, Deutscher Taschenbuch Verlag, 1988, 10. Auflage, Mai 2004, at 104)

THE PROTECTION OF AMBIENT AIR IN INTERNATIONAL AND EUROPEAN LAW

Edited by

HARRY POST

eleven
international publishing

Published, sold and distributed by Eleven International Publishing
P.O. Box 358
3500 AJ Utrecht, The Netherlands
Tel.: +31 30 231 0545
Fax: +31 30 225 8045
info@elevenpub.com
www.elevenpub.com

Sold and distributed in USA and Canada
International Specialized Book Services
920 NE 58th Avenue, Suite 300
Portland, OR 97213-3786, USA
Tel: +1 800 944 6190 (toll-free)
Fax: +1 503 280 8832
orders@isbs.com
www.isbs.com

Printed on acid-free paper.

ISBN: 978-90-77596-63-0

Cover picture: NO_2 concentration over Europe, courtesy of ESA (www.esa.int)

Printed in The Netherlands

Table of Contents

Preface

Concern with the protection of air quality in a trans-boundary context has been at the origin of the modern development of international environmental law. The 1941 arbitral award in the Trail Smelter dispute between Canada and the United States established the principle that states have the responsibility to ensure that activities within their territory do not cause damage through air pollution to the environment of other states. The arbitral tribunal formulated criteria for the quantification of damage and payment of compensation. Perhaps most importantly, it developed for the first time scientific criteria for the progressive abatement of noxious emissions so as to prevent or minimise future damage.

In spite of this early impulse, later developments in international environmental law have fallen short of effectively counter-acting the progressive degradation of ambient air. On the one hand, the focus of environmental law and diplomacy has shifted gradually from ambient air to the upper strata of the atmosphere with the ozone layer and climate change becoming the center pieces of environmental negotiations and of multilateral conventions in the past twenty years. On the other hand, even where international instruments for the protection of ambient air have been adopted – as in the area of prevention of acid rain – no effective mechanism of judicial enforcement of such standards has followed. An emblematic case of this shortcoming is the note added to the 1979 Geneva Convention on Long Range Trans-boundary Air Pollution with it express disclaimer that the "… Convention does not contain a rule on State liability as to damage."

To compensate for this lack of judicial enforcement at the international level, judicial practice in the field of international economic law has recognised the importance of air quality and the relevance of its protection in the process of settlement of economic disputes. In the 1996 Re-formulated Gasoline case, brought before the Dispute Settlement Body of the World Trade Organisation (WTO) by Venezuela in a dispute with the United States over the latter's import restriction on gasoline, the Appellate Body of the WTO recognized the importance of ambient air protection on the grounds that air is an exhaustible resource the conservation of which may justify the imposition of non-discriminatory standards for gasoline to be sold and used in the territory of the importing country.

Going beyond this patchwork approach of international environmental law, European Union law has addressed ambient air protection in a much more coherent and effective way within the framework of the EU environmental principles laid down in Article 174 of the EC Treaty. It has acted on the basis of the principle of direct effect and supremacy of EU legislation in domestic law and, when necessary, by resorting to the Article 226 infraction procedure against those Member States which violate the Community's environmental standards. The European Union's action in this field has culminated in the adoption on 21 May of Directive 2008/50/EC by Parliament and Council on ambient air quality and cleaner air for Europe. This Directive will provide the legal framework for the implementation of a Community wide policy of environmental and public health protection through the imposition of pollution limits and of sanctions for non complying Member States.

Given this diversified and complex background, the current book is a timely and welcome contribution to the analysis of the problem of ambient air degradation in Europe and to the widening of our knowledge of the normative instruments and scientific-technical approaches adopted to counter such degradation. I very much enjoyed the workshop of March 2007 in Modena, to which I was invited to chair a session, and the debates that followed. I must congratulate Professor Harry Post and the other contributors to the book for having turned the papers of the workshop into a coherent book. I am confident that it will make a positive impact on the doctrine and practice of international and European environmental law and will contribute to the raising awareness of the importance of the irreplaceable public good that is represented by the air we breathe.

Francesco Francioni
Fiesole, February 2009

List of Contributors

Vittorio Boraldi
Direttore della sezione provinciale di Modena dell'Agenzia Regionale Prevenzione e Ambiente dell'Emilia-Romagna (Director of ARPA, Section Province of Modena)

Vanni Bulgarelli
Presidente Hera Modena (Chairman of the Management Board of Hera Modena)

Francesco Francioni
Professor ordinario di diritto internazionale, Università di Siena, Professor of International Law and Human Rights, European University Institute, Florence

Marco Gasparinetti
Head of Sector, Directorate General Environment, European Commission, Brussels

Luisa Guerra
Responsabile Ecosistema Urbano, Servizio Sistemi Ambientali, Sezione provinciale di Modena dell'ARPA (Responsibile for Urban Ecosystems, Environmental Systems Service of ARPA, Section Province of Modena)

Massimiliano Montini
Professore associato di diritto internazionale, Università di Siena

Phoebe Okowa,
Reader in Public International Law, Queen Mary, University of London

Giovanni Franco Orlando
Assessore alle politiche ambientali del Comune di Modena (Councillor for Environmental Policy of Modena City Council)

Harry Post
Professore di diritto internazionale, Università di Modena e Reggio Emilia

Arie Trouwborst
Associate Professor of Public International Law, Utrecht University

Lino Zanicchelli
Assessore all'ambiente e sviluppo sostenibile della regione Emilia-Romagna (Councillor for Environmental and Sustainable Development of Emilia-Romagna)

Abbreviations

ARPA	Agenzia Regionalc Prevenzione e Ambiente dell'Emilia-Romagna (Regional Agency for Environmental Protection)
CAFE	Clean Air for Europe (EU programme)
CO	Carbon Monoxide
CO_2	Carbon Dioxide
CSCE	Conference on Security and Co-operation in Europe (1973-75)
DPSIR	Driving forces-Pressures-State-Impacts-Responses (Model)
EC	European Community
ECE	Economic Commission for Europe (or UNECE)
ECJ	European Court of Justice
EEA	European Environmental Agency
EIA	Environmental Impact Assessment
EIB	European Investment Bank
EMAS	Eco-Management and Audit System
EMEP	European Monitoring and Evaluation Program
ENEA	Ente Nazionale per l'Energia
EP	European Parliament
EPA	Environmental Protection Agency (US)
EU	European Union
FER	Ferrovie Emilia Romagna
HCNG	Hythane
IARC	International Agency for Research into Cancer
INEMAR	Inventory of Emissions in the Air
LRTAP	Long-Range Transboundary Air Pollution
NGO	Non-Governmental Organisations
NO_x	Nitrogen Oxides
O_3	Ozone
PM	Particulate Matter
POP	Persistent Organic Pollutants
SCI	Site of Community Importance
SO_2	Sulphur Dioxide
SPA	Special Protection Area
TEC	Treaty of the European Community
UNECE	United Nations Commission for Europe (or ECE)
VOC	Volatile Organic Compounds
WHO	World Health Organisation
WTO	World Trade Organisation

Introduction

This book aims to explain a complicated subject: the state of the air that we breathe. Or, in the terminology of the European Union: the state of the ambient air. However, its level of ambition is considerably diminished by the fact that it only aims to elucidate the state of the ambient air from the legal perspective, more precisely from the international and European legal perspective.

We will be discussing the lower levels of the atmosphere. In the last few decades these lower levels of the atmosphere have been much less of a concern in law and politics than the higher levels. The quality of the latter much more esoteric areas, has become so problematic that climate change is occurring as a result of their deterioration. In particular since human activities have authoritatively been identified as the major cause of damage to the ozone layer and of a rise in global temperature, attempts to improve the quality of the atmosphere have become a top item on the list of international political concerns.

In comparison the state of the lower levels of the atmosphere has been much less politically topical, it seems. Regional and local politicians and civil servants, and increasingly their national counterparts as well, may see this slightly differently. In the last decade, particularly in Europe under pressure of the European Community, they were forced to devise and 'sell' to their citizens complicated and not very popular policies aiming at improving air quality. Ordinary citizens, particularly those living in urban areas, had become concerned and even more so by scientific reports telling them how bad the air had become and how detrimental that was for their health and that of their families, even if they were not yet suffering from respiratory or cardial problems. This kind of information became increasingly alarming and so were the measures that were subsequently taken to reverse this trend of the deterioration of the air. The effects on daily life were ever more direct: inner cities were closed off for traffic, certain forms of fuel and transportation were restricted, construction works were suspended due to the levels of dust, of particulate matter (PM_{10} or $PM_{2.5}$). The area of Beijing in China and parts of Europe like The Netherlands, the Ruhr area in Germany and the Po river basin in Northern Italy, have been identified as the areas in the world most negatively affected by air quality problems. There in particular, bad air quality

Harry H. G. Post (Ed.), The Protection of Ambient Air in International and European Law, 1-4.

is a major cause of poor health.[1] In this book the Po River basin has been taken as the starting-point and major example for the examination of the protection of ambient air under international and European law.

Air pollution is a complex topic, particularly for non-scientists. Part I of this book opens with a chapter scientifically introducing the state of the lower parts of the atmosphere. It explains the different components and causes of the gradual deterioration of the ambient air and illustrates the measures issued and policies undertaken to assess it and to improve its quality. The main example in this first chapter as in the whole of Part I is the region of Emilia Romagna and one of its middle-sized towns, Modena. In Chapter 2, the Assessore (Councillor) for environmental policy of Modena explains the local approach to assess and fight the deterioration of air quality in his town. In the executive sphere of these urban policies a rather particular Northern Italian company operates, Gruppo Hera spa. The Chairman of Hera Modena introduces his company and presents its special position in the execution of the air quality policies in the towns and the region. The Assessore responsible for the environment and sustainable development of Emilia Romagna elucidates more in particular the regional perspective and the measures taken to implement the EC directives on air quality thereby concluding Chapter 2 and Part I on Practice.

In Part II the legal perspective is explained, firstly, as it has developed at the general international level. A rather unique and somewhat curious international treaty that somewhat surprisingly perhaps emerged in Europe during the Cold War, the 1979 Geneva Convention on Long-Range Transboundary Air Pollution has served as the authoritative source -and example in the world- for legally addressing deterioration of the ambient air. In Chapter 3 Phoebe Okowa examines this prime and rather successful example of what is occasionally called a 'Treaty-Protocol' approach, up to its most recent 2004 Protocols.

The European Community in its measures to fight air pollution has gone its own way, issuing directives and other forms of communitarian legislation since the early seventies, but this legislation was at times also clearly inspired by the progressive steps taken in the context of the Geneva Convention. However, in particular since issuing the 1996 Framework Directive on Ambient Air Quality Assessment and Management the EC has taken centre stage in this field. In Chapter 4, Massimiliano Montini explains and criticizes the Community's 'Mother-Daughter' approach as it has developed in the first years of this century when ever more detailed rules to be implemented in the Member States were issued. He evaluates the instruments the Community has launched and expresses considerable doubts about their effectiveness.

In Chapter 5, Arie Trouwborst analyses in detail two essential aspects relative to the effectiveness of the Community approach: direct effect and the ever stronger emphasis on criminal sanctions in the EC's environmental

[1] *See* World Health Organisation, *Health Aspects of Air Pollution. Results From the WHO Systematic Review of Health Aspects of Air Pollution in Europe*, June 2004.

legislation, initiated in particular in respect to the protection of the ambient air. Both Montini's and Trouwborst's assessment of the state of EC law in respect to the effective protection of the ambient air anticipate and partly introduce already the latest phase of Community activity in this area: a comprehensive overhaul of the legislation.

Part III of this book discusses the potential of the future contribution, again from the legal perspective, of the most recent EC effort to protect air quality: the 2008 Directive on ambient air quality and cleaner air for Europe, agreed upon on 14 April 2008. The grand aim of EC policy is "… to cut the annual number of premature deaths from air pollution-related diseases by almost 40% from the 2000 level." The number of premature deaths related to PM and (low-level) ozone in 2000 was estimated by the European Commission to be about 370,000 a year, by 2020 that number should be reduced to 230,000.[2] Marco Gasparinetti has worked on drafting the new directive for many years. He explains the instrument, what the national, regional and local policy makers have to implement and what the EU citizens may perhaps expect in terms of their future air quality. Gasparinetti's evaluation is quite positive on what has been achieved here, but the results, of course, depend also on economic and political forces beyond the structure of the law. The concluding Chapter 7 of this book summarizes and critically reflects upon the future of ambient air management in view of the choices the European policy makers have made. The author confesses that he is not always able to understand the reasoning stated in the documents leading to the rather fundamental choices between life and death here at stake.

On 9 March 2007 an International Conference on 'The Protection of Ambient Air in International and European Law/La protezione dell'aria ambiente nel diritto internazionale e communitario' was organized in Modena by the Facoltà di Giurisprudenza and the Dipartimento di Scienze Giuridiche of the University of Modena and Reggio Emilia. It was a highly successful gathering and debate between those in town and region who have to decide in practice on how to control and manage air quality and a selected group of prominent Italian and international legal scholars. This meeting of practice and academia and the discussions between these legal experts and important policy makers, proved to be most fruitful and mutually inspiring. This book is to quite some extent the result of the reports and comments presented by the participants at the Modena Conference.

The editor of this book wishes to express his gratitude to each one of them and also to those who so generously supported him in the organisation of the conference and the publication of the book. I would like to thank besides the authors of this volume, in particular, the President of the Facoltà di Giurisprudenza, Professor Alessandra Bignardi, and the Director of the

---

[2] *See* the Explanatory Memorandum to the 2005 Proposal for the Directive (SEC (2005)) 1133, 1. Context of the Proposal.

Dipartimento di Scienze Giuridiche, Professor Maria Cecilia Fregni, for their great co-operation and efforts. Without their consistent and enthusiastic support there would neither have been the conference nor this book. I would further like to express my gratitude to the Comune of Modena, the Fondazione Cassa di Risparmio di Modena and Hera Modena for their generous financial support; to Professor Giorgio Pighi, Mayor of Modena, Professor Andrea Lanzi, Presidente of the Fondazione and Dott. Vanni Bulgarelli, Presidente of Hera Modena for their confidence in this research project. My colleagues Professors Maria Grazia Scacchetti and Andrea Gioia, Dott. Ivana Palandri, Dott. Federico Casolari, Dott. Barbara Viaro, Dott. Chiara Bursi and Dott. Gabriella Liberatori have all specially contributed to the success of this project. Vi ringrazio molto!

I would also like to thank the staff of Eleven International Publishing, in particular Mirjam van der Heide and its Director Dott. Selma Hoedt for their great patience, help and competence in the publication of this book. Finally, for her support and thorough language revision, I would like to express my warmest gratitude to Carol Post.

Harry H. G. Post
Bologna, December 2008

PART I

Practice

VITTORIO BORALDI AND LUISA GUERRA

A Scientific Introduction to the Management of Ambient Air: From SO_2 to $PM_{2.5}$

The Principal components of atmosphere

GAS	FORMULA	P.M	COMP. IN VOLUME %	COMP. IN VOLUME PPM*	COMP. IN PESO %	COMP. IN PESO PPM	G
Nitrogen	N_2	28.0	78.09	780 900	75.51	755 100	38 648 x 10^{20}
Oxygen	O_2	32.0	20.95	209 500	23.15	231 500	11 841
Argon	AR	39.9	0.93	9 300	1.28	12 800	0.6555
Carbon dioxide	CO_2	44.0	0.03	300	0.04	460	0.0233
Neon	NE	20.2		18		12.5	0.000636
Helium	HE	4.0		5.2		0.72	0.000037
Methane	CH_4	16.0		2.2		1.2	0.000062
Krypton	KR	83.8		1		2.9	0.000146
Nitrogen dioxide	N_2O	44.0		1		1.5	0.000002
Hydrogen	H_2	2.0		0.5		0.03	0.000002
Xenon	XE	131.3		0.08		0.36	0.000018

(ex DPR 203/88).

Air pollution: every change of the normal conditions or physical state of atmospheric air, caused by the presence of one or more pollutants with the quantity and features that modify normal ambient and health air conditions, in a way that becomes harmful, directly or indirectly, for human health

The atmospheric system is physically and chemically dynamic

A DEFINITION OF POLLUTION

The atmosphere is mainly made up of hydrogen, oxygen and noble gases.

Although air concentrations of its main components have not really changed in recent times, the atmosphere is a dynamic system in continuous evolution, because of its interaction with vegetation, oceans and living things, and especially with human beings.

HARRY H. G. POST (ED.), The Protection of Ambient Air in International and European Law, 7-29.

Gases are generated by biological activities: volcanic fumes, human activities and chemical processes which take place in the atmosphere.

There are mechanisms that are balanced between the addition and the removal of substances: they leave the atmosphere in a stationary condition or almost do. In the last two centuries concentrations of some components have greatly and rapidly changed: constant increases of certain emissions interfered with the complex atmospheric system. They have caused changes in oxidative capacity of the atmosphere itself bringing concentrations of some substances to harmful levels for human health. The result is what we call air pollution. In figure 1 you can see a definition of atmospheric pollution as it is described in the Italian law DPR 203/88.

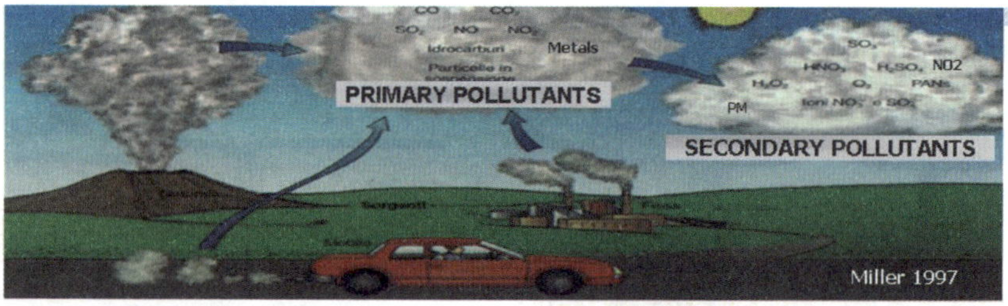

PRIMARY POLLUTANTS: they are directly put into the atmosphere, because of both anthropogenic and of natural processes;

SECONDARY POLLUTANTS: they are generated by chemical-physical reactions among primary polluting substances or within the atmosphere, sometimes activated by solar energy;

Primary pollutants		Atmospheric Components		Secondary pollutants	Reaction
Acid gas	+	Basic particles	=	Salt particles	Acid-base reaction
NH_3	+	H_2SO_4	=	$(NH_4)_2SO_4$	
SO_2, H_2S, cat. partic. atmosf.	+	O_2, H_2O	=	H_2SO_4	oxidation
NO	+	O_2, O_3	=	NO_2	
VOCs	+	NO, O_3	=	NO_2	Photochemical reaction
		O_2, Solar rad.	=	O_3	
		NO_2, O_2, Solar rad.	=	NO	
		O_3	=	Free radicals	

PRIMARY AND SECONDARY POLLUTANTS

Pollutants can be primary or secondary, apart from their natural or human origin.

Primary substances are put directly in the environment by the process that generated them; while secondary substances derive from primary ones through chemical reactions and physical processes which, in many cases, depend on atmospheric oxygen and light.

The main polluting substances are emitted during combustion processes. They are in particular Carbon monoxide, Carbon dioxide, Nitrogen Oxides (especially Nitrogen monoxide), particulate matter and unburnt hydrocarbons. If the combustible substances contain sulphur, there will also be an output of Sulphur Dioxide.

After their emission in the atmosphere, primary polluting substances are transformed by chemical-physical processes which can lead to the generation of new chemical species. The result is often more toxic and has a greater range of action than the original compound (NO_2, O_3, PAN – PeroxyAcetylNitrate).

The following figures give a description of the main features of polluting substances. Their emissions are monitored and regulated in Italy by specific laws.

CO - Carbon Monoxide

Colourless and odourless Gas, lighter than air, can cause asphyxia

CHARACTERISTICS:

It is a primary polluting substance.

It presents a strong spatial gradient: its concentration quickly decreases moving away from the generating source

SOURCES:

Most of all road traffic

HOW IT IS GENERATED:

Incomplete reaction between fuel and oxygen

POLLUTANTS

Carbon oxide (CO) or *carbon monoxide* is a colourless, odourless, inflammable and very toxic gas. It is generated by incomplete combustion of organic substances or in processes at high temperature.

The most important source is road traffic, in particular the fumes from cars even though in the last years the quantity of CO emitted from the discharge system of cars has decreased thanks to technological improvement of engines and to obligatory checks of emissions.

Other sources are industrial processes such as cast iron and steel production and petrol refineries.

Carbon oxide smog is a typical urban pollution. Its concentrations are higher close to roads where traffic is most intense. Its concentration trend follows that of traffic, showing a strong spatial gradient when we move away from the sources where the CO has been generated.

The effects for the environment may not be very important at actual levels but they are for human health. The possible reaction between CO and blood haemoglobin is especially dangerous, giving birth to a physiologically inactive compound, called *carboxyhaemoglobin*, which does not allow the oxygenation of tissues. At low concentrations, it causes migraine, spreads weakness and dizziness; at higher concentrations it can cause death.

SO_2 - Sulphur dioxide

Colourless gas, pungent smelling

CHARACTERISTICS:

- it is a primary pollutant
- It reacts in the atmosphere, generating small drops of sulphuric acid and sulphate, which are precursors of secondary particulate matter

SOURCES:

Combustion processes of fuels containing sulphur

Coal> Oil comb. ATZ> Oil Comb. BTZ> Gas oil 0,3%> methane

HOW IT IS GENERATED: reaction between fuels (containing sulphur) and oxygen

POLLUTANTS

Sulphur dioxide is a colourless gas, irritant, not inflammable, very soluble in water and sharp smelling. It comes from sulphur oxidation in combustion processes of substances containing this element, whether as an impurity (fossil combustibles) or as a basic component.

Oxidation of sulphur dioxide gives origin to sulphur trioxide. When it reacts with water vapour it generates sulphuric acid which is mainly responsible for acid rain. It is also a precursor of secondary particulate matter.

Principal human sources are combustion systems that use fossil fuels (power stations, foundries, etc.). Road traffic is not the main source; its input is low.

Replacement of fossil combustibles with a low sulphur content, like methane, greatly reduces the levels of this pollutant in the environment.

SO_2 is an irritant for respiratory tracts and it may cause bronchus constraint at high doses. Moreover it is responsible for damage to plants and materials.

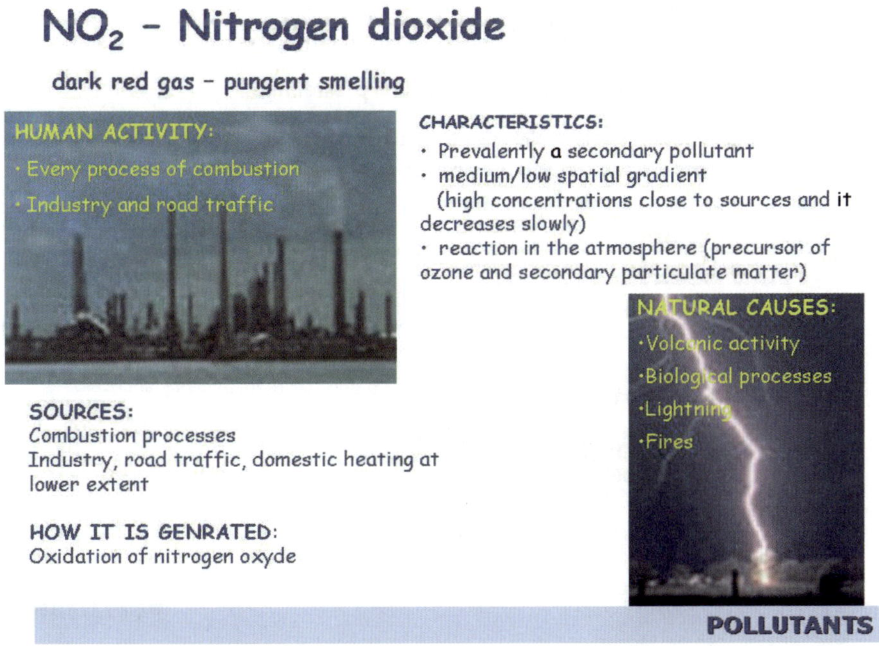

Nitrogen dioxide is a yellow-red sharp smelling toxic and strongly irritant gas; it is a very reactive oxidative and is therefore highly corrosive. It is generated in outdoor ambient air by oxidation of nitrogen monoxide and for this reason it is classified as (mainly) a secondary pollutant. Moreover, it contributes to photo-chemical smog; in fact ultraviolet radiation is able to separate NO_2 molecules and to generate NO and very reactive oxygen. The reactions that take place in the atmosphere lead to the production of secondary pollutants such as ozone, nitric acid, nitrous acid, alkylnitrates, peroxyacetylnitrate, etc.

Principal human sources of nitrogen oxides are combustions at high temperature, like the ones that take place in car engines, in particular diesel ones: the high temperature during combustion bursts leads to a reaction between nitrogen in the air and oxygen. This reaction generates nitrogen monoxide which can transform then into NO_2.

Other important sources of nitrogen oxides are thermo-electric stations and to a smaller extent, heating systems. Anthropogenic sources are further: the production of nitrogen fertilizers and of nitric acid for ammonia oxidation and the production of explosives.

The main natural sources are from bacterial action.

Nitrogen dioxide at high concentrations is an irritating substance for the respitory system, but the biggest danger for man is its contribution to the formation of photochemical oxidants.

O_3 - Tropospheric Ozone

Light blue gas, very reactive and sharp smelling

At ground level ozone molecules are generated when other pollutants, mainly **nitrogen oxides** and **volatile organic compounds**, react because of sun light.

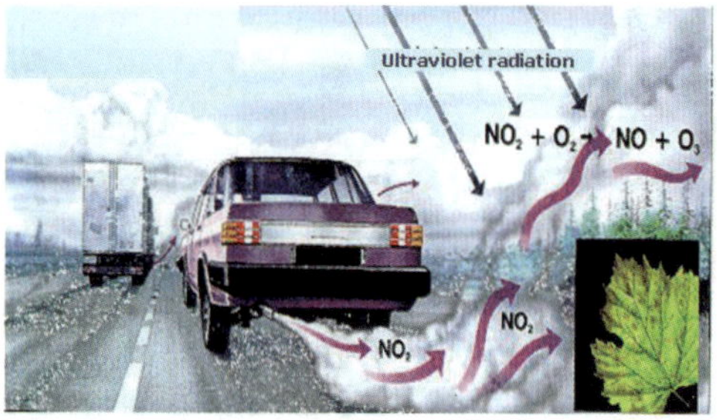

CHARACTERISTICS:

- It is a completely secondary pollutant
- It presents a weak spatial gradient (highest concentrations are in open plain, far from primary sources)

HOW IT IS GENERATED:

Photochemical reaction that involves NO_2,VOCs, sun light

POLLUTANTS

Tropospheric ozone is a toxic blue gas, formed by instable molecules of three atoms of oxygen (O_3). These molecules split up easily into one oxygen molecule (O_2) and one oxygen atom that is extremely reactive ($O_3 \rightarrow O_2+O$). It is a highly oxidative and aggressive compound and because of its chemical characteristic it doesn't stay in the atmosphere for long, even if it can be transported over long distances by masses of moving air.

In the troposphere (the part of the atmosphere that is closer to the ground), ozone is generated by photochemical reactions favoured by sun radiation, which involve primary pollutants as Nitrogen Oxides and non-methane hydrocarbons. These primary pollutants, known as precursor gases, are produced during the combustion of fossil fuels and are thus associated with industry and the transport sector. Virtually none of the ozone in the troposphere is emitted directly from natural (including human) sources. Therefore this ozone is considered a *secondary pollutant*, formed in the atmosphere from chemical precursors.

In urban areas, where there is more atmospheric pollution, ozone is formed and reacts very rapidly (primary compounds that take part in its origin are the same that can cause its quick destruction). If ozone generated in urban areas is physically removed by transporting it towards suburban areas and the countryside, it gets a longer life because of the smaller presence of NO. In this way, it can accumulate reaching concentration levels higher than in urban areas.

The effects on human health caused by excessive exposure to ozone essentially regard our breathing system and our eyes. With regard to vegetation, damage caused by ozone is so great that this gas is considered, together with sulphur dioxide, as one of the main causes of forest destruction (acid rain). Ozone is also very harmful for materials and for historic buildings.

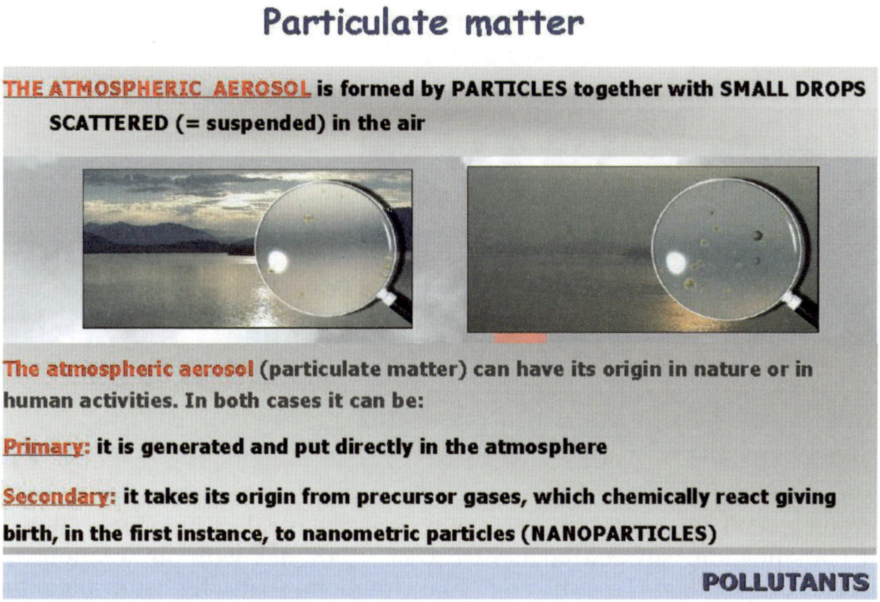

Suspended PM is a complex mix of organic and inorganic substances, which are present in liquid and solid state, with a variable chemical composition according to size characteristic and to the source that generates it.

Particulate matter is divided in classes according to particle size

PTS: total PM – the first to be regulated and measured – industrial emissions are still expressed as total PM

PM10 : European and Italian reference valid for air quality

PM2,5: proposed as for a European standard

PM1: it will be subject to a standard in the U.S.A.

PM0,1: ultra-fine particles, the frontier of research

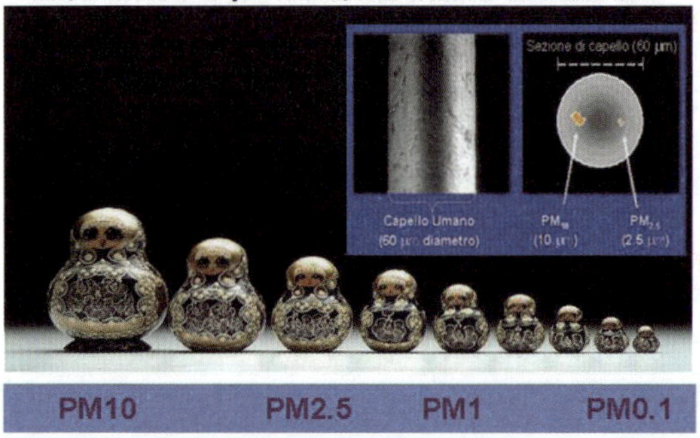

CHARACTERISTICS:
- It has an important secondary component
- It presents very low spacial gradient (uniform concentrations in the whole plain of the Emilia-Romagna)

SOURCES:
- Combustion processes (industry and road traffic)
- Soil erosion - Yards
- tyre and brake lining wear

L. Tositti – Modena 15/3/2006 **POLLUTANTS**

The size of Particles varies in a range from some nanometers to dozens of micrometers. The most important physical-chemical differences allow a first classification between coarse fractions (particles with an aerodynamic diameter bigger than 2,5 µm) and 'fine' fractions (particles with diameters equal or smaller than 2,5 µm ($PM_{2,5}$). This distinction depends mainly on the different origin of particulate matter.

The class of 'fine' particles is principally generated by secondary particles and primary particles produced by combustion reactions. They are the result of several chemical processes with a natural or anthropogenic origin. The class of bigger particles (with diameters greater than 2.5 µm) is constituted by crust materials, powders made out and/or lifted off the ground by car traffic and dust produced by industry.

The different origins of particles cause their morphology and chemical composition: fine particles were found to consist primarily of nitrate, sulfate and ammonium ions which, together with elemental and organic carbon made up 70-80% of the total $PM_{2.5}$ mass. In contrast, these components made up only about 10-20% of the coarse fraction between 2.5 and 10µm. The coarse fraction was dominated by aluminium, silicon, sulfur, potassium, calcium and iron, which made up 40-50% of its mass.

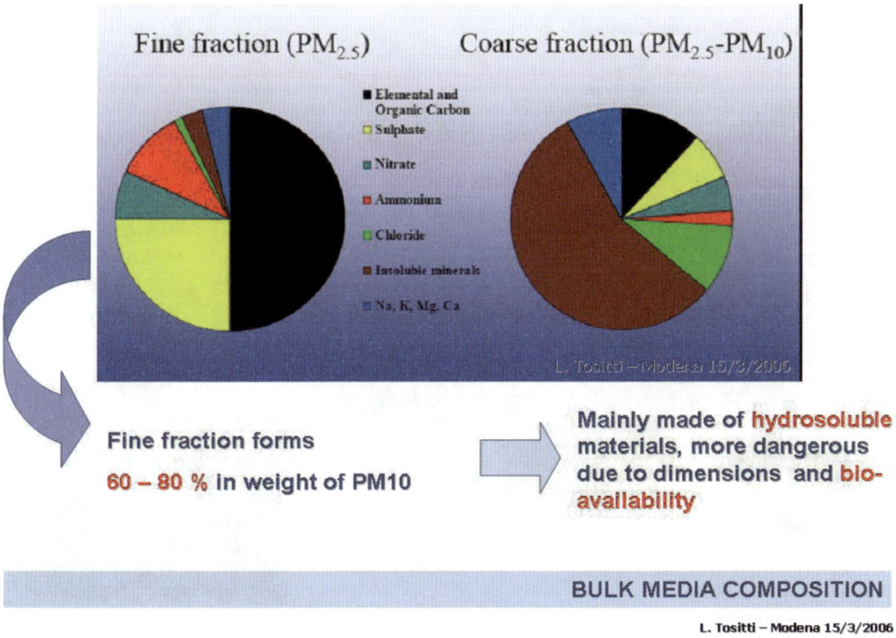

Principal *natural sources* of primary particulate are volcanic eruptions, wood fires, the erosion of rocks, plants (pollens and vegetable residues), spores, sea spray and insects rests.

Secondary natural PM is formed by fine particles which have their origin in the oxidation of various substances, such as: sulphur dioxide and hydrogen sulphide emitted by fires and volcanoes, nitrogen oxides emitted from the soil and terpenes (hydrocarbons) emitted by vegetation.

Anthropogenic sources of primary particles include combustion from car engines, solid-fuel combustion in households, industrial activities, erosion of the pavement by road traffic and abrasion of brakes and tyres, work in caves and mines. Secondary anthropogenic particles are formed in the air, usually by chemical reactions of gaseous pollutants, and are products of atmospheric transformation of nitrogen oxides mainly emitted by traffic and industrial processes, and sulfur dioxide resulting form the combustion of sulphur-containing fuels.

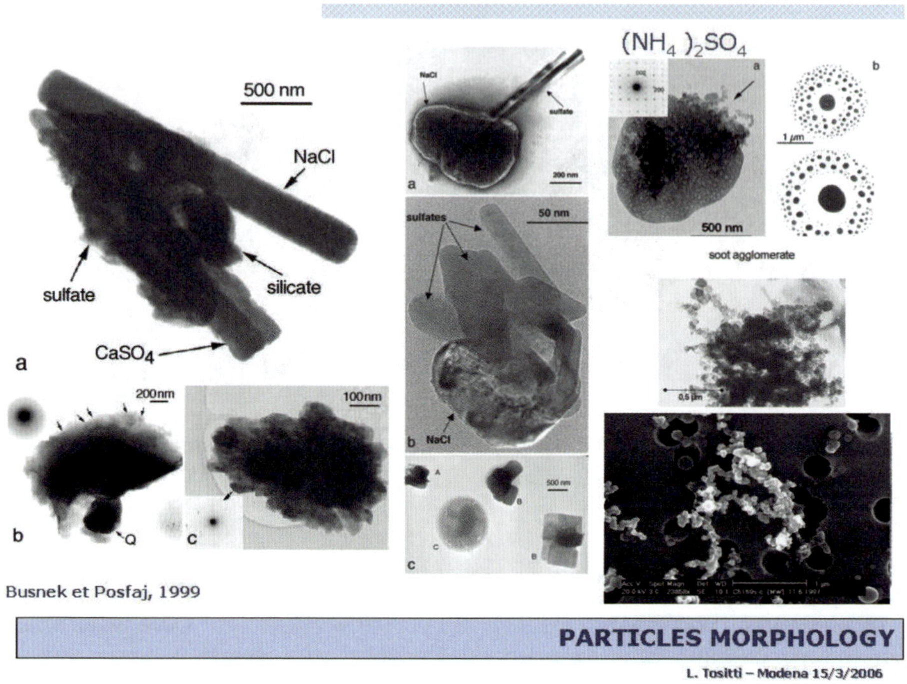

Large amounts of PM can also originate from agricultural activities.

Particle size is considered to be the most important parameter in characterising the physical behaviour of particulate matter in the atmosphere.

Particles in the size range of 0.1-2.0 μm can remain in the atmosphere for days to weeks, because atmospheric removal processes are eventually efficient in this size range. Dry deposition and precipitation are the processes by which these fine particles are removed from the atmosphere.

Particles larger than 2.0 μm are efficiently removed by gravitational settling and therefore remain in the atmosphere for periods of a few hours to a few days.

Extremely small ('ultrafine') particles of less than 0.1 μm in diameter are subject to random motion and to coagulation processes in which particles collide quickly and yield larger particles. Consequently these tiny particles have short atmospheric residence times

The problem of atmospheric pollution is not new especially considering that since the last century in some countries, such as the United Kingdom, laws were promulgated in order to fight it. In fact the Clean Air Act was already issued in 1956 by the British government in order to limit domestic and industrial fumes, which damaged the health of London citizens and even limited visibility, not only in the capital but also in many other industrial cities.

Clean Air Act: **issued by the British Government in 1956 in order to limit domestic and industrial fumes, which damaged the health of London citizens and even limited visibility.**

(In December 1952, an estimated 4000 citizens died because of atmospheric pollution)

AMBIENT AIR QUALITY MANAGEMENT

Italy waited until 1966 to enact the framework law about atmospheric pollution, which was called 'Anti-smog Law'. This law was issued in order to limit damages to public health due to fumes, gas powders and exhalations. It was the first step towards the protection of the atmospheric environment. Previously, the law on this matter was laid down in instruments on health, hygiene and security protection (damage protection), rather than in the regulation of the protection of air quality. The 1966 law was limited, first of all in that it was not applicable in the whole national territory.

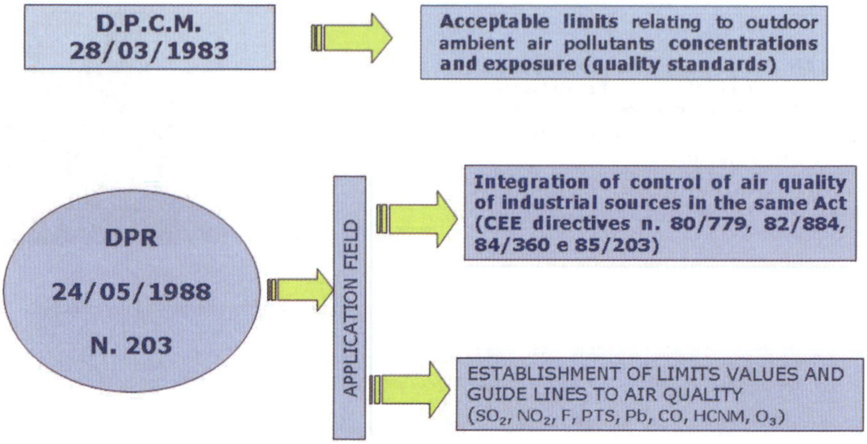

AMBIENT AIR QUALITY MANAGEMENT : DPCM 28/3/1983 and DPR 203/88

Changes in the law, which occurred in the 1980's, followed legislative progress in the European Community, in addition to increasing environmental consciousness. Laws produced in these years, ranging from DPCM 28/3/1983 ("Maximum limits of acceptability of concentrations and exposure with regard to air pollutants in the outdoor environment"), up to DPR 24/05/1988, n. 203 (implementating EEC Directives 80/779, 82/884, 84/360 and 85/203), form the basis of all the Italian legislation up to the 1990's.

Finally, from 1999 on, the implemenation of the European directives issued in 1996 and thereafter was the turning point and lead to the current system of laws.

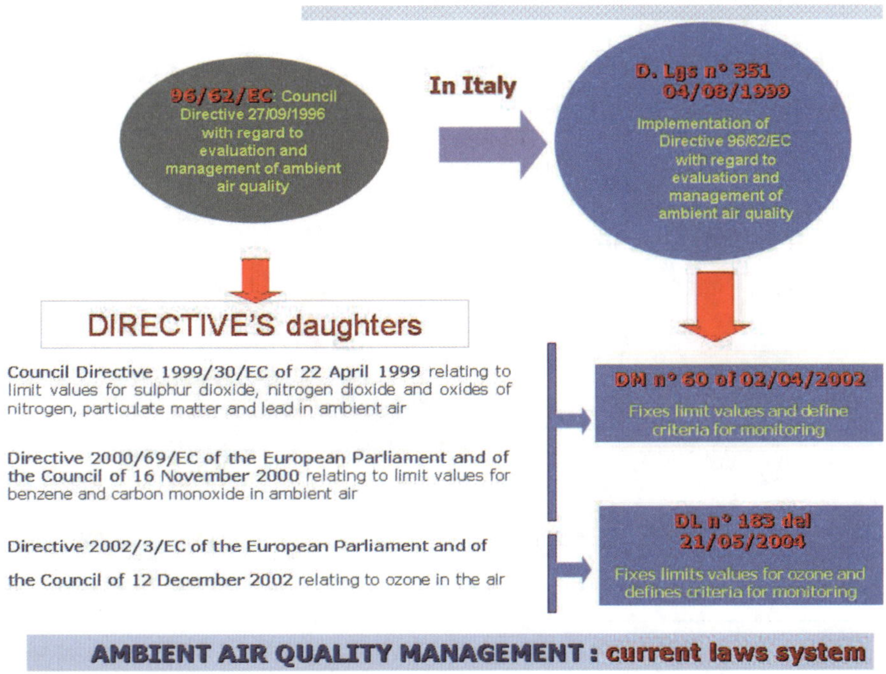

In September 1996 the Council of the European Union adopted Directive 96/62/EC on ambient air quality assessment and management, in order to define the fundamental principles of a common strategy. This Framework Directive was to:

- define and establish objectives for ambient air quality in the Community designed to avoid, prevent or reduce harmful effects on human health and the environment as a whole,
- assess the ambient air quality in Member States on the basis of common methods and criteria,
- obtain adequate information on ambient air quality and ensure that it is made available to the public, inter alia by means of alert thresholds,
- maintain ambient air quality where it is good and improve it in other cases (see, in detail, the contributions in Part II of this book).

This 'Framework' Directive is transposed in national Italian rules through D.Lgs. 4/08/1999, n. 351.

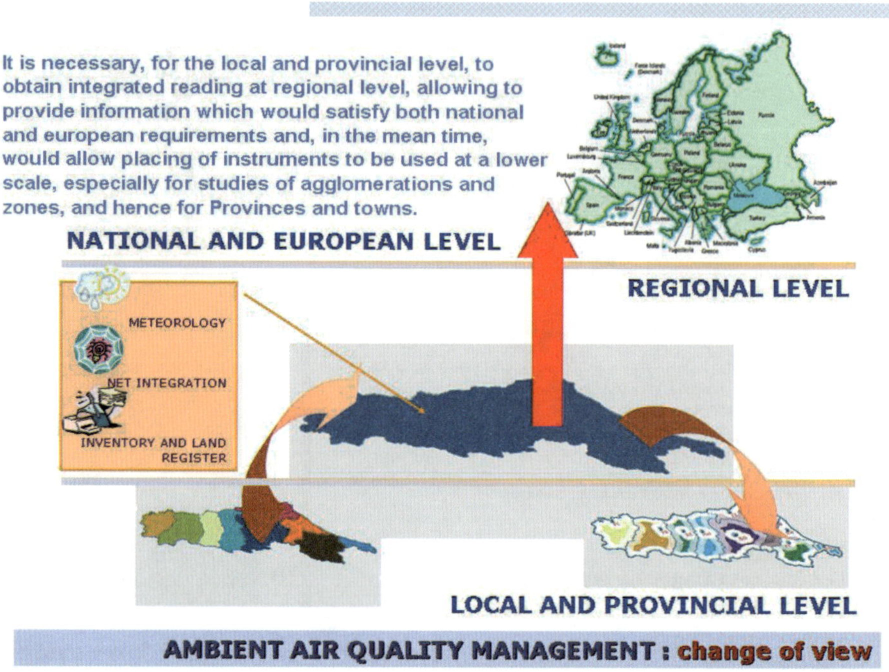

The main new element is the definition of a 'common strategy' in the European Community, with regard to the evaluation and management of ambient air in the whole territory of the Member States. The common strategy would make sure that limit values would be respected and that common criteria and methods are used that allow the exchange of consistent information among different levels: local/provincial, regional, national and European.

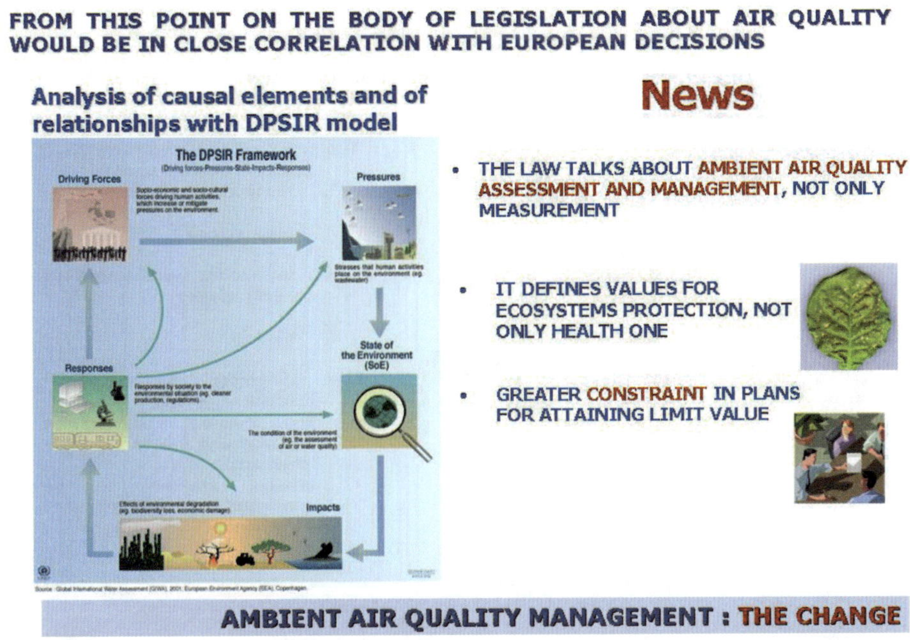

In addition, the Italian Framework Law modifies the concept of measurement changing it to 'assessment of air quality'. This is seen as integration between monitoring and the use of modelling techniques in order to ensure knowledge of ambient air in the whole territory. This means in practice that 'the ambient air quality management' is laid down in a set of actions and measures, which allow to prevent or to decrease the harmful effects on human health and on the environment as a whole.

The basis of this strategy is therefore, the analysis of the correlations among environmental conditions, pressures and political answers, such as is represented in the well-known DPSIR model.

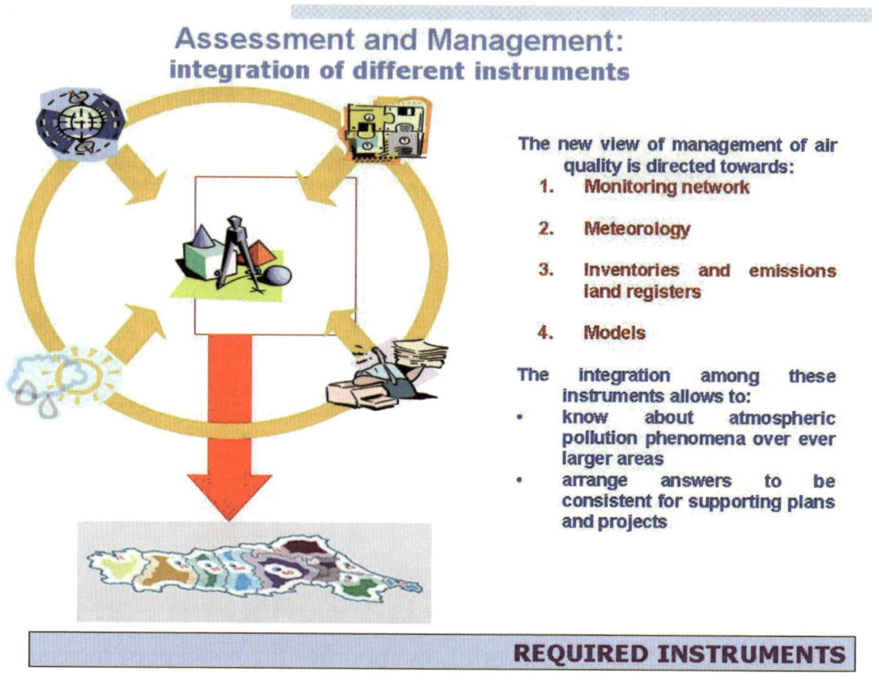

Ambient air quality assessment is necessary in the cognitive stage to identify priority actions and to monitor the effects of the actions accomplished. Now it is carried out with all available means. *Measuring*, the only instrument provided by the previous directives, is supplemented therefore with *other instruments*, such as *emission inventories and modelling techniques*.

Supporting this strategy, the European Commission says in the report which explains the so-called Daughter Directives to the Framework Directive (see Part II of this book) that even a relatively dense monitoring network cannot fully gage and represent the air quality in quite a large area. Moreover, measuring by itself is not sufficient to find the correlation between concentrations and emission sources and does not allow toe estimate the likely results of the actions and measures taken.

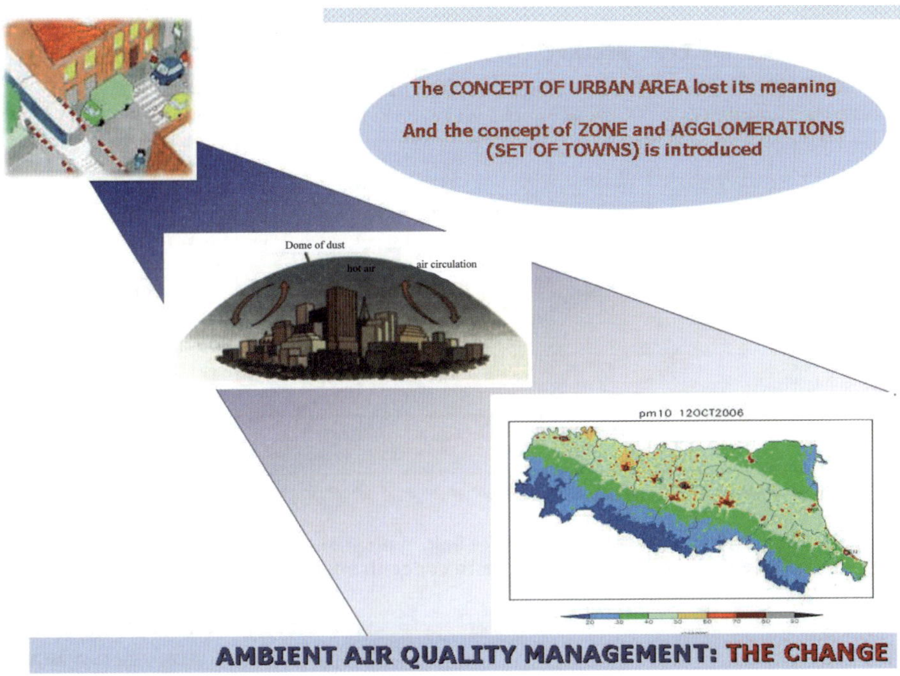

Air quality assessment begins with the *classification of territory in zones and agglomerations* in order to *manage* them. Zones and agglomerations consist of towns which share the risk of breaking limits values.

Therefore larger contexts of action are defined than urban areas which were considered in previous laws. Furthermore, monitoring is not related to single points, although often the critical ones, but it aims at representing the quality of the air over wide areas.

The shift to an ever bigger scale is also caused by the necessity to consider that, in recent years, quality and quantity characteristics of environmental pollutants produced by human sources, and scientific knowledge of their effects on human health, has changed.

At the beginning of the 1980's the most frequent pollutants were the primary ones – sulphur dioxide, carbon monoxide, particulate matter, lead – emitted directly from combustion processes, road traffic, industry and heating systems.

Currently, indeed, the biggest environmental problems are determined by secondary pollutants, such as nitrogen oxides and, most of all, PM_{10}, $PM_{2.5}$, as you can see from the graphics which follow.

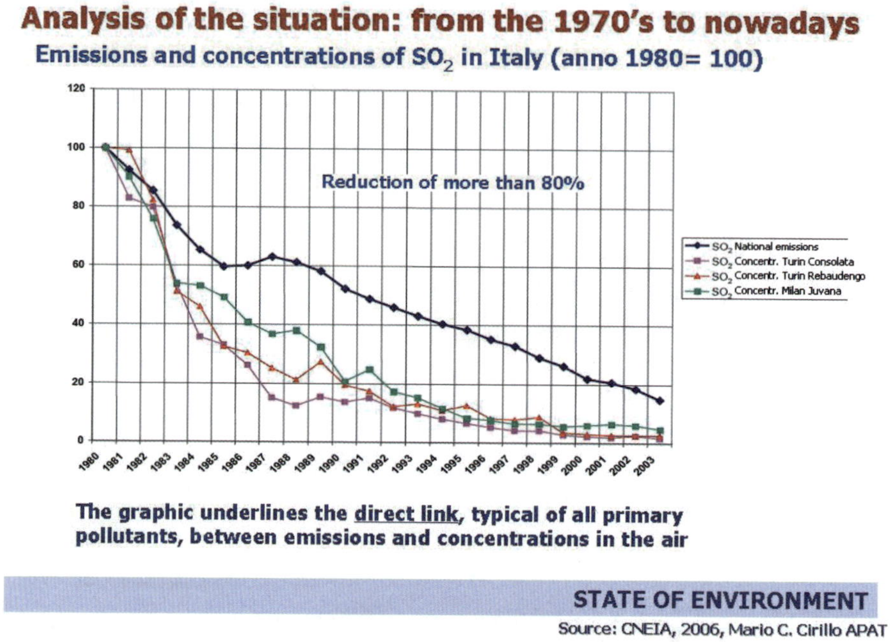
Analysis of the situation: from the 1970's to nowadays
Emissions and concentrations of SO_2 in Italy (anno 1980= 100)
Reduction of more than 80%
SO_2 National emissions
SO_2 Concentr. Turin Consolata
SO_2 Concentr. Turin Rebaudengo
SO_2 Concentr. Milan Juvana
The graphic underlines the direct link, typical of all primary pollutants, between emissions and concentrations in the air
STATE OF ENVIRONMENT
Source: CNEIA, 2006, Mario C. Cirillo APAT

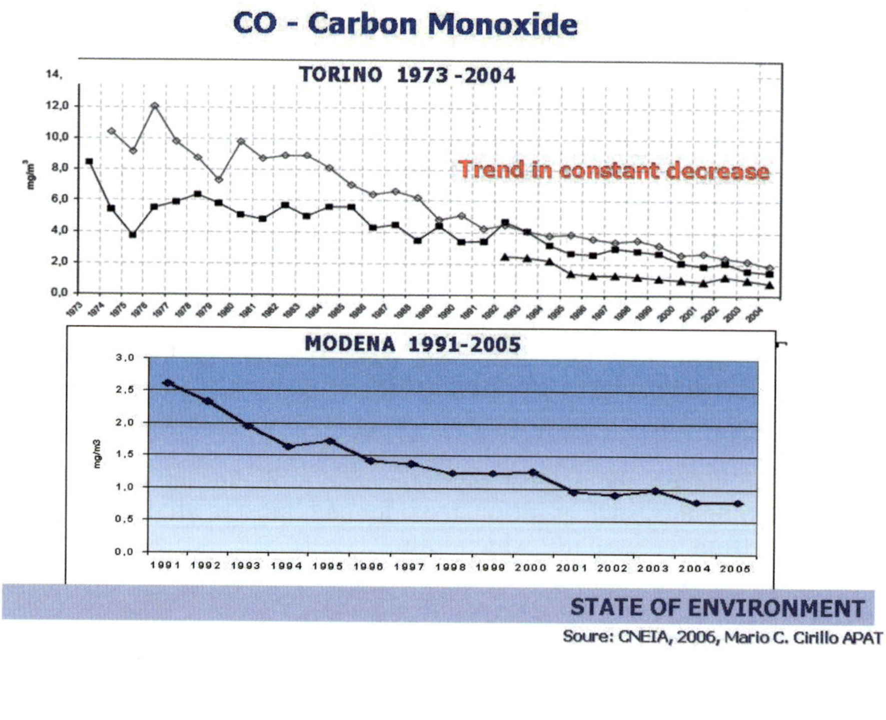
CO - Carbon Monoxide
TORINO 1973 -2004
Trend in constant decrease
mg/m³
MODENA 1991-2005
mg/m3
STATE OF ENVIRONMENT
Soure: CNEIA, 2006, Mario C. Cirillo APAT

During the 1990's there was a consistent decrease in emissions of principal atmospheric pollutants in Italy. It was mainly thanks to technological improvements made in the field of transportation and to the widely spreading of the use of methane in domestic and industrial combustion heating.

Conforming with this reduction of emissions, there was a great decrease of primary pollutants in atmospheric concentrations (SO_2, Pb, CO and benzene): they got lower below reference values practically in the whole national territory (as is shown in the above figure on measurements made from the 70's to nowadays).

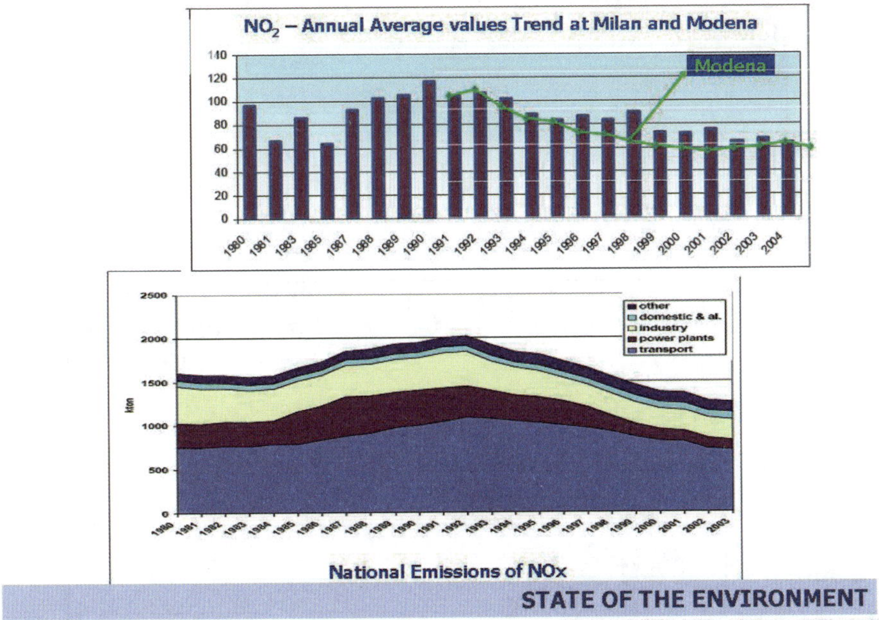

Source: CNEIA, 2006, Mario C. Cirillo APAT

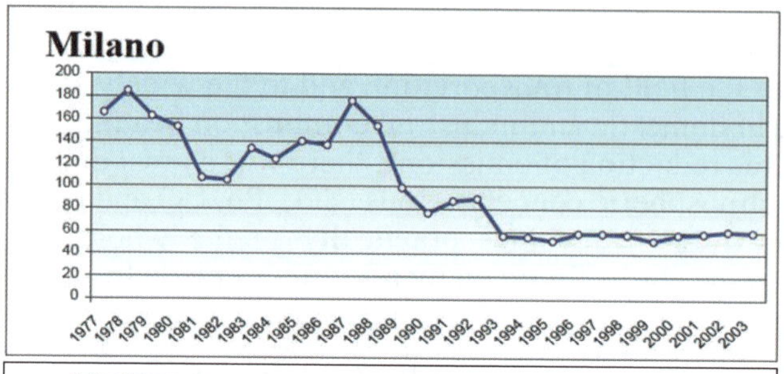

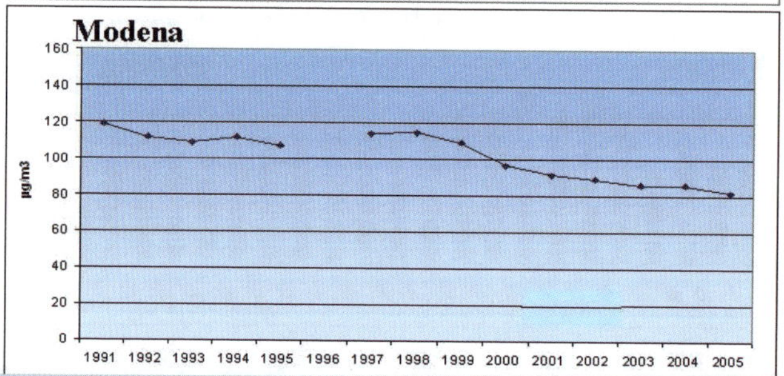

PTS

PM, Particulate Matter situation: the origins are partly primary, partly secondary or

There is a decrease of total PM (PTS) concentrations

STATE OF ENVIRONMENT

Source: CNEIA, 2006, Mario C. Cirillo APAT

PM10 Modena

Limited historical series

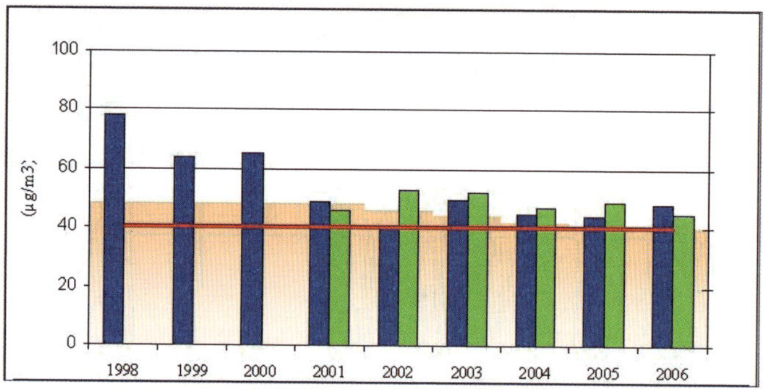

STATE OF THE ENVIRONMENT

The situation of pollutants that have got both a primary and a secondary origin, as PM_{10} and NO_2, is more complex. We have registered significantly decreasing values of atmospheric concentrations, but not sufficient to ensure the attainment, over the whole national territory, of reference levels fixed by laws, especially not in urban areas. In particular, in the last years, PM_{10} concentrations seem to be quite stable.

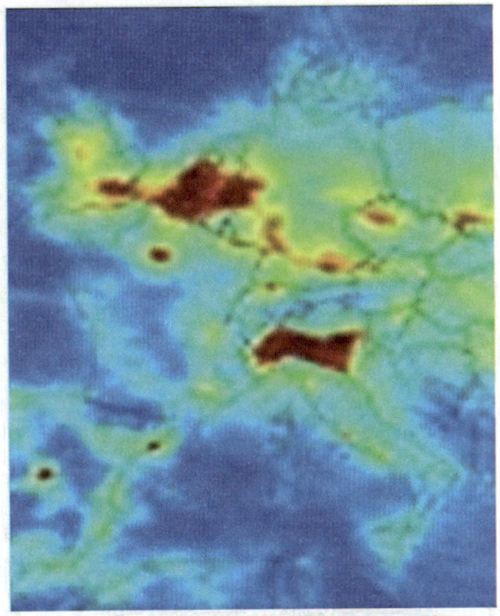

Concentrations of NO_2 measured at ground level by satellite

AMBIENT AIR QUALITY MANAGEMENT

This change in types of current critical pollutants brings different problems in preparing measures to attain limit value or improve air quality. Success obtained with primary pollutants was due to the relatively easy identification of emission sources and their low reactivity in the atmosphere. Secondary pollutants are involved in large scale processes in the whole Po valley. Therefore the measures taken must also be at a wide scale.

Sceneries: Emilia Romagna zero emission, PM10

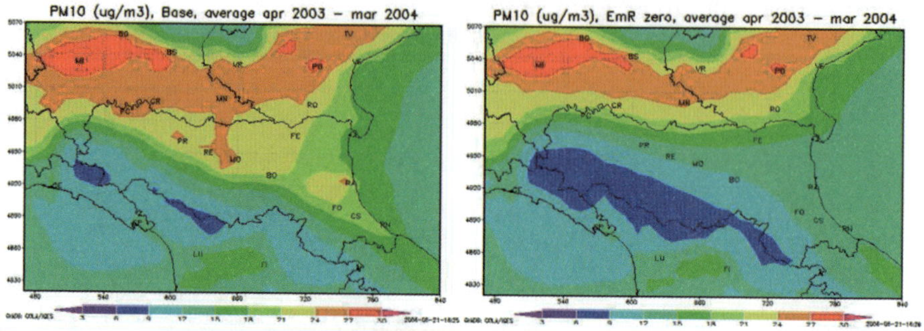

PM10, annual average concentration, basic situation (left) and EMR scenery zero (right)

- Zero Emission in the Emilia Romagna, corresponding to a reduction of emissions in the whole Padan plain of about 13%
- The annual average of PM10 (far from regional borders) decreases by 40-50% - at the border by only 20-30%
- The number exceeding the threshold of 50 $\mu g/m^3$ is practically reduced to zero
- Ozone: reduction of the numbers of those exceeding the level for health protection is about 20%

AMBIENT AIR QUALITY MANAGEMENT: spatial scale of action

An example of this different approach is represented in the figure above, where two sceneries (realised with prevision models) are compared: they show the current situation of PM_{10} concentrations (on the left) and a hypothetical situation with all emission sources in the Emilia-Romagna (road traffic, heating systems, industry, etc.) turned off. The latter correspond to 13% of the total emissions in the whole Po valley.

The result shows the large spatial scale of this phenomenon. The annual average of this indicator decreases with percentages between 20 and 50% according to the distance from the regional borders, relative to the higher or lower impact of neighbouring regions.

The reduction is much more evident for ozone levels.

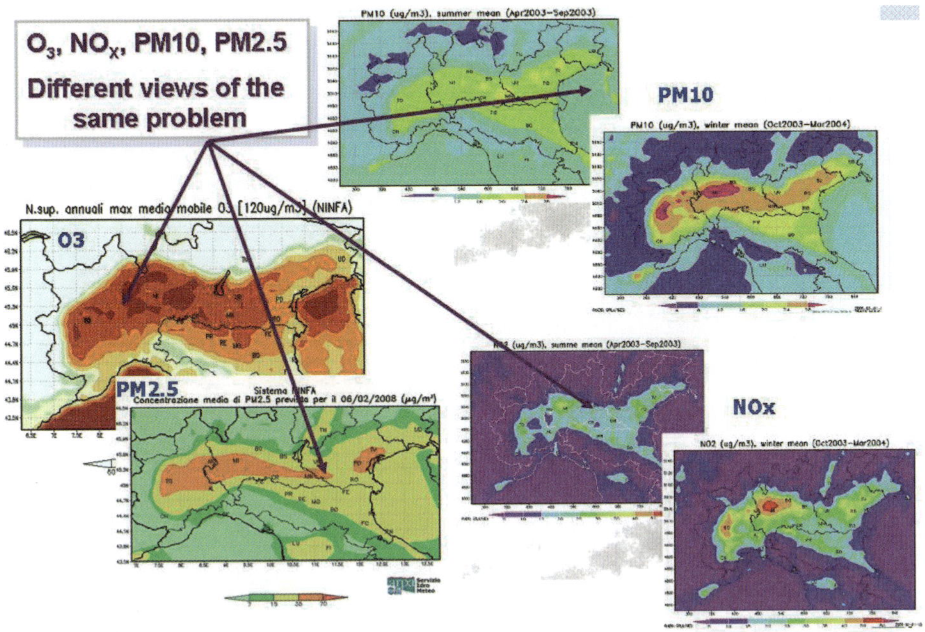

From the analysis of the behaviour of pollutants and of their mutual interactions, it is possible to understand that the problem is a general one all over the Po valley. It requires coordinated actions in order to prepare plans for attaining the limit values that would be effective.

Giovanni Franco Orlando

The Protection of Air Quality in the City of Modena

Environmental Protection is a very important and complex subject. It is widely discussed at local levels, as it is often confined to a limited territorial dimension. But the systems of local government (town councils, provinces and regions) are – if you will – often 'left to their own devices' to deal with and take decisions in regard to environmental matters: decisions which affect the day to day lives of our cities and our citizens. Ever more, we are witnessing a somewhat paradoxical situation. The now widespread awareness of the fact that environmental pollution has a vast, one might even say 'global' scope is counterbalanced by the limited means and fragmentary and uncoordinated intervention mechanisms available for more limited areas.

Recently, there have been a number of cases across Italy of magistrates taking action against the Mayors of several Italian cities. These Mayors were legally charged insofar as they were held responsible for not having done everything in their power to safeguard and protect the health of their citizens as regards the ever more worrying phenomenon of air pollution. This is clearly an exasperated (yet emblematic) reaction to the helplessness of local governments with the means at their disposal, in the face of a highly complicated phenomenon.

Italy is a country where, as you know, football is very widely followed – there is no Italian citizen who does not believe to know far more about the game than the current trainer of the national team or of their own home team for that matter. As well as being a nation of supposed experts on football, we also seem to be a nation of experts on PM_{10} levels and nano-particles. Not a day goes by without some fellow citizen pulling a miraculous idea out of a hat, the magic formula, the solution that will allow us to drive around town as we always have done and at the same time breath clean air. Unfortunately, this is a field in which opinions are ten a penny, as are the arguments, the

Harry H. G. Post (Ed.), The Protection of Ambient Air in International and European Law, 31-37.

undeniable data and the absolute truths. Rather than helping us come to terms with the matter, often they end up discouraging even the most tenacious of administrators in his or her attempt to stymie the problem and limit the damage caused with the few means available. This is why it is of the utmost importance to have input from the world of science, both in terms of research as well as a clear cognitive framework of the situation which may identify responsibilities and thus determine choices when drawing up a regulatory outline.

Here in Modena, part of the so-called 'Po Basin', we live in an area that looks onto the Po Plain, which lies across all the main regions of Northern Italy (as well as the Emilia-Romagna, so do also the Veneto region, Piedmont and Lombardy). As may be seen from satellite photos from some time ago, along with a part of Germany and another of China, the Po Plain is among the most polluted parts of the planet.[1] Due to its meteorological and climatic conditions, its great anthropisation, the widespread presence of production plants and of major transport communication networks (linking Italy to the rest of Europe), this unfortunately is the situation in which we find ourselves.

Bad quality of air means bad quality of life. And this link between air and life standards constitutes one of the key issues that must be dealt with in the short term. In order to reduce the risks and the damage, both for our health and our environment, we clearly need to use new technologies: first and foremost those regarding our mobility systems and our use of energy.

Biased and impartial opinions aside, the main cause of atmospheric pollution in Modena are the emissions generated by the transport system, responsible for at least 80% of the pollution registered, albeit to varying degrees depending on the type of pollutant considered. Production activities have relatively little impact on air quality (having been subjected to national and regional laws on the matter ever since the '70s), and neither have domestic heating systems, which in Modena – unlike in many other Italian cities – today operate almost exclusively on natural gas.

Monitoring of air quality by Modena City Council began at the beginning of the '70s with the analysis of sulphur dioxide. Today this is carried out by an automatic data-gathering system consisting of three monitoring stations run by the ARPA (Regional Agency for Environmental Protection) placed at different points across the council's territory: two on roads carrying high levels of traffic (Via Nonantolana at the 'Torrenova' shopping centre, and Via Giardini at the 'Guidotti-Mistrali' middle school), and one in a large city park near the town centre (Parco Enzo Ferrari).

The monitoring network has undergone various changes and modifications over the years, especially in terms of broadening the range of parameters monitored in keeping with the changing legal regulations. The most recent modifications, which date back to 2005, meant coming into line with the Ministerial Decree No. 60/2002. It lead to a reduction in the number of

[1] *See also*, e.g., the map in the contribution by Boraldi and Guerra in Chapter 1, at 27 above.

monitoring stations (from five to the current three) and to the relocation of these stations to more strategic areas of the local territory. They now provide a guarantee of information comparable over a wider scale and thus constitute a more reliable source of information for citizens. The Parco Ferrari station, which supplies data on the city centre, has also been equipped for the experimental monitoring of $PM_{2,5}$ levels, a pollutant which by law is not yet required to be monitored, but which has attracted a great deal of attention from the responsible bodies.

From an analysis of the data gathered in the monitoring stations across Modena Town Council's territory, it appears that over the last few years, the most *critical factors* are represented by the presence of fine particles (PM_{10}), of nitrogen dioxide (NO_2) and, in the summer months, of ozone (O_3). I want to sum up briefly the effects of these pollutants on our health. Local health service studies highlight the fact that respiratory illnesses constitute the third cause of death in the province of Modena, just as in Emilia-Romagna and Italy as a whole. In that light we should realise that:

- the *PM_{10}* and *$PM_{2,5}$ fine particles* found in urban areas contain substances of a toxic and mutagenic nature. When inhaled given their tiny size, they may reach the pulmonary alveoli and may thus provoke lung inflammations;
- *nitrogen oxides* may cause irritations to the eyes and the respiratory tracts as well as acute respiratory intoxication;
- *ozone*, the dangers of which are due to its great oxidising power and its ability to quickly reach the alveolar level, may cause irritations to the eyes as well as breathing disorders. After prolonged exposition they may lead to phenomena of over-sensitisation and permanent irritations.

Alongside these pollutants, which are responsible for the most critical issues, we should also bear in mind the presence in vehicle exhaust fumes of:

- *carbon monoxide*, which is toxic and may lead to respiratory failure; and
- *benzene*, a compound recognised by the International Agency for Research into Cancer (IARC) as carcinogenic.

Analysing the *trends* of the three key pollutants in Modena (PM_{10}, nitrogen oxides and ozone), we should notice that pollution conditions are closely linked to meteorological parameters like wind speed, sunlight irradiation, rainfall, the vertical temperature gradient, conditions of atmospheric turbulence or stability. Considering the geographical position and characteristics of the Po Plain, these parameters are unfortunately hindering the dispersion of the pollutants, especially during the winter months which then lead to the building-up of these elements. The situation is further worsened by long dry spells and low wind speeds.

As far as the PM_{10} levels are concerned, the critical aspect comes to a head particularly during certain peak moments. These, although still well beyond the legal limits, are linked to the daily averages being exceeded rather than to dangerously high averages throughout the year. Around the end of the '1990s, we witnessed a decrease both of the average annual levels of $PM_{10,}$ and of the occurrence of excessive peak levels. This may clearly be attributed to the improved emission standards of new car engines. However, the rise in the number of vehicles in general and the increased share of diesel engines over the last few years are seen as the main causes of this positive trend being reversed again after 2001. The percentage of diesel vehicles out of the total number of vehicles circulating was e.g., over 25% in 2005, compared to under 10% just a few years before. In fact, from the year 2001 on, the average annual concentrations of PM_{10} have been largely stationary. Furthermore, in 2006, there was a sharp increase in the number of days in which the maximum threshold of average daily concentrations was exceeded compared to the year before (130 days in 2006 compared to the 35 days allowed in the Ministerial Decree No. 60/2002).

As for Nitrogen Dioxide, the other pollutant typical of the winter season, the critical aspect emerges in its average annual levels, which have always been above the maximum threshold, set at 40 $\mu g/m^3$. This threshold will come into force in 2010. The trend of the presence of nitrogen dioxide over time is very similar to that of the PM_{10} levels, albeit less accentuated, with two concentration peaks: one in the morning and one in the evening. They correspond to rush-hour traffic and greater atmospheric stability. There is a drop in levels at weekends and public holidays, attributable to the reduction of traffic volume. Average annual levels remained at a more or less stationary high level from 2001 to 2005; in 2006 however, there was a positive and notable drop, reaching the level of 56 $\mu g/m^3$.

Ozone represents the main pollutant in the summer period. The concentration of ozone is higher in the hotter months and during the day when solar irradiation levels are at their highest. The trend over time in ozone levels is so closely linked to weather conditions that it is not possible to recognise any specific trend. Although the maximum threshold is exceeded a limited number of times, the most critical aspect remains that of respecting the target threshold of the long-term objective.

In the face of these data and trends, as well as Community legislation which is ever more demanding and severe,[2] over the years a number of measures have been adopted aimed at reducing atmospheric pollution, both on a local level and on a wider, regional level. Over the last few years the regional and provincial governments and the local town councils with populations above 50,000 inhabitants have devised a common Programme. The Programme includes an overall range of different measures to adopt in order to renew the quality of the air with particular reference to levels of PM_{10}. In compliance with this agreement, the town councils of Modena and Carpi (the only other

2 *See* Montini's contribution in Chapter 5 of this book.

town in the territory with more than 50,000 inhabitants) and to a lesser extent also the other councils in the Province, have adopted planned restrictive measures of traffic circulation. These measures apply across a large part of the urban area in autumn and winter, the period in which the most critical pollution situations in respect to PM_{10} occur. The agreement signed as part of the Programme, prescribes limitations on traffic circulation for long periods of the year for the most polluting vehicles including outright traffic blocks (with some exceptions) one day per week from January to March when no rain is forecasted and PM_{10} pollution levels above 50 $\mu g/m^3$ are expected.

The agreement signed by Modena Town Council and the other town councils – together with those councils representing more than 50,000 inhabitants – also commits the signatories to implement initiatives in favour of sustainable mobility, logistics and sustainable housing. Given the need to introduce coordinated policies applicable across a vast area in order to deal with the problem of atmospheric pollution, and bearing in mind that the European Commission itself has invited pollution prevention and reduction measures to be defined and implemented harmoniously and coordinated across the Po Basin. In October 2005, Emilia-Romagna, Lombardy, Piedmont and the Veneto regions also signed a special agreement to coordinate their own policies in this field. They have set up a technical think-tank in order to identify possible common actions to be undertaken. This agreement now also involves the Autonomous Provinces of Trento and Bolzano and, more recently, the Ticino Canton of the Swiss Confederation.[3]

Beyond the measures that have been implemented an initiative of great symbolic and also political value has been taken: on 25 February 2007, in all the above-mentioned regions there has been a total traffic block for private vehicles. The approach adopted by these regions is finally taking us towards approaching the issue of atmospheric pollution in a correct, more realistic and effective manner. In my opinion, this set of commitments and coordination of initiatives concerning ever wider territories now requires measures to ensure that the policies implemented in single areas are spread and coordinated regardless of the number of inhabitants. They should involve all the local councils across the territory and not just the largest ones.

Another theme of great importance which should not be considered secondary is the active involvement of the motorway companies in the policies of environmental protection and renewal. Modena, like much of Emilia-Romagna, is crossed by large road infrastructures which reach well into the urban area itself, causing the addition of external air pollution into the territory. Theoretically, it might thus be possible to close off the city completely to traffic but, given unfavourable wind conditions, we still would find ourselves burdened with air pollution problems caused exclusively by passing motorway traffic.

---

3 *See*, furthermore, Zanicchelli's contribution, *infra*, in Chapter 3 of this book..

Incisive initiatives (and opportunities for comparison) are therefore also needed on a national and Community level in order to deal with the specific problems of the Po Basin. Policies should be designed and supported by economic and financial means aiming at providing structural innovations, not simply emergency remedies. Likewise, it is also of fundamental importance to exploit technological innovation and the spread of new and experimental practices that allow us if not to eliminate, at least to lessen the devastating consequences of these terribly high pollution levels.

Alongside the limitation of traffic measures in the most critical periods, and the various initiatives undertaken to raise awareness among the general public as to the benefits of more sparing use of the car, there have also been a number of other measures put in place by the local administration. Of these, I might mention a few that have been implemented over the last few years:

- The compulsory exhaust-fume check for cars, which has been carried out here since 1992, and which is done on over 90% of the vehicles required to do so. This check aims to identify those vehicles whose emissions exceed the maximum thresholds set by the regulations. These vehicles are then subjected to the maintenance work necessary to bring the emission levels back to within the norm. This practice thus leads to a reduction in the emission of atmospheric pollutants as well as a reduction in the vehicles' fuel consumption.
- To encourage citizens to make use of public transport systems, not only through the creation of public transport lanes and a ticketing policy convenient for season-ticket holders, but also by way of night-time services (the Taxi BUS service) and other innovative services to satisfy particular needs (for example the ProntoBus service that, on call, links various outlying districts to the centre of town). Furthermore, a car-sharing project has been set up, with a fleet of 17 vehicles.
- The promotion of transport by bicycle and on foot, with projects like *C'entro in bici* which offers the chance to hire council-owned bicycles for free, picking them up from various points around town throughout the day, or the *Pedal* project, promoted by the Regional Government encouraging bicycle transport between home and school. The project *vado a scuola con gli amici* aimed at primary school children and promoted by *Circoscrizione* No. 3. As a matter of fact, Modena lays claim to a good 110 km of footpaths and cyclepaths, allowing for sustainable mobility in complete safety.
- Initiatives for energy saving, both in terms of reducing the consumption of electricity and of promoting the adoption of renewable energy sources such as thermal solar energy (already in use in a number of council sports centres including the *Dogali* and *Pergolesi* swimming pools and the baseball field) and photovoltaic energy (installed in various schools and in the trade fair area).

- The numerous communication and education projects that concern schools in particular, such as: *L'ora d'aria* ('Time for Air') for primary and middle school pupils to examine the theme of atmospheric pollution. *Insieme in bicicletta* ('Together on the bicycle'), the *Festa dell'aria* ('Air Party') and *Raccogliamo miglia verdi* ('Let us collect thousand times green') aim at raising awareness of and encouraging sustainable mobility. *Curiamo il nostro quartiere* ('Let us cure our district') provides pupils with an insight into the field of sustainable town planning. Finally, not to forget the European *Display* project which encourages and improves the energy efficiency of buildings up to 'class A' level.
- Discount season tickets for public transport for those who possess a pre-Euro car or a Euro 1 diesel car.
- Financial incentives for the purchase of electric vehicles (bicycles).
- Contributions towards the installation of LPG or methane gas fuel systems in more polluting vehicles.

I would like to conclude by reminding you again that we are facing here a complex issue for which there is not necessarily one simple answer. Although much has already been done in this field, there is still a lot left to achieve and more than anything else, we need to keep public opinion focused on these themes.

VANNI BULGARELLI

Ambient Air Quality in Town and Region: The Role of a Special Company

Hera Modena is one of the operating territorial companies of the Hera Group spa, a Holding for environmental and energy services. The Hera group was founded in 2002 after the successive fusion of 14 municipal utilities in the 6 provinces of the Emilia Romagna region. Hera Modena became part of it in 2005. Now Hera Modena provides services in the areas of environmental hygiene (the complete recycling of waste), water and water purification, electricity (production and distribution), gas and water systems and public illumination for over 2.7 million citizens. Hera shares are traded on the Italian stockmarket and are for 58% in public hands (municipalities and other public entities). Institutional investors own 10% and 32% is privately owned. The company employs over 6000 people, and its 2007 balance showed returns of over €2,863 million. Over 4 million tons of waste are treated per year, 3.000 Giga Watts of electric energy is sold together with over 2,400 million m^3 gas and 243 million m^3 of water is distributed and purified. In size Hera Modena is the second largest (after Bologna) of the participating societies in the Holding. It is a (very) prominent operator and stakeholder in the conduct of environmental policy in Emilia Romagna, including in respect to air pollution.

There is increasing awareness and great concern about air quality by the public, in the scientific world and among the authorities of states and cities. In areas where high economic development takes place which are characterized by specific geo-climatic conditions, air-quality has reached such a critical level that permanent negative effects for human health and ecosystems are the result. Air pollution is an indication of energy inefficiency and of low-quality socio-economic management of a territory, i.e., of limited sustainability. As is well known, there is a close relationship between air pollution and climate

HARRY H. G. POST (ED.), The Protection of Ambient Air in International and European Law, 39-41.

change. Emissions of green-house gases (mainly due to the consumption of fossil fuels) have a local impact on air quality and, at a global scale, on CO_2 concentrations.

For the protection of air quality European Community (EC) legislation is decisive. It is essential to act on a supra-national scale with coherent and efficient technical regulations, tuned to technological innovation. Community legislation also expresses, in juridical terms, the demands by citizens for a better environment, for health and security. The EC's environmental law has compelled Italy to improve its juridical instruments and its socio-economic organization, strongly stimulating innovation in many sectors of the country's civil life. It has helped to fill a gap which it could hardly have narrowed itself. The many infraction procedures (of European environmental legislation) initiated against Italy confirm how much resistance and negligence still persist in our country. There is resistance particularly in production sectors but more and more frequently also among public services (for instance in respect to waste management). There are attempts to escape social responsibility by businesses who try to reduce competitive limits by way of environmental dumping. However the lack of competitiveness is the result of a lack of innovation of products, of production cycles and of system inefficiencies.

Italy's cultural, political and economical delays in respect to environmental quality and sustainable development in addition to the resistance from the industrial world, have prevented our country from playing a propulsive role in the development of the Community's environmental legislation. Neither has it managed to play a role in the creation of norms that possibly could have been closer to our juridical culture and to our industrial systems. We mainly have passively followed the Community's norms, paying higher prices to keep the pace, mainly running behind innovation not anticipating it. This being the situation, the application of norms is now very difficult without a coherent structural strategy for sustainable development. An example of this is provided by Modena's choice in 1959 as one of the first towns in Italy to supply natural gas to private households and industries through its net. This choice structurally reduced air pollution.

Emission sources must be controlled according to legislation. Important (commercial) benefits can be achieved by introducing new and more advanced technologies. A new structuring of economic and productive models is fundamental. Likewise technological innovation, other consumption patterns, life styles and social organization are essential to reduce emissions. To support this commitment, a reinforcement of the juridical and technical-scientific culture, in addition to a more diffuse general sensitivity are needed for a new responsibility to be shared by citizens. It is, in fact, from citizens that a stronger consensus must come to innovate the economic development mechanisms on which the wealth of our country is partly based.

For the formation of this awareness a higher level of knowledge of citizens, based on adequate economic, juridical and technical information that is scientifically verified, is needed. In Italy we observe, with increasing frequency, the opposition of groups of citizens to environmental choices that are technically and juridically correct and fully in line with the policies of the European Community. At the same time, more serious phenomena are neglected due to ignorance or simple laziness. For instance, CO_2 emissions from cars recorded in Modena in 2005 were 44.370 tons/year, while only 1.784 tons/year were produced by industries, mainly by tile factories. PM_{10} produced by cars was 849 tons/year, while 315 tons/year came from industrial activities of which 248 from the tile sector. Nevertheless, the attention of public opinion is not focused on a reduced use of the (personal) car, but on other less relevant sources.

Hera Modena has decided on a twofold commitment: firstly, to make important investments and provide services for sustainability and for transparency of all technical-economical parameters, and, secondly, to support all the initiatives, above all among young people, that could be useful to promote a scientific, economical and juridical culture directed towards environmental quality.

LINO ZANICHELLI

Implementing European Policy and Law: Emilia Romagna

1. The Context of the Po River Basin and Emilia-Romagna

In respect to the bad condition of the ambient air the valley of Ruhr and Rhine/Mosel in Germany and the Po basin are the two most seriously affected areas in Europe.[1] We are dealing here with highly complex situations. The Po plain is located in a stable anticyclonic area where a thermal inversion causes pollutants generated at low altitudes to accumulate over the earth: mostly suspended particles and nitrogen oxides. In the summer the concomitance of weather conditions characterized by high pressure and intense solar radiation, subsequently causes the production and concentration of nitrogen. These pollutants have serious consequences for the health of the citizens and their life expectancy and calls for action that addresses the gravity of the problems we are facing. However, we do not intend to resign to the difficulty of the circumstances, nor to be paralysed by panic. A mixture of more incisive regulations and technological innovations can help us to govern the situation according to a sustainable development approach that must combine development, social cohesion and the protection of natural resources.

1.1. Emilia-Romagna

Emilia-Romagna is a region that traditionally has had quite a 'virtuous' management policy. Territory and urban planning have been carried out with a network of services for people and for small and medium-size businesses

1 *See* the map in Chapter 1, *supra*, at 27.

HARRY H. G. POST (ED.), The Protection of Ambient Air in International and European Law, 43-49.

that places the region at the forefront in Europe. The high number of industrial patents and level of (secondary) education illustrate the region's position in view of the Italian average (although Italy is behind compared to the EU of the 15).

In any case, the Emilia-Romagna region is in a very delicate position: It consumes a lot of natural resources which is not compatible with current environmental policy. The increasing production of special and urban waste, of energy consumption and of the number of cars in circulation over the years are signs of growth and expansion.

Geographically our region is located in the heart of the Italian north-south, east-west system. In the northwest it faces the EU of the 15, in the northeast the EU of the 25 and to the south the Mediterranean. Its links with emerging countries such as China and India provide great opportunities but could also be a threat if not correctly managed. Even today, 35% of all Italian heavy goods pass through the Emilia-Romagna.

There are local problems of dust (particulate matter – PM) and atmospheric pollution in the region that are directly linked to issues of climate change and greenhouse gases. To solve these problems will require an integrated initiative. There is a growing trend towards the rise of temperature caused by various factors on all of which greenhouse gases have a direct impact. A portion of pollutants directly concern man's activities in main industries: the percentages differ, but the cause of pollution of PM_{10} and those of CO_2 more or less originate from the same agents.

1.2. Regional Legislation Concerning Air

For all the above reasons, topics such as the quality of water, earth and air resources are an essential aspect of our policy. Since the seventies the Emilia-Romagna has paid great attention to atmospheric pollution. An example of this is the initiative (of national importance) concerning the quality of the environment in the ceramics producing area of Sassuolo-Scandiano which is in the provinces of Modena and Reggio Emilia. The project's objective was to take emission limits well below those of the current laws. As a result the district has obtained EMAS certification.

The presence of important chemical and energy plants in the region (in Ferrara, Ravenna and Piacenza) has given great input to initiatives in regional legislation.

The region's conversion to methane in energy production has helped to contain pollutants in the energy sector but it hasn't solved all the problems.

2. New European Legislation

Since the mid-nineties, European Community legislation in respect to the environment has been strongly developed and been implemented in and recognised by national legislation. Examples are Council Directives 1999/30/EC, which limits values for sulphur dioxide, nitrogen dioxide and oxides of nitrogen, particulate matter and lead in the air, and 2000/69/EC which limit values for concentrations of benzene and carbon monoxide.

These directives have set the limits that have been central to our initiatives in recent years. As regards particulate matter (PM_{10}), this must not exceed a 50 micrograms/normal cubic metre limit over 35 times a year and must not exceed an annual average of $40mc/Nm^3$.

We soon realised the difficulty of realising this standard but we did make real commitments in the first place by implementing the standards set forth in national and European legislation in regional legislation.

In 1999 the regional administration approved law n. 3 on '*regional and local system reform*'. Articles 121 and 122 of that law define a regional strategy (followed by a subsidiarity principle). The region determines criteria and policies in order to identify areas where pollution is to be limited or prevented. It sets restrictive limits, defines aims and provides monitoring and control systems. Following guidelines, the provinces will identify zones that require a plan of action for their recovery and the administrative power for system equipment.

Other regions have chosen a different approach. We remain convinced that, on the one hand, our strength lies in looking at the whole Po basin and, on the other hand, on focusing on whenever we can request participation in taking concrete action. We have done this with planning policies in the sector of waste, but we have also done so in relation to planning in emerging areas such as electromagnetism and light and sound pollution. We are sure that the regional system will prove to be strong if all those concerned continue to play their part in the overall scheme.

Currently all provincial air quality plans in the region have been adopted. They define the framework of reference and the necessary actions to be taken in the most sensitive areas. These plans are also in response to the request of the EU Commission, which has launched infringement procedures against Italy for having disregarded the aforementioned directives. There has been much participation in drawing up the plans, following the inspiration of the Agenda 21 process.

3. Regional Measures

In the meantime, we have worked on creating voluntary programme agreements between the region, its provinces and main towns with over 50,000 inhabitants.

We have reached 5 programme agreements which introduced regulative actions in respect to traffic: Circulation is now limited for the most polluting vehicles, on Thursdays there is a general ban in force for all private vehicles in the centres of towns and pedestrian areas and restrictive traffic areas will be enlarged .

Alongside this initiative we have undertaken various actions to support sustainable policies. In the mobility sector we have begun the renewal of local public transport, upgrading buses and re-launching minor railways by setting up a regional company (FER-Ferrovie Emilia Romagna), which re-launched some minor rail links (i.e. Bologna-Vignola).

In 2006 we increased cycle lanes to cover around 1,000 km, compared to 491 km in 2000.

At the same time, in towns affected by the agreement, limited traffic areas (excluding pedestrian areas) grew from 7,1% to 9,8% with an increase of around 10 km^2.

Furthermore, we wanted to examine the 'balance' of these agreements concluded in our Region in order to measure their effectiveness and find positive as well as some critical aspects that have emerged from the experience. The critical aspects are mainly related to the reduction of lanes reserved for public transportation, which has slowed down public transport making it less competitive with private transport.

Another important aspect of the measures we have taken has been to update monitoring technology with a notable investment in the upgrade of monitoring equipment for measuring fine and ultra fine PM, ensuring that it conforms with European regulations.

The citizen information and service campaign entitled '*Liberiamo l'aria*' (free the air) has been of particular importance to communicate and explain the measures taken; it has increasingly been taken on board.

4. Co-operation and Agreement in Emilia-Romagna

Five years of intense dialogue and concluding agreements have nevertheless left us with a situation that is still uncertain.

Our research has supplied us with very worrying data. If we 'switched off' Emilia-Romagna and brought emissions to zero, we would improve conditions by 20-30% in areas close to the border, such as Piacenza, and by 40-50% in central areas and the coast.[2]

For this reason, we have given ourselves a new aim: to work for the whole basin area and coordinate the initiatives. The car-free day of 25 February 2007 was not designed to change atmospheric pollution but to send out a message about the commitment required for the basin area.

The protocol on the quality of the air in the area of the Padana ('*La qualità dell'aria nell'area padana*') includes :

1) to adopt progressive limits regarding the circulation of the most polluting vehicles in order to increase the renewal of vehicles and direct the market towards types that will have a lower impact on the environment;
2) to define and adopt common emission 'standards' for production activities and for civil sources, within the autonomy granted to the subscribing entities by current national regulations;
3) to promote and facilitate the installation of filters against PM and similar devices that reduce emissions, on new vehicles and progressively on existing vehicles;
4) to define and adopt regulations for the use of combustibles, including ligneous biomasses for heating, for which the spreading of better technical solutions is required;
5) to share and technically improve the Inventory of Emissions in the Air (INEMAR) and the model supporting the elaboration and inspection of regional plans and programmes.

Our regional actions and measures are moving in the same direction

5. Actions in Particular Areas

5.1. Energy

A regional Energy Plan has been approved by the regional council. It is 'a new generation' plan that bases its actions on fossil fuel with a low environmental impact, especially natural gas.

The focus has been placed on energy saving and renewable sources which, in Emilia-Romagna, can yield great results. By 2010 we wish to achieve notable energy savings within the main industries of transport, civil consumption and production.

2 *See* the figures and tables in chapter 1, *supra*.

5.2. Production

Production companies have already made significant investments. We are by far the best Italian region for EMAS (Eco-Management and Audit System) and Ecolabel quality certifications, a demonstration of our desire for environmental quality. Strengthening 'system' policies will be of the utmost importance. We have approved guidelines for Ecologically Equipped Areas that we wish to upgrade in terms of technological innovation, networks and environmental quality. Environmental integration procedures concerning companies represent an opportunity to improve all system performances.

5.3. Mobility

Mobility is a very demanding sector where full scale action must be taken. We do not oppose the construction of infrastructures that are essential for high-speed rail links (which are reaching completion), the '*cispadana*' and '*pedemontana*' networks, and south-north and south-northeast road links.

The problem lies in constructing a transport system that is far more integrated than it is today. For this reason we have asked the Government to use resources that can be obtained from the rigorous policy it has adopted in order to accelerate the development of public rail and road transport.

The new Operational Plan for European structural funds gives many resources to systems that have an environmental spin-off in the areas of research, technology networks, logistics, energy saving and qualification.

5.4. Research and Innovation

An essential topic for the future will be research and innovation in the environmental field. A good example is provided by the research and innovation network of Emilia-Romagna's industrial system, notably in respect to the use of Hythane (HCNG). We must continue to make investments in this direction. The agreement signed on 28 September 2006 with, inter alia ENEA (*Ente Nazionale per l'Energia*) is relevant to this area of intervention. Experiments using hythane, a new hydrogen/natural gas blend fuel that creates less pollution than methane, may lead to fuel buses circulating in the region as well as certain private vehicles.

5.5. Sustainability Education

Last but not least we have addressed sustainability education and citizen behaviour. This is one of the most difficult and delicate topics to deal with.

On 21 March 2007, the first day of spring, we initiated the air festival, in agreement with the Regional School Office and the schools. Each class will be able to count the CO_2 savings obtained using sustainable mobility, bicycles, buses or pedestrian routes. Last year this event took already place in some provinces, one of which was Modena; a 70-ton saving of CO_2 was recorded there in just two weeks.

6. Conclusion

> Thus, astride our bucket, we shall face the new millennium, without hoping to find any more in it than what we ourselves are able to bring to it.
>
> Italo Calvino, American Lectures

PART II

Law

Phoebe Okowa

The Legal Framework for the Protection of the Environment Against Transboundary Air Pollution:

A Reflection on Customary and Treaty Law

1. Customary Law and the Trail Smelter Decision

Although the protection of the environment against air pollution has largely been eclipsed by global problems in the areas of climate Change and protection of biodiversity resources,[1] it retains a unique place as having provided the occasion for the articulation of international law rules that apply in the field of environmental protection. The dispute leading to the Trail Smelter Decisions of 1938 and 1941 provides a useful starting point from which to assess the framework of accountability that exists in international law for transboundary air pollution damage.

This was a dispute concerning transboundary air pollution between the United States and Canada. A Canadian Company at Trail in British Columbia was emitting sulphur dioxide fumes, which as the tribunal found were causing damage to crops and timber in the state of Washington. In reaching its decision the tribunal was considerably influenced by a compromissory agreement between the two parties, in which the responsibility of Canada as the defendant state was assumed. It was therefore primarily concerned with the apportionment of damage and not with the formulation of general rules.

However, the tribunals' famous pronouncement, that

1 *See* Sustainable Development: the UK Strategy (CM2426), Ch. 6; D. French, *1997 Kyoto Protocol to the 1992 UN Framework Convention on Climate Change*, 10 JEL 227 (1998).

Harry H. G. Post (Ed.), The Protection of Ambient Air in International and European Law, 53-71.

> under the principles of international law, as well as the law of the United States, no State has the right to use or permit the use of its territory in such a manner as to cause injury by fumes in or to the territory of another or the properties of persons therein, when the case is of serious consequence and the injury is established by clear and convincing evidence

in many ways irrevocably confirmed that transboundary environmental damage and specifically transboundary air pollution entailed state responsibility.[2] The principle itself was by no means novel nor remarkable, for international law had always held states accountable for damage resulting from activities on their territory, on the basis of the presumed territorial control that a state exercises.[3] There were already variants of its application in the context of the law on the non-navigational uses of international watercourses.[4] For instance in the San Juan River Case,[5] an arbitral tribunal was established by Costa Rica and Nicaragua to delimit the common boundary with Nicaragua in accordance with the terms of an applicable treaty. Although concerned with the interpretation of the terms of a water treaty, a number of pronouncements were made by Grover Cleveland, president of the United States, acting as arbitrator which are relevant to the present inquiry. He observed that:

> The Republic of Costa Rica cannot prevent the Republic of Nicaragua from executing … within her own territory … works of improvement provided such works of improvement do not result in the occupation or flooding or damage of Costa Rican territory, or in the destruction or serious impairment of the navigation of the said river or any of its branches at any point where Costa Rica is entitled to navigate the same. The Republic of Costa Rica has the right to demand indemnification for any lands on the same bank [of the River San Juan] which may be … flooded or damaged in any other way in consequence of works of improvement. The natural rights of the Republic of Costa Rica … are not to be deemed injured in any case where the territory belonging to the Republic of Costa Rica is occupied or flooded.[6]

Although the tribunal was not strictly speaking concerned with the determination of general principles that would apply across the board in all cases of transboundary damage, nevertheless, the passage was couched in the most general terms and must be taken to be a reflection of the applicable principles of general international law especially given the status of the

---

2 *Trail Smelter Arbitral Decision*, 35 AJIL 684, at 716 (1941).

3 *Alabama Claims Arbitration (1872), in* J. B. Moore, History and Digest of International Arbitrations Vol. 1 (1898), at 495; I. Brownlie, System of the Law of Nations: State Responsibility (1983); P. Okowa, State Responsibility for Transboundary Air Pollution in International Law 65 (2000).

4 *See* S. C. McCaffrey, The Law of International Watercourses – Non-Navigational Uses 211 (2001).

5 *The San Juan River Case (Costa Rica v. Nicaragua), Award of 22 March 1888, in* J. B. Moore, History and Digest of International Arbitrations Vol. 2 (1898).

6 *Id.*, at 1964-1966.

arbitrator.[7] It would therefore not be overstating the case to say that the novelty of the Trail Smelter arbitration lay in contextualising the application of the 'no harm principle' to the field of industrial pollution. The *compromis* concluded by the two litigant states had itself envisaged this by empowering the tribunal to

> apply the law and practice followed in dealing with cognate questions in the United States of America as well as international law and practice and shall give consideration to the desire of the High Contracting parties to reach a solution just to all parties concerned.[8]

A number of problems identified by the tribunal were to resonate in unexpected ways in the context of the much more complex problems of long-range transboundary air pollution. First is the question of scientific uncertainty. The tribunal awarded compensation for damage in the face of much scientific uncertainty. The first question submitted to the tribunal required it to determine "[w]hether damage caused by the Trail Smelter in the State of Washington has occurred since the first day of January 1932?" The tribunal had to find an answer to this question in the face of divergent and contradictory scientific opinion. Evidence of widespread damage due to the fumigations was presented by US scientists, but those engaged by the Canadian government treated the damage as insignificant. In many ways, the dispute was as much about the content of the applicable law as it was about the appropriate scientific basis for apportioning of damage. Significantly, the tribunal decisively rejected the 'invisible injury claim' put forward by American scientists as not appropriately substantiated.[9] The tribunal concluded:

> The contention made by the United States that fumigation prevents germination of seed is, in the opinion of the tribunal, not sustained by the evidence .... The tribunal is of the opinion that it is not proved that fumigation prevents trees from producing sufficient trees.[10]

The limitation to damage quantifiable in economic terms was to prove a lasting limitation of the liability model, especially, when applied to the new and more complex problems of long-range transboundary air pollution. As discussed below, the hallmark of the problems associated with long-range pollution is that the resulting harm is usually undetectable owing to the complex processes that pollutants undergo before causing damage. Not surprisingly, the bulk of the international effort in dealing with transboundary air pollution has been

---

[7] S. McCaffrey, *Fifth Report on the Law on Non-Navigational Uses of International Watercourses*, 1989 (II, Part I) YILC 91, at 113.

[8] Convention on Damages Resulting from Operation of the Smelter at Trail, British Columbia, 5 June 1935, US-Canada, Art IV, 49 Stat. 3245.

[9] J. D. Wirth, Smelter Smoke in North America 38 (2000); For a recent account of the background and history of the dispute, *see* R. M. Bratspies & R. Miller, Transboundary Harm in International Law; Lessons from the Trail Smelter Arbitration (2006).

[10] Trail Smelter Arbitratal Decision, *supra* note 2, at 204.

directed to co-operative and regulatory models rather than the liability model. Moreover, in the Trail Smelter case both the source of harm and the receptors were clearly identifiable; in the problems of long-range pollution that emerged in the 70's and early 80's a straightforward relationship of cause and effect was not always possible. In Europe, the complexity is compounded by the phenomenon of globalization and the needs of regional economic integration, both making it difficult to locate the activities of a company or industrial plant with one particular state.

The tribunal awarded an indemnity of $78,000 dollars for damage between 1932 and 1937. However this victory was hedged with the very significant restriction that the obligation to pay compensation would only arise when the resulting harm is of serious consequence and established by clear and convincing evidence. The third question under the 1935 treaty required the tribunal to propose a regime that would reduce the amount of pollutants to one that was scientifically acceptable. The tribunal thus also established a permanent regime, with aim of reducing the amount of sulphur pollutants released to a level that was deemed least injurious to the interests of the American farming community.

The general principle in the *Trail Smelter Case* has also received the explicit endorsement of the International Court of Justice in its recent jurisprudence. In its *Advisory Opinion on the Legality of the Threat or Use of Nuclear Weapons*, the Court noted that the existence of the general obligation to ensure that activities within their jurisdiction and control respect the environment of other states or of areas beyond national control is now part of the corpus of international law relating to the environment.[11]

Notwithstanding its limitations, the arbitral award was to prove of lasting significance in so far as it emphasised the responsibility of states to prevent activities on their territory from causing harm to the territory of others. Thus, even when the imposition of liability has not been the preferred model, the existence of an obligation of prevention has proved invaluable in the negotiation of more concrete regimes such as those taken under the auspices of the 1979 ECE Convention and its Protocols (see Section 3, below). It has provided the incentive to negotiate, and given legal imprimatur to treaty making processes, as well as influencing the content of the emerging regulatory regimes.

2. Long-Range Transboundary Air Pollution

Before discussing the treaty framework for the regulation of long-range pollution it is useful to give a brief account of the nature of the problem. Unlike

[11] Advisory Opinion on the Legality of the Threat or Use of Nuclear Weapons, 1996 ICJ Rep. 226, at 241 para. 29; *See also* Gabčíkovo-Nagymaros (Hungary/Slovakia), 1997 ICJ Rep. 7, at 81-82.

the localised problem in the *Trail Smelter Case*, a distinctive feature of long-range transboundary air pollution is the general inability to trace the precise sources of pollutants that eventually cause damage.[12] This is largely due to the fact that owing to the large number of possible sources in different states, as well as the complex chemical processes that pollutants undergo before eventually causing damage, the determination of a cause/effect relationship is in most cases elusive.[13] These complexities have not only influenced the form of regulatory regimes, it also poses a unique problem for the rules on state responsibility and the conditions for their availability. Many of these rules have largely been concerned with discrete bilateral disputes where the source of harm and victim were clearly identifiable. Their application to a cumulative and multilateral problem has never really been tested.

Long-range transboundary air pollution has been defined as:

> air pollution whose physical origin is situated wholly or in part within the area under the national jurisdiction of one state and which had adverse effect in the area under the jurisdiction of another state at such a distance that it is not generally possible to distinguish the contribution of individual emission sources or groups of sources.[14]

The pollutants responsible for long-range transboundary air pollution have the capacity to remain airborne for several days and travel over thousands of kilometers before being deposited. The spatial scale of these problems can range from hundreds of thousands to a million square kilometers. Although the level of emissions contributed by particular states can now be measured using monitoring techniques, these are in almost all cases dependent on data supplied by States, and other variables such as weather patterns.[15] The precise contribution of individual states to the problem remains elusive.

Long-range pollution invariably involves a multiplicity of states in a complex relationship either as source or receptor states. The behaviour of long-range pollutants, notably their transportation over long-distances, chemical transformation, interaction with other compounds and subsequent deposition is well documented. Indeed, air pollution monitoring programmes in Europe have been able to point out that the problem of transboundary air pollution is a regional one, in which all European States are both 'exporters'

[12] A. Record, Acid Rain Information Book (1982), Sec. 2, at 31.

[13] J. M. Alcamo & E. Runca, *Some Technical Dimensions of Transboundary Air Pollution*, *in* C. Flinterman, B. Kwiatkowska & J. G. Lammers (Eds.), Transboundary Air Pollution 235 (1986).

[14] 1979 Geneva Convention on Long-Range Transboundary Air Pollution, 1302 UNTS 217, in force 16 March 1983.

[15] T. Iversen, *et al.*, *Airborne Transboundary Transport of Sulphur and Nitrogen over Europe-Model Descriptions and Calculations*, EMEP/MSC-W Report 2/89 (1989); Calperine, *Trajectory Model of Long-Range Air Pollutant Transport for the Calculation of Deposition and Concentration*, WMO/TD No. 187 (1987); UNECE, Impacts of Long-Range Transboundary Air Pollution 201 (1982).

and 'importers' of pollutants. Every European country, for instance, receives and sends acidifying compounds across its borders. In most of the European countries monitored through the co-operative programme for the monitoring and evaluation of long-range transboundary air pollution (EMEP), the majority of the pollution was found to be the result of emission from foreign sources.[16] For instance, more than 60% of the sulphur deposition in Norway, Sweden, Switzerland, Austria, the Netherlands, and Eastern Canada originates in other countries. Countries such as Switzerland suffer almost exclusively from foreign emissions

At the 1984 Munich Multilateral Conference on the Environment, the delegation of Denmark observed that approximately 75% of the sulphur dioxide emitted in Denmark is transported to other countries. At the same time about 65% of the total deposits of Sulphur compounds in Denmark were foreign in origin.[17] The fact that some states receive more pollutants than they emit has led to an underlying tension between those who are mainly recipients of pollutants and net emitters. In the negotiations leading to the 1979 ECE Convention on Transboundary Air Pollution, the principal recipients of pollution, most notably the Scandinavian Countries and Canada, would have preferred concrete emission standards. Countries such as the United Kingdom and the United States, who are mainly emitters, on the other hand were reluctant to accept stringent commitments that would have resulted in reduced industrial output. The underlying tension between recipients and emitters explains the qualified nature of the legal regimes, since a compromise had to be reached between the extreme positions advocated by the two groups of states.[18]

3. The 1979 ECE Convention on Transboundary Air Pollution[19]

This is perhaps the most comprehensive treaty directly regulating transboundary air pollution. Negotiated under the auspices of the United Nations Economic Commission for Europe (ECE), it is a framework convention outlining a set of agreed general principles, as well as mechanisms for negotiating more specific

[16] EMEP/MSC-W Report 1/88 Estimates of Airborne Transboundary Transport of Sulphur and Nitrogen over Europe, Oslo, August 1988; EMEP/MSC-W Report 1/89; UN ECE, Effects and Control of Long-Range Transboundary Air Pollution Studies No. 10 (New York 1994).

[17] Multilateral Conference on the Environment, Munich 24 May-7 June 1984, Ann. 5.11. For similar claims by Norway, *see* statement by the Norwegian Minister for the Environment and Housing Division to the ECE Special Group on Long-Range Transboundary Air Pollution at 2 (Text supplied by the ECE Secretariat).

[18] *See* for instance R. R. Churchill, K. Kutting & L. Warren, *The 1994 UNECE Sulphur Protocol*, 7 JEL 169, at 169-179 (1994).

[19] Geneva Convention on Long-Range Transboundary Air Pollution, *supra* note 14.

and concrete standards for the abatement of transboundary air pollution. Protocols lay down relatively specific standards for the control of sulphur, nitrogen, and volatile organic compounds. Thus while the Convention sets broad goals for reducing transboundary air pollution, the Protocols address specific sources of pollutants and lay down concrete remedial measures.

Although the idea of a Convention to control transboundary air pollution had been put forward by Scandinavian countries at the 1972 Stockholm conference on the Human Environment, a more direct impetus can be traced to the Conference on Security and Co-operation in Europe which took place from July 1973 to August 1975. The final Act of the Conference reiterated a commitment to the prevention of pollution beyond national limits. It required states to co-ordinate their efforts to control pollution. The participating states were exhorted to promote:

> the progressive development, codification and implementation of international law as one means of preserving and enhancing the human environment, including principles and practices as accepted by them, relating to pollution and other environmental damage caused by activities within their jurisdiction or control of their states affecting other countries.[20]

It is against this background that the Convention was negotiated under the auspices of the ECE, an umbrella organisation whose membership includes east and west European states, as well as Canada and the United States.

According to Article 1(b), the Convention is directed at the regulation of:

> Air pollution whose physical origin is situated wholly or in part within the area under the national jurisdiction of another state and which has adverse effects in the area under the jurisdiction of another state at such a distance that it is not generally possible to distinguish the contribution of individual emission sources or groups of sources.

This definition is comprehensive in terms and some writers have suggested that it applies to all forms of transboundary air pollution including nuclear pollution.[21] With respect, this is difficult to justify. The negotiation and debates that preceded the adoption of the convention leave no doubt that it was aimed at the reduction of pollutants that are the main precursors of acid rain, notably sulphur and nitrogen oxides. Thus in keeping with the maxim inclusion *unius est exclusion alterius*, it may be presumed that since the definition of air pollution was stated for a particular purpose, it is meant for that purpose only.[22]

[20] Conference on Security and Co-operation in Europe, Final Act, 14 ILM 1292 (1975).
[21] P. Sands, Chernobyl Law and Communication 36 (1988).
[22] A. McNair, The Law of Treaties 399 (1961).

3.1. Substantive Provisions

The substantive obligations of the states parties to the Convention are to be found in three key Articles. Article 2 provides that:

> The contracting parties, taking due account of the facts and the problems involved are determined to protect man and his environment against air pollution and shall endeavour to limit, and, as far as possible, gradually reduce and prevent air pollution, including long-range transboundary air pollution.

And under Article 3:

> The contracting parties, within the framework of the present Convention, shall by means of exchanges of information, consultation, and research and monitoring, develop without undue delay policies and strategies which shall serve as a means of combating the discharge of air pollutants taking into account efforts already made at national and international levels.

Finally Article 6 concerning air quality management provides that:

> Taking into account Articles 2 to 5, the on-going research, exchange of information and monitoring and the results thereof, the cost and effectiveness of local and other remedies and, in order to combat air pollution, in particular that originating from new or rebuilt installations, each contracting party undertakes to develop the best policies and strategies including air quality management systems, and as part of them, control measures compatible with balanced development, in particular by using the best available technology which is economically feasible and low- and non-waste technology.

There is little doubt that these obligations are general in character and do not lay down any concrete standards to be observed. However, they create obligations of result, an expectation that pollution strategies will be put in place. In each case a state party is required to achieve a reduction in the level of emissions, but is left a wide margin of appreciation as to the exact modalities of doing so. States are thus only required to exercise due diligence and to that extent mirror an emerging principle of customary law, under which states are only responsible if they fail to take all practical and necessary measures to prevent pollution.[23]

It has nevertheless been suggested by a number of writers that the obligations in the 1979 ECE treaty are no more than a political commitment without any binding effect breach of which could not be an appropriate basis for imposition of liability.[24] These writers suggest that the open ended character of the obligations precludes any external verification of compliance, and that in so far as each state party is free to determine for itself whether the

---

[23] *See* American Law Institute, *Third Restatement* (St. Paul 1987) Sec. 601 and accompanying commentary; P. Birnie & A. Boyle, International Law and the Environment 389 (1992).

[24] I. Van Lier, Acid Rain and International Law (1981); J. Brunnee, Acid Rain and Ozone Depletion 113 (1988).

measures taken are in keeping with conventional obligations, the provisions are devoid of legal character and must be seen as purely programmatic and aspirational. However the interpretation of the 1979 ECE treaty in its context and in light of its object and purpose as required by Article 31 of the Vienna Convention militates against any conclusion that the treaty is a political instrument devoid of legal effect. The generality of the provisions is not so much a lack of intention to create legal relations, but rather the result of an attempt to accommodate the different interests of the states parties who were reluctant to accept more definite commitments.[25]

A number of other reasons may also be proffered for the open-ended character of these provisions. In the first place, it has been noted that the scientific uncertainty surrounding the causes and effects of transboundary air pollution made many states reluctant to accept concrete commitments. They questioned the necessity of taking measures that would result in reduced industrial output in the absence of concrete evidence that reduction of emissions would stop acidification of lakes and forests. Secondly, a number of less-developed European States such as Ireland, Greece and Portugal were not prepared to accept stringent anti-pollution measures that would significantly hamper their industrial development.

Thirdly, it is generally accepted that a certain amount of flexibility is required in formulating environmental obligations. For while the setting of specific goals such as ambient air quality standards or acceptable loads of pollutants that can be tolerated by the environment, may be a more effective means of realising environmental objectives, changing scientific evidence as to the nature of pollutants and their effects means that fixed obligations concerning emission levels quickly become outdated. As a result many treaties regulating pollution invariably start with a framework convention, which may then be followed with more specific obligations in an annex or a Protocol in light of new evidence and advances in technology.[26] The adoption of a framework Convention has the distinct advantage of creating a mechanism for on-going negotiation, enabling the parties to adjust or amend their obligations according to changes in scientific knowledge.

The challenge to the legal quality of the provisions of the 1979 Convention has also been grounded on the fact that a footnote to Article 8 of the Convention

---

[25] A Nordic Proposal which would have required the Convention to impose emission limits and lay down concrete reduction targets was rejected by negotiating parties, especially the main pollution exporting countries – the United Kingdom and the Federal Republic of Germany. *See* the Draft Convention for the ECE Region on the Reduction of Emissions Causing Transboundary Air Pollution, 4 EPL (1978). A draft Canadian proposal that would have required the States parties to observe agreed air quality standards based on a dose/effect relationship was also rejected (Proposal submitted by the delegation of Canada to the ECE, 11 January 1979). Text supplied by the Air pollution Division of the ECE.

[26] *See* the 1985 Vienna Convention for the Protection of the Ozone Layer, 24 ILM 1529 (1985), in force 22 September 1988.

expressly provides that the present Convention does not contain a rule on state liability as to damage. It is then argued that the footnote was inserted to make it clear that the state parties to the convention did not intend it to attract any legal consequences. This argument is in many ways a non-sequitur. Many treaties of undoubted legal quality do not contain any provisions on sanctions. Yet the absence of such provisions has never been cited as detracting from their legal quality.

It is true that the negotiating history was strongly influenced by a desire to reduce pollution through co-operation rather than the imposition of liability. But there is nothing to suggest that the intention was to exclude the application of the regime of state responsibility, or the normal remedies for breach of international law altogether. In many ways the provision itself is superfluous, since it is clear from the text of the convention that it does not as such contain provisions on responsibility of liability. Under the normal rules of treaty interpretation, issues of responsibility fall to be determined in accordance with customary law principles, unless the treaty expressly provides for consequences of breach

3.2. The 1985 Helsinki Sulphur Protocol[27]

The resolution adopted by the signatory states at the time of the adoption of the ECE Convention attached priority to the abatement of pollutants caused by sulphur compounds. Two subsequent ministerial conferences strongly urged the adoption of more concrete measures to curb the ever-increasing effects of acidification. As a result the 1985 Sulphur Protocol was adopted under the auspices of the executive body, the principal supervisory body established under Article 10 of the 1979 ECE Convention.

The Protocol's key provision is to be found in Article 2. It required the States Parties to reduce "… their national annual sulphur emissions or their transboundary fluxes by at least 30% as soon as possible and at the latest by 1993, using 1980 levels when as the basis for calculation of reductions." For those States that acceded to the Protocol after 1990, the date for complying with the reduction could have been later than 1993, but in all instances the reduction levels had to be achieved by 1993.[28] This arrangement enabled the many states that were either unwilling or unable to ratify the Protocol to do so at a later date when domestic circumstances permitted. The obligation to reduce emissions on the basis of the 1980 levels implicitly meant that the

[27] 1985 Helsinki Protocol on the Reduction of Sulphur Emissions or their Transboundary Fluxes by at Least 30 Percent, 27 ILM 698 (1988), in force 2 September 1987.
[28] Art. 10(3).

Convention imposed a moratorium on further emissions. This obligation left a wide discretion as to the precise modalities of implementing it and to that extent, it too can be characterised as an obligation of result.

It is generally agreed that a reduction of 30% was on all accounts modest, and unlikely to have any real impact on the acidification of Lakes and forests across Europe.[29] By introducing a flat rate for emissions, the convention failed to take into account variations in emission levels and effects between the different countries. This was in fact the main reason why the less developed states of Europe, notably Ireland, Greece and Portugal refused to ratify the Protocol.[30] These States argued that their own contribution to sulphur emissions was insignificant and that reductions on their part were therefore not warranted. A 30% reduction was nevertheless adopted as an acceptable compromise since those ratifying the Protocol were not prepared to accept more stringent commitments.

A large number of states, some of them with a significantly high level of emissions, failed to ratify the Protocol, thus minimizing its impact.[31] These States include the United Kingdom, the United States, Yugoslavia, Portugal, Poland, Romania, Spain, Turkey, Greece, Iceland, and Ireland. Of this group, the United States, the United Kingdom, Poland, and Spain contribute appreciably to the total emission levels.

Some of the States, such as Poland, felt that they lacked the technological capacity to meet the obligation stipulated in Article 2. The United States and the United Kingdom were of the view that the decision to base reduction of emissions on the 1980 levels failed to take into account the very significant reductions they had made before 1980. They also argued that a 30% reduction level was both onerous and unnecessary in light of the scientific uncertainty surrounding the link between emissions and acidification of lakes as well as forest damage.[32]

It is undeniable that the obligation assumed by the parties to the Protocol was not necessarily the most effective way of protecting the interests at stake. A more effective means would have been based on the capacity of the environment to tolerate pollutants without causing significant damage, the so called 'critical loads approach'. The Scandinavian countries would have preferred a more stringent agreement but had to compromise in view of the fact that most states are reluctant to make extensive commitments.[33]

---

[29] J. G. Lammers, *The European Approach to Acid Rain, in* D. B. Magraw (Ed.), International Law and Pollution 275 (1991).

[30] *See* Statement by the Head of the Delegation of the Republic of Ireland at the Third Meeting of the Executive Body of the Convention on Long-Range Transboundary Air Pollution (Helsinki 1985 – Texts supplied by the Air Pollution Division of the ECE).

[31] D. Woolley *et al.*, Environmental Law 101 (1999).

[32] *Id.*

[33] Okowa, *supra* note 3, at 38.

It is also significant that although there was already a marked downward trend in sulphur emissions, the commitment in the Protocol gave a legal force to this trend, and effectively acted as a barrier against the resumption of increased emissions in the event of changed economic circumstances. In any event, within the terms of its provisions, the Protocol must be hailed as a success as all the parties were able to achieve the 30% reduction target, and overall a 50% reduction in the emission of sulphur oxides has been achieved.[34]

3.3. The 1994 Oslo Sulphur Protocol[35]

The legal regime envisaged by the 1985 Sulphur Protocol was intended to remain in operation until 1993, after which it was hoped that it would be replaced by a new and more stringent Protocol. After protracted negotiations, the second Sulphur Protocol was opened for signature in 1994. It is clear that the many shortcomings of the 1985 Protocol led to a completely new approach being adopted in its successor. The new Protocol avoids many of the shortcomings of the previous Protocols. In particular, the flat rate of emission reduction has been replaced by a set of varied flexible targets, taking into account the different levels of state contributions to the Sulphur problem.

The main obligation of the parties is that contained in Article 2 which requires them to ensure that their emissions in the long term do not exceed the critical loads for sulphur given in Annex I.[36] Annex II specifies the levels and timing of reductions to be achieved by each of the states parties annually. These levels have been specifically varied to take into account the different state contributions to the air pollution problem as well as the different effects of sulphur emissions in the contracting states. A further flexibility built into the Protocol is that it allowed the parties to vary reduction levels within different areas under their jurisdiction.[37] The flexibility allows states to concentrate on those areas that have significantly high proportions of sulphur emissions, thus avoiding the need to adopt uniform measures throughout the whole of their country.

An additional improvement in the new Protocol is that the parties were given guidance as to the measures that may be adopted in order to accelerate the realisation of their emission targets. These include, *inter alia*

---

[34] *See* UNECE Air Pollution Studies, *The State of Transboundary Air Pollution Studies*. No. 12, (1996).

[35] 1994 Oslo Protocol on Further Reduction of Sulphur Emissions, 33 ILM 1540 (1994), in force since 5 August 1998.

[36] Ann. 1 of the Protocol defines 'critical load' as a quantitative estimate of an exposure to one or more pollutants below which significant harmful effects on specified sensitive elements of the environment do not occur according to present knowledge.

[37] Art. 2(3). *See generally* Ann. II.

- Measures to increase energy efficiency
- Measures to increase the use of renewable energy
- Measures to reduce the sulphur content of particular fuels and to encourage the use of fuel with a low sulphur content, including the combined use of high sulphur with low-sulphur or sulphur free fuel
- Measures to apply the best available control technologies not entailing excessive cost.
- In addition the parties are encouraged to apply economic incentives and disincentives as part of the methods for realising cost-effective reduction of sulphur emissions.

Although the obvious effectiveness of some of these measures had been known for some time, their formal inclusion in the Protocol was welcomed, for it underscored the importance of extra-legal procedures as a means of realizing the parties' formal commitments.

More specific provisions related to the reduction of emissions from large-scale combustion plants and the sulphur content of gas oil. Under Article 2(5), all new combustion plants are to be subjected to the stringent emission standards contained in Annex V. However the parties had some degree of flexibility in relation to existing plants; these did not have to conform to the stringent standards specified in Annex V until 1 July 2004. Within two years after the entry into force of the Protocol, the parties were required to apply national standards for the sulphur content of gas oil at least as stringent as those specified in Annex V. However, in those instances where compliance with these provisions may entail difficulties, the parties could extend the period of compliance for a further period of ten years.

A number of the provisions of the Protocol were also a marked improvement on the 1985 Protocol. As part of the ongoing review of the measures adopted, the parties are required to put in place ongoing monitoring procedures. The collection of information on the actual levels of emissions and the effects of the depositions on the environment proved invaluable in assessing the effectiveness of the Convention.[38] Article 5, like its predecessor in the 1985 Sulphur Protocol contained the reporting obligations of the parties. A new provision in Article 7 provided for the monitoring of compliance. This article established an implementation committee whose primary task was to review the extent of compliance with the Protocol's provisions based on reports submitted. Although the provisions did not envisage measures of a coercive nature, the Committee had powers to recommend measures that were likely to ensure that a party fulfilled its obligations under the Convention. Article 8 envisaged review of the parties' obligations as well as the progress made at periodic meetings of the executive body. At such review meetings parties are expected to take into account changes in technology and economic conditions

[38] Art. 4(2).

as well as the extent to which they have complied with obligations under the protocol.[39] It has been suggested that as a result of undertakings in this Protocol, European sulphur emissions will likely to be reduced by 60% by 2010 as from 1980 [40]

3.4. The 1988 Sofia NO_x Protocol[41]

Since Sulphur and Nitrogen are the main precursors of acid rain, it is not surprising that as soon as agreement was reached on the reduction of sulphur emissions, oxides of nitrogen became the immediate object of attention. In 1988, a Protocol to the Convention was adopted at Sofia. Under the Protocol, the State parties undertook to stabilize their nitrogen emissions. Under Article 2(1) the parties undertake to:

> take effective measures to control and or reduce their national annual emissions of nitrogen oxides or transboundary fluxes so that these, at the latest by 31 December 1994, do not exceed their national annual emissions of nitrogen oxides or transboundary fluxes of such emissions for the calendar year 1987 or any previous year to be specified upon signature of, or accession to, the Protocol, provided that in addition, with respect to any party specifying such a previous year, its national average annual trans-boundary fluxes or national average annual emissions of nitrogen oxides for the period 1 January 1987 to 1 January 1996 do not exceed its transboundary fluxes or national emissions for the calendar year 1987.

In the second instance, the parties agreed progressively to reduce emissions from new as well as existing stationary and automobile sources of nitrogen pollutants. The obligations here, like those under the Sulphur protocol may be characterized as requiring the exercise of due diligence. Although the parties were under a duty to apply national emission standards to new mobile and stationary sources, this was only in so far as such measures were economically and technologically feasible. The State party was not however, the final arbiter of the economic feasibility or otherwise of the measures adopted under the Convention, and the measures adopted may under appropriate conditions be the subject-matter of scrutiny by the Executive body, the principal supervisory organ under the Protocol.

The Protocol allowed States parties to it to select a year previous to 1987 as the reference point for the stabilization of emissions. As Lammers has pointed

---

[39] Art. 9 contains non-mandatory provisions on dispute settlement which are not different in form or substance from those contained in previous Protocols. However, an important innovation is to be found in Art. 9(6) which establishes a Conciliation Commission with power to make recommendatory wards which parties are expected to consider in good faith.

[40] *See* Birnie & Boyle, *supra* note 23, at 510.

[41] 1988 Sofia Protocol Concerning the Control of Emissions of Nitrogen Oxides or Their Transboundary Fluxes, 28 ILM 212 (1989), in force 14 February 1991.

out, the ability to select a year previous to 1987 introduces a flexible element in the Convention, allowing the parties whose emissions have declined as a result of reduced economic activities to select a year during which their emissions were at their highest.[42] In this way the obligation was deemed not too onerous should the state in question resume a high level of economic activity.

Apart from stabilization of emissions, the parties were also required to apply national emission standards to new or substantially modified stationary sources, and new mobile sources, having regard to the best available technology and the economic feasibility of the measures to be taken. In applying these standards the parties were to take into account the technical Annex, and in respect of mobile sources, the relevant decisions taken within the framework of the Inland Transport Committee of the ECE.

Three other Articles elaborate the substantive obligations of the parties. Article 4 requires the parties to make unleaded fuel sufficiently available no later than two years after the entry into force of the Convention. This is to facilitate the circulation of vehicles with catalytic converters. Like the provision in Article 2, this too may be characterised as an obligation of result. The parties are left a wide margin of appreciation as to the exact modalities of compliance. Articles 6 and 7 of the Protocol required the parties to initiate a number of measures with a view to reducing the emissions of nitrogen oxides. In particular, Article 6 required the parties to identify the effects of nitrogen emissions on humans, plant, and animal life, waters, soils and materials, as well as the geographical distribution of such pollutants. Article 7 required the parties to:

> … develop without undue delay national programmes, policies, and strategies to implement the obligations under the present Protocol that shall serve as a means of controlling and reducing emissions of nitrogen oxides or their transboundary fluxes.

These Articles also left the states parties free to determine the precise modes for implementing the obligations assumed. Despite the general flexibility in the Protocol's provisions, a 1996 survey indicates that most parties to the Protocol have achieved their goals, and overall compliance with the Protocol has resulted in reduction in the level of emissions. For instance, eighteen of the twenty five parties to the Protocol had stabilized their NO_x emissions at the 1987 level by 1990, and by 1993 all parties had reduced NO_x emissions by 6%.[43]

[42] Lammers, *supra* note 29, at 279.
[43] UNECE Air Pollution Studies, *supra* note 34.

3.5. 1991 Geneva Protocol on Volatile Organic Compounds[44]

This was the third Protocol to be negotiated under the 1979 ECE Convention. Volatile Organic compounds may react with oxides of nitrogen to form tropospheric ozone (ground level ozone) leading to the formation of smog. Like other air pollutants, ozone has the capacity to drift across international borders causing damage at distances far removed from the source of the emissions.

In 1991 this Protocol, which creates a framework for the reduction of volatile organic compounds, was adopted. The basic obligation under the Protocol is to be found in Article 2(1). It requires the parties to:

> Control and reduce their emissions of VOCs in order to reduce their transboundary fluxes and the resulting secondary photochemical oxidant products so as to protect human health and the environment from adverse effects. Under the Protocol, the first obligation of the parties was to reduce national emissions of VOCs by at least 30% by the year 1999, using 1988 levels as the basis for the calculation of reductions or any annual leave during the period 1984 to 1990.

In the alternative, they were required to ensure that their total national annual emissions of VOC's by the year of 1999 do not exceed 1988 levels. The flexibility in the determination of the base year was adopted at the insistence of the United States which had substantially reduced its base emissions as a result of the passing of the 1990 Amendments to the Clean Air Act. The second alternative, requiring the stabilization of emissions by 1999 instead of a 30% reduction was agreed upon at the insistence of a number of Eastern European States, who felt that a 30% reduction in emissions would severely constrain their industrial development.

In addition, each state party was required progressively to adopt emission standards in existing as well as new mobile sources, using best available technology that is economically feasible. There was also a commitment under Article 2(6) to commence negotiations within 6 months after the entry into force of the Protocol to review the efficacy of measures taken in light of science and technological developments.

The provisions of Article 3(3) establish mechanisms for monitoring compliance. Like the two Protocols on Sulphur and Nitrogen Oxides, the supervision of compliance is entrusted to the executive body. The method of supervision is nevertheless unique in one respect; it provides for an inter-state complaints procedure. Article 3(3) states that:

> The parties shall establish a mechanism for monitoring compliance with the present protocol. As a first step based on information provided pursuant to Article 8 or other information, any party which has reason to believe that another party is acting or has acted in a manner inconsistent with its obligations under

[44] 1991 Geneva Protocol Concerning the Control of Emissions of Volatile Organic Compounds or their Transboundary Fluxes, 31 ILM 568 (1992), in force 29 September 1997.

> this Protocol may inform the executive body to that effect, and simultaneously the parties concerned. At the request of any party, the matter may be taken up at the next meeting of the executive body.

Although there is little evidence that it was actually used in practice, its existence provided a positive step in the evolution of normative regimes for the monitoring compliance with obligations negotiated under the auspices of the ECE.

3.6. 1998 Aarhus Protocols on Persistent Organic Pollutants[45] and on Heavy Metals[46]

These later protocols reflect in their content the significant advances in the normative framework of international environmental law. The protocols reflect a commitment that measures taken to reduce pollution should not be trade restrictions in disguise The 'Pop' Protocol is directed at the sources of air pollution

> ... contributing to the accumulation of persistent organic pollutants, in particular the use of certain pesticides, the manufacture and use of certain chemicals and the unintentional formation of certain substances in waste incineration, combustion, metal production and mobile sources.

The Heavy metals Protocol is directed at reducing emissions to the atmosphere of heavy metals in particular cadmium, lead, and mercury. Both Protocols contain a progressive commitment, in each case the parties are required to do no more than is scientifically and economically feasible. To that extent their substantive provisions are broadly in line with the commitments undertaken in earlier protocols.

3.7. 1999 Gothenburg Protocol to Abate Acidification, Eutrophication and Ground-Level Ozone[47]

This is the most recent agreement under the LRTAP Convention. It came into force on 17 May 2005 following the ratification of Portugal. Like the previous Protocol's the Convention reaffirms the basic principle of international law that the exploitation of a state's resources carries with it the obligation to ensure that the activity undertaken does not cause damage to the territory of other states.

---

[45] 1998 Aarhus Protocol to Control Persistent Organic Pollutants, 37 ILM 505 (1998), in force 23 October 2003.

[46] 1998 Aarhus Protocol on Heavy Metals, http://www.unece.org/env/lrtap/status/llrtap-s.htm, in force 29 December 2003.

[47] 1999 Gothenburg Protocol to Abate Acidification, Eutrophication and Ground-Level Ozone, Document EB.Air/1999/1&2, in force 17 May 2005.

Crucially it reiterates a commitment to the precautionary principle as found in principle 15 of the Rio Declaration. The Protocol also anticipates the possible effects of pollution control measures on trade in an increasingly globalized economy and reaffirms that measures taken should not be discriminatory or be deliberately directed at restrictions on trade.

It is called multi-effect or multi-pollutant, because it aims to cut emissions of four pollutants, sulphur dioxide, nitrogen oxides, volatile organic compounds and ammonia. The emission targets which are designed to be environmentally sensitive are set on a country by country basis with each country expected to achieve emission ceilings by the year 2010.[48] The targets were also assigned and intended to be cost effective, the idea in each case being to achieve the lowest overall cost for Europe as a whole. It was envisaged that these reduction targets would be revised in 2008 and 2009. The Protocol also enacts emission limit values for stationary and mobile sources as well as fuel standards. An Annex to the Protocol aims to reduce ammonia emissions from agricultural sources. Other provisions of the Convention contain obligations on exchange of information and monitoring of compliance under the auspices of an implementation Committee. These provisions are broadly similar to those contained in the early protocols discussed previously. The Convention's measures have proved popular with signatory states because they are perceived as sensitive to local needs and are cost effective.

4. The Conventions and its Protocols: An Evaluation

There is little disagreement from the fact that cumulatively the Convention and its Protocols have had a decisive positive effect on the reduction of transboundary air pollutants. Annual review of strategies and policies taken under the auspices of the ECE demonstrates that most parties to the Convention have taken positive measures to reduce the emissions of sulphur dioxide. State practice confirms that the parties have interpreted the provisions of the Convention as requiring the adoption of specific measures aimed at the control of pollution. Before international conferences on air pollution, states have consistently asserted that the obligations assumed by them under the Convention require the adoption of anti-pollution measures, strategies or policies. The work plan for the implementation of the Convention on Long-Range Trans-boundary Air Pollution requires the States Parties to submit information annually on recent developments in national strategies and policies which are utilized in the reduction of emissions. The information is also required to include actual levels of sulphur compounds, nitrogen oxides, and other agreed pollutants.

48 The Swedish NGO Secretariat on Acid Rain, *The Convention on Long-Range Transboundary Air Pollution*, available at www.acidrain.org, at 13(3).

It would be myopic to suggest that the measures adopted under the Convention and its Protocols are stringent enough for purposes of effective environmental protection. They are invariably the result of compromise between States at different stages of economic development, and to that extent are considerably weaker than is desirable in light of the scientific evidence available. Although the obligations assumed by the parties may seem open-ended, it has been noted that they are in fact broadly similar to those found in most contemporary treaties in the environmental context. This serves to reinforce the fact that obligations for the protection of the environment cannot be absolute and that in any case, law and legal instruments are just one aspect of the measures needed to reduce transboundary air pollution.

It is suggested that notwithstanding the soft wording of its provisions, the 1979 Convention is intended and does impose restraints on unilateral state action. Perhaps the most significant contribution of the Convention to the problem under consideration is the creation of a framework for the on-going negotiation of more concrete anti-pollution measures contained in the Protocols. It is particularly significant that the Gothenburg protocol with its multi-pollutant and multi-effect approach is firmly grounded on sound environmental principles. Second, the EC's ratification of the Convention has facilitated adoption of directives aimed at the reduction of sulphur and nitrogen emissions. The participation of the EC is particularly significant, since many of its member states are in one form or another affected by transboundary air pollution. These directives are considered in detail elsewhere in this volume.

Finally, the reports submitted to the executive body indicate that on the whole and as a result of measures taken under the Convention, emission levels are decreasing throughout the territories of member states. Although other factors including reduced industrial output have been identified, it is clear that the existence has not been without consequence.

Massimiliano Montini

EC Legislation on Air Pollution: From Guidelines to Limit Values

1. The Guidelines: The Framework Directive

The air pollution issue became a dramatically urgent priority in the EC context in the 1980s and early 1990s. This happened when the 'ambient air quality' emergency exploded, as an evident consequence of the progressive environmental degradation calling for immediate and effective reaction both at European and at Member State level.[1]

The worsening of the ambient air quality was mainly due to the increasing rate of emissions deriving from several different sources such as industrial activities and mobile sources. It was also due to the uncontrolled deforestation activity and all the related factors leading to the depletion of the ozone layer and to climate change.

After a first legislative response at the EC level, characterized by incoherent and dispersed actions,[2] the Fifth EC Action Programme of 1992 on the Environment envisaged amendments to the existing legislation on air pollutants particularly recommending the establishment of long term air quality objectives.[3]

[1] On this issue *see* H. Jans, European Environmental Law 359 *et seq.* (2000); L. Kramer, EC Environmental Law 305 *et seq.* (2007); *see also* EEA report no. 2/2007, *Air Pollution in Europe* available at www.reports.eea.europa.eu/eea_report_2007_2/en: the report analyses air pollution changes in Europe as well as their impacts on the environment and human health.

[2] *See* EC Directives on sulphur dioxide and particulate matter (80/779/EEC), OJ 1980 L229/30; on lead (82/884/EEC), OJ 1982 L378/15; on nitrogene dioxide (85/203/EEC), OJ 1985 L87/1; on ozone (92/72/EEC), OJ 1992 L297/1.

[3] For more details on the 5th Action Programme (OJ 1993 C138/1) *see* the EC official website www.europa.eu.int.

Harry H. G. Post (Ed.), The Protection of Ambient Air in International and European Law, 73-87.

Despite the growing concerns about air pollution it was only in 1996 that the EC, responding to the call of the Fifth Action Programme, finally reached agreement on Council Directive 96/62, the Framework Directive on ambient air quality assessment and management.[4]

This Directive embraces an omni-comprehensive approach, addressing both integrated environmental protection (related to air, water and soil) as well as safeguarding human health.[5]

Moreover the Directive reveals a broad scope, covering the entire outdoor air in the troposphere. Only working places are excluded. That is to say: It applies to all ambient air with the only exception of air within working places.[6] More specifically, it identifies 13 atmospheric pollutants listed in Annex I of the directive. These are to be taken into consideration to make it fully operational and effective by assessing and managing ambient air quality.[7]

Directive 96/62 has to be read together with its four 'Daughter' directives, issued between 1999 and 2004.[8] The overall impression is that the Framework Directive introduces the basic principles and guidelines useful to identifying the EC Member States commitments for ambient air quality assessment and management. The daughter legislation integrates them particularly by setting concrete prescriptions and methods of measurement for the emissions as well as specific limit values and thresholds. However, they are always taking as a reference point what was envisaged in the 'Mother' Directive.

A confirmation of this way of reading the ambient air quality legal system can be found, first of all, in Article 1 of the Framework Directive, which states that this piece of legislation introduces the "basic principles of a common strategy to define and set objectives for ambient air quality" with the ultimate aim "to avoid, prevent or reduce harmful effects on human health and the environment."[9]

Coupled with this general aim, Directive 96/62 also endorses the following objectives: "assess ambient air quality in Member States on the basis of common methods and criteria, obtain adequate information on ambient air quality and ensure that it is made available to the public, inter alia by means of alert thresholds." Lastly, the Directive is to "maintain ambient air quality where it is good and improve it in other cases."[10]

In order to achieve these objectives, the Directive relies on the commitment of the Member States to measure and monitor ambient air quality throughout

[4] EC Directive 96/62 in OJ 1996 L296/55.
[5] *See id.*, particularly recitals and art. 1.
[6] *See id.*, art 2.1 'definitions'.
[7] *See id.*, Ann. I for the complete list of pollutants.
[8] On the four Daughter directives *see* the next section.
[9] *See* Directive 96/62, *supra* note 4, art. 1.
[10] *See id.*, art. 1.

their territory. This is to be done by means of methods, criteria, devices and equipments that have to be accurate, uniform, reliable and comparable.[11]

To realise this, the Directive requires Member States to actively cooperate with the work carried out by international scientific groups in this field. They must also continuously update the techniques and instruments of measurement and assessment. In this way they will confirm the latest approach of EC environmental law and policy to overcome the traditional contrast between technical and scientific improvement and environmental protection. This approach suggests instead the possibility of a parallel growth of them both, one at the beneficial service of the other.

After having set its objectives and scope, the Framework Directive imposes a general obligation on the Member States, requiring them to comply with the emission limit values set by the EC legislation for the sake of ambient air quality improvement.[12]

On the basis of this general requirement, the Framework Directive introduces another key provision, stating that "limit values" and "alert thresholds" are to be set for all of the 13 pollutants covered by the Directive in order to allow the consequent and following step of ambient air assessment and management throughout the EC territory against the EC values and targets.[13]

It is evident how fundamental the concepts of 'limit values' and 'alert thresholds' are in the architecture of the ambient air Framework Directive, since several important commitments are linked to their fulfilment (or violation).

First of all it is important to define these two key terms, and indeed the Directive itself provides that:

a) 'limit value' shall mean a level fixed on the basis of scientific knowledge, with the aim of avoiding, preventing or reducing harmful effects on human health and/or the environment as a whole, to be attained within a given period and not to be exceeded once attained; and,
b) 'alert threshold' shall mean a level beyond which there is a risk for human health from brief exposure and at which immediate steps shall be taken by the Member States as laid down in the directive.[14]

It can easily be inferred from the definitions given above that specific and tailor-made actions are connected respectively with the 'limit values exceed' and the 'alert threshold crossed' scenario.

[11] For more details *see id.*, art. 3.

[12] *See id.*, art. 7.

[13] *Id.*, art. 4 provides that the EC Commission shall submit to the EC Council proposals for setting limit values and alert thresholds. The Council and the EC Parliament did set such values and thresholds for specific pollutants via the daughter directives. They will be analysed here, *supra* in the text. Ann. II of the Directive specifies the factors to be taken into consideration when setting limit values and alert thresholds.

[14] *See id.*, arts. 2.5, 2.7 'definitions'.

Indeed in case of measurements and assessment revealing that in a certain zone the given limit values levels are exceeded, Article 7 of the Framework Directive requires the Member State concerned, firstly, to list the zones and agglomerations[15] where the levels detected are higher than the allowed ones. And, secondly, to react effectively against these emission levels by drawing up adequate plans and programmes to attain the limit values prescribed by the EC legislation within a set deadline. Furthermore, it specifies that when the level of more than one pollutant among the 13 covered by the Directive is being exceeded, such plans/programmes have to be 'integrated' ones.[16] It is then the EC Commission's task to 'regularly check' the implementation and progress of the above plans and programmes and to ensure that they are made publicly available.

In the event of alert thresholds being crossed, the Member State concerned shall inform the public through all adequate means and, within three months, forward to the EC Commission any relevant information and data related to the levels recorded and the emission episode.[17]

Apart from these two extreme cases the Framework Directive also considers two other scenarios: the case of zones where emission levels are lower than those presented by the limit values, and the case where there is a risk of the limit values/alert thresholds being exceeded.[18] In the former case the Directive prescribes to the Member State concerned to maintain such values below the limits and to put in place all efforts to preserve 'the best ambient air quality'.[19]

In the first of these scenarios the Framework Directive envisages a self explanatory commitment for the Member States concerned, who should obviously be in charge of avoiding any increase of the values below the prescribed ones. In the latter scenario where there is a risk of limit values and/ or alert thresholds being exceeded, Article 7.3 of the Directive does not show any satisfactory approach.

It calls for the Member State to draw up action plans indicating the measures to be taken in the short term in order to reduce the risk, but it completely fails to give any further element or criteria to determine whether and under which circumstances the 'risk' in question can be regarded as real or at least as a probability to occur.

At the same time Article 7.3 of the Framework Directive fails to mention any EC environmental law principle, first and foremost the 'precautionary' one, which could be particularly useful when dealing with 'risk-management'.

[15] For a definition of 'agglomeration' *see id.*, art. 2.10.

[16] For more details on the event of limit values being exceeded *see* art. 8, Framework Directive; for details concerning the content and nature of the plans and programmes *see id.* Ann. IV.

[17] *See id.*, art. 10.

[18] *See id.*, art. 7.3.

[19] *See id.*, art. 9.

This would have strengthened the ratio of such a provision by giving it a precise legal basis in the Treaty and would probably have allowed a less controversial interpretation and a more effective enforcement of this provision.[20]

In more practical terms, it is very likely that the lack of any precise criteria and guidelines for the identification of such a risk occurrence, can offer a 'side exit' for the Member States willing to avoid the costly and challenging commitments of drawing up and enforcing plans and programmes mentioned in Article 7.3. For this reason too, a clearer approach would have been preferable.

As previously mentioned in this paragraph, the latest trend revealed by the development of EC Environmental Law shows how the EC legislator resolved the idea of a complete separation and conflict between the scientific world and environmental protection. By the sharing of knowledge and information among all the parties involved in the 'management of the environment', he enhanced the opportunities of improvement offered.

In this respect the Framework Directive relies on a strong and pro-active duty of co-operation and exchange of information between Member States and scientific groups as well as on the co-operation and exchange of information among Member States themselves,[21] especially in case of emission limits being exceeded as a result of 'transboundary pollution'.[22]

Such a system is completed by the Member States duty of mandatory transmission to the Commission of reports and information on measurement, assessment and management, and also through the plans and programmes mentioned in Article 8.[23]

The EC Commission will then try to 'link' all the subjects involved in the exchange of information by publishing every three years a report on ambient air quality. This report will be drafted on the basis of the Member States reports and the information provided by the European Environment Agency.

The main features of the framework legislation for ambient air quality assessment and management that have been described so far, represent a relevant reference, especially in terms of guidelines, to the more detailed 'Daughter' legislation.

In particular because that the latter introduces specific provisions related to air assessment and management commitments, methods and criteria of measurement, obligations related to limit values and alert thresholds and the exchange of information duties.

---

[20] On the precautionary principle *see* in general Jans, *supra* note 1, at 33 *et seq.*; Kramer, *supra* note 1, at 23. *See also* EC Commission Communication COM (2000) 1; Judgment of 26 November 2002 in *Joined cases T-74/00 and others*, *Artegodan GmbH and others v. Commission*, [2002] ECR II-4945.

[21] *See* Council Decision 97/101 establishing a Community-wide procedure for exchanging information and data on ambient air quality in the EC, OJ 1997 L35/14.

[22] *See* Directive 96/62, *supra* note 4, art. 8.6.

[23] *See id.*, art. 11.

As said above, the strategy designed by the Framework Directive is applied to the specific groups of pollutants identified in its Annex I by means of the four Daughter directives analysed in the following section.

2. The Limit Values: the Four Daughter Directives

Article 4 of the Framework Directive requires that the European Commission submit proposals to the Council for setting the limit values for the 13 pollutants covered by Annex I of the Directive.

As already anticipated many times in the previous section, such limit values, as well as a more detailed and tailored legislation for the above pollutants, are contained in the four Daughter directives issued so far, namely Directive 1999/30,[24] Directive 2000/69,[25] Directive 2002/3[26] and Directive 2004/107.[27]

Each of the four Daughter directives supplement and integrate the Framework Directive by setting exact limit values against which Member States must measure and assess ambient air quality for the respective pollutants. It also specifies for the group of various pollutants covered by each of the directives, the methods and requirements for their assessment, as well as the criteria for locating, classifying and using the sampling points for their measurement and assessment.[28]

The Framework and the Daughter directives are conceived as an exhaustive and mutually integrated legislative resource to effectively tackle the ambient air degradation issue. Therefore, quite unsurprisingly, the Daughter directives restate the Framework Directive in more than one aspect. Beginning with their objectives, as stated in their Articles 1: They exactly mirror the four objectives endorsed by the Framework Directive.

The same can be said regarding the general aim of the entire daughter legislation, namely the protection of both human health and the environment as a whole[29] and about the basic structure related to Member States obligations.

Accordingly, each of the Daughter directives commits the Member States to assess ambient air in their territory by the common methods prescribed in the Annexes to the directives, and to ensure compliance with the limit values (also

[24] Directive 1999/30 relating to limit values for sulphur dioxide, nitrogen dioxide and oxides of nitrogen, particulate matter and lead in ambient air ('Daughter Directive one'), OJ 1999 L8/30.

[25] Directive 2000/69 relating to limit values for benzene and carbon monoxide in ambient air ('Daughter Directive two'), OJ 2000 L23/76.

[26] Directive 2002/3 relating to ozone in ambient air ('Daughter Directive three'), OJ 2000 L2/17.

[27] Directive 2004/107 relating to arsenic, cadmium, mercury, nickel and polycyclic aromatic hydrocarbons in ambient air ('Daughter Directive four'), OJ 2004 L32/11.

[28] For details *see* the Anns. to the single Daughter directives.

[29] *See* the Preambles of the Daughter directives and their Arts. 1.

set in the Annexes). To this effect, they must take all the necessary measures, included the drafting and performance of adequate plans and programmes. These must be publicly available in order to restore the status quo ante in case of limit values and alert thresholds being exceeded, as stated in Article 8 of the Framework Directive.

It may be important to underline once again that the relationship between the Framework Directive and the daughter ones is not of strict subordination of the latter to the former. Rather it is of a more detailed integration and completion achieved by the daughter legislation starting from the guidelines, the principles and the structure provided by the Framework Directive.

This is evident if one draws the many interesting parallels which can be established between the mother and the daughter directives. This relates not only, as already pointed out, to their respective objectives, aims and basic structure, but also to the specific commitments of the Member States.

In fact, just as the Framework Directive does, requires Member States to improve the ambient air quality so do the daughter ones. Particularly where air quality is not in compliance with the specific standards given in the Annexes, or to maintain it where it corresponds to a 'good status'.

Also in the section regarding the exchange of information between the Member States and their commitments on reporting to the Commission, the daughter provisions restate the Framework Directive, confirming the importance of the establishment of a network to forward and exchange data. This is useful not only for monitoring enforcement but also for assessing any improvement of the Member States performances and to test the effectiveness of the legislation in force.

Apart from the above described basic structure, which stems from the Framework Directive and is resembled in all of the four Daughter directives, some specific features of the latter ones need to be mentioned.

Firstly, as far as the 'second' Daughter Directive is concerned, the one related to benzene and carbon monoxide, the EC legislator puts an additional requirement on the Member States. They should routinely inform the public, consumers and environmental organisations included, on updated ambient air concentrations of these two pollutants, regardless of any event of limit values being exceeded.[30]

Secondly, regarding the 'third' Daughter Directive, the one on ozone, probably due to the particular sensitivity and social alarm caused by this pollutant, the legislator felt the necessity to add a fifth objective beside the four 'basic' ones shared by all the four directives. It sets 'long term objectives' in terms of achieving ozone concentrations below which the negative effects on environment and human health are unlikely and related to the acidification

[30] *See* Directive 2000/69, *supra* note 25, art. 7.

abatement strategy. In addition by 2010 'target values' are to be achieved likely to ensure that no harm is done to human beings and the environment as a whole.[31]

Moreover, the long term objectives listed above, as stated in section III of Annex I to this Directive, should comply with the World Health Organisation's guidelines on ozone.[32]

In addition to that, given the particular formation mechanism of ozone, if a target value fixed for this pollutant is exceeded, the Commission, upon information forwarded by the Member State(s) concerned, shall evaluate whether some additional measures are needed at community level. These measures must be on top of those already taken by the interested Member States via specific plans and programmes.[33]

Thirdly and finally, the 'fourth' Daughter Directive, on arsenic, cadmium, mercury, nickel and polycyclic aromatic, presents some specific peculiarities that are worthy of analysis.

It has been mentioned from the very beginning of the present contribution that all the EC legislative framework related to ambient air quality aims at protecting both the environment as a whole and human health.[34] This by means of the provisions contained in the mother Directive supplemented by those embodied in the daughter ones. Therefore 13 pollutants have been identified by Directive 96/62 that also set the core structure, objectives and commitments to adequately pursue and ultimately achieve the above mentioned overall aim.

Given this, the peculiarity of the 4 pollutants covered by the fourth Daughter Directive lays in the fact that they are human carcinogens and that there is no identifiable threshold below which they pose a 'zero risk' to human health.[35]

Thus the directive at stake, unlike its three 'sister' ones, applies the principle of the lowest possible exposure to such pollutants. Instead of fixing any specific limit value for them, as the other three Daughter directives do for the specific pollutants they cover, it prescribes to use benzo(a)pyrene as a marker for these pollutants and sets a target value not to be exceeded for this substance.[36]

The fourth Daughter Directive particularly underlines the strong link between scientific knowledge and human and environmental protection mentioned here more than once. It does so by explicitly stating that there

---

[31] *See* Directive 2002/3, *supra* note 26, Preamble and arts. 2.9, 2.10 (definitions), 3, 4 as well as, for more details Ann. I.

[32] The WHO guidelines are available at www.euro.who.int/Document/E87950.pdf.

[33] *See* Directive 96/62, *supra* note 4, art. 4.1.

[34] *See* Art. 174 TEC.

[35] *See* on this line of reasoning, related to the 'zero risk' for human health, the findings of the WTO Appellate Body in the EC Asbestos case, in Report of the Appellate Body, WT/DS/135/AB/R (2001).

[36] *See* Directive 2004/107, *supra* note 27, art. 3 and Ann. I.

is scientific evidence of the carcinogenic potential of the pollutants covered by it and that their impact on human health and environment occurs via concentration in ambient air and deposition.

However, this Directive also reveals that, following the same scientific basis, there is not currently any certainty about an identifiable threshold below which they no longer pose risks.

In this context, again, the EC legislator cautiously avoids supporting its reasoning by involving the precautionary principle. It fails to seize the opportunity of consolidating the 'authority' of such a useful general environmental principle, which could justify protective measures not supported by full scientific certainty, provided that proper 'risk assessment' and consequent 'risk management' have been performed.[37]

Speaking in broader terms, the precautionary principle is still surrounded by a certain degree of scepticism and controversy, being sometimes in need of confirmation. The entire ambient air quality legislation, dealing with an extremely sensitive and socially affecting issue and, at the same time as seen above, very often leading to problems regarding 'risk assessment' and 'risk management', could have been a good and effective ground to test and eventually assert the legislative and 'moral' authority of the principle.

It is a pity that the EC legislator completely neglected to do so.

3. The Framework and the Daughter Legislation: Some Outstanding Issues

The EC legislator conceived Directive 96/62 and the four Daughter directives as the most appropriate response to the continuous and dynamic problem of ambient air degradation.

The choice of setting basic principles, commitments and guidelines by means of a framework legislation to be furthered by virtue of a more detailed sectoral daughter legislation is not new neither at a national level nor at a European level. Provided that coherence and consistence are achieved, this choice is likely to ensure an effective and omni-comprehensive action to satisfy the desired objectives, usually stated in the mother piece of legislation.

However, the legislation on ambient air quality described above has failed to successfully reach the desired objective of preserving ambient air quality

[37] On the precautionary principle and risk management *see* M. Lee, EC Environmental Law 97 *et seq.* (2005); A. Trouwborst, *The Precautionary Principle in General International Law: Combating the Babylonian Confusion*, 16 RECIEL 185, at 192-193 (2007); Judgment of 11 September 2002 in *Case T-70/99, Alpharma Inc. v. Council*, [2002] ECR II-3495, paras. 162-169 and Judgment of 11 September 2002 in *Case T-13/99, Pfizer Animal Health SA v. Council*, [2002] ECR II-3305, paras. 149-156.

and, hence, to avoid and reduce harmful effects on environment and human health. Sharp and persistent evidence of progressive ambient air degradation can still be perceived.

The question is whether the directives analysed above reveal significant shortcomings responsible for the ineffectiveness of the EC response to such degradation.

The very first impression is that globally and generally this legislation is quite coherent and satisfactory. It imposes upon the Member States the specific task of assessing ambient air quality by means of a common method prior to taking any further action and couples this requirement with the setting, at European level, of specific limit values and thresholds, for each specific pollutant, that Member states have to comply with.

However, once the attention is shifted from the 'declaration of principles' perspective to the implementation and enforcement one, it is self evident that neither the framework legislation nor the more detailed daughter ones are capable of seriously and effectively reverting the present negative trend in the quality of the ambient air.

It has already been said about the directive's 'missed chances' of stating and enforcing important general principles of EC Environmental Law, in particular the precautionary principle, that would otherwise have conferred more authority and power to the entire set of directives.[38]

Beside that, one of the main weaknesses of the legislation in question is the too generic wording used in some very relevant provisions. Even if it were acceptable that the directives use vague and general wording when referring to the 'plans and programmes' that have to be devised by Member States in case of limit values being exceeded in order to attain the limit values again,[39] the same cannot be said with regard to the Annexes to the directives. They should put some light on the real content and value of such plans and programmes, but they fail to do so.

Analogous reasoning can be followed when referring to the alert threshold crossing scenario. To this the directives only, and inadequately, react by simply committing Member States to "inform the interested inhabitants and forward the Commission the relevant information."

Such limited strength and clarity cannot be justified by simply referring to the very nature of a directive as a European legal act binding only with respect to the results that have to be achieved, but leaving the addressees free of choosing the preferred methods and forms to reach its objectives.[40]

[38] *See* the previous sections.

[39] That is to say in case of serious danger of non-achievement of the directives objective (*see* the previous sections).

[40] *See* Art. 249 TEC.

Indeed, it rather appears to be a symptom of the forced and distorted use of the subsidiarity principle.[41] This leads to a paradoxical situation in which the EC takes action claiming to regulate the matter at the European level without effectively regulating it in a strong and straight forward way.

It can be supposed that this happens when a very sensitive area with a pure transboundary 'social and environmental' relevance, such as the ambient air quality sector, interlinks with sectors of high economic interest such as transport, industry and commerce. That leads to mandatory targets and commitments which are reluctantly accepted by the Member States because of their repercussions for such national economic interests.

One may now question what could be the real and concrete strength and effectiveness of this kind of use of the subsidiarity principle justifying a supranational EC action of particular scale and effects vis-à-vis the Member States. In fact it hides some discontent of the latter ones to abide by compulsory emission limits, thresholds and other commitments imposed by the EC.

The result is weak legislation formally regulating the matter by imposing precise tasks, obligations and limit values to be attained but concretely failing to impose structures and procedures to ensure an effective compliance with all of this.

Indeed, in the directives described above there is no trace of sanctions to be issued in case of non compliance with the limit values and alert thresholds set at EC level. Basically, neither serious deterrent from infringement nor any serious mechanism of stimulating compliance is envisaged for the Member States.[42]

It should be kept in mind that in this respect the EC has no general power of regulating criminal matters by inflicting penal sanctions.[43] This notwithstanding, the absence of any reference to penalties and compliance, not even in the usual form of an invitation to the Member States,[44] appears to be unjustifiable. Particularly in such a controversial and sensitive field as environmental protection and especially in a very socially alarming area such as ambient air quality preservation, this is detrimental.

In other terms, it seems unsatisfactory to rely only on the time consuming, slow and weak infringement procedure of 226-228 TEC to ensure an effective reaction against non compliance with the legislation on air quality.

---

[41] *See* Art. 5 TEC.

[42] On the implementation of the obligations deriving from the Treaty and from secondary legislation *see* Jans, *supra* note 1, at 135 *et seq.*; Kramer, *supra* note 1, at 418 *et seq.*

[43] On this issue *see* Kramer, *supra* note 1, at 439 *et seq.*; *see also* Judgment of 13 September 2005 in *Case C-176/03, Commission of the European Communities v. Council of the European Union*, [2005] ECR I-7879.

[44] *See* Art. 28 of the new Directive 2008/50/EC on ambient air quality and cleaner air in Europe (OJ 2008 L152/1), Appendix, *infra.*, and, more generally, the next section as well as Trouwborst's contribution in Chapter 5.

The infringement system should at least have been strengthened by the directives, especially by the Framework one, possibly by referring to the so called 'duty of loyal cooperation' of the Member States.[45] This duty underlines their necessary obligation of precise and prompt fulfilment of the binding undertakings arising from the legislation on ambient air quality because of their general commitments as EC Members.

However, about a set of directives so rich in formal commitments and declarations of guidelines and principles but concretely reaching such limited results, it is natural to question their capability of being effectively 'binding' for the Member States who are ultimately responsible for their application.

4. The Latest Stage: The Thematic Strategy on Air Pollution and the New Directive on Ambient Air Quality and Cleaner Air for Europe

The concrete but still weak improvements reached at EC level by means of the application of the sectoral legislation analysed so far, give evidence of the fact that ambient air quality still is one of the major concerns among the environmental and human health protection issues. It causes both local and transnational problems and has significant negative impacts such as increasing mortality rates, ecosystem damage and biodiversity loss ('*eutrophication*') and is even detrimental for the preservation of monuments and artistic heritage.[46] Current legislation is clearly in need of improvement.

It was against this scenario that the Community's Sixth Environmental Action Programme identified ambient air quality as one of the seven significant thematic areas. It called for the development of a specific Thematic Strategy on air pollution in the perspective of attaining "levels of air quality that do not give rise to significant negative impacts on, and risks to human health and the environment."[47]

To this end the Strategy proposes to supplement, simplify, streamline and modernise the existing air quality legislation by introducing specific emission reduction targets for the main pollutants as well as by setting general objectives to be delivered in stages and eventually achieved by 2020.[48]

These main outcomes of the Strategy, as well as its concerns and priorities, can be summarised in the two actions to improve regulation and integration

[45] *See* Art. 10 TEC.

[46] For more specific estimations *see* COM (2005) 446 final.

[47] Thematic Strategy for Air Pollution, *id.*

[48] The Strategy has been drawn up with the support of the CAFE (Clean Air For Europe) programme, which tasks are precisely to develop, collect and validate scientific information on the effects of air pollution and support in monitoring, implementing and reviewing the existing air quality legislation as well as to develop structural links with the relevant policy areas.

of air quality concerns in other policy sectors. The Commission proposal for a Directive on ambient air quality and cleaner air for Europe, which was presented in 2005[49] and finally approved in April 2008[50] demonstrates these two actions.

Keeping in mind the main goal of this new piece of legislation namely the one of attaining "levels of air quality that do not give rise to significant negative impacts on, and risks to human health and the environment" it is possible to check whether it is really capable of achieving this through the better regulation and integration devices.

As far as streamlining and simplifying the current legislation to improve the regulatory scenario, the new directive simply, and disappointingly, suggests merging into one single legislative instrument the Framework Directive, the first, second and third daughter ones[51] and Council Decision 97/101 on the exchange of data on air pollution.[52] The idea is to improve the current monitoring and reporting system as well as the ambient air assessment by disseminating best practices and strengthening the dialogue between the parties.

Although this step is regarded by the Commission as a crucial one in making air quality legislation work better, it seems largely unsatisfactory. Especially considering that the new Directive does not seem to contain either any innovative features or any improved opportunities for implementation and enforcement.

Indeed, even at a first glance, the objectives of the new Directive would still remain the same as the previous directives.[53] This is also true for the basic obligations for the Member States relating to air quality assessment, measurement and management, in terms of the drawing up of air quality plans and programmes in cases of limit values and target values being exceeded (while maintaining the status quo where air quality is good).[54]

Even the existing limit values will remain unchanged, with the possibility of amendments by the EC Commission under a specific procedure.[55]

Therefore the newly approved legislation is most probably not well suited to remedy the gaps and vagueness of the one repealed. It will neither bring any further clarity on the specific and concrete actions, 'plans and programmes', that the Member States should draw up for ambient air protection.

[49] *See* COM (2005) 447 final.

[50] The new Directive was finally approved on 14 April 2008 and it is published in the Official Journal, *see supra* note 44, and the Appendix, *infra*.

[51] The Commission proposes to merge the 4th Daughter directive at a later stage through a simplified process.

[52] *See supra* note 16.

[53] *See* new Directive, *supra* note 44, art. 1.

[54] *See id.*, arts. 21 *et seq*.

[55] *See id.*, art. 28.

However, it is worth mentioning two interesting features of the new Directive.

The first one is the increased attention given to the issue of control of particulate matter. It aims to lower human exposure to $PM_{2.5}$, considering its particularly dangerous nature for human health. This despite the fact, that there is still some scientific uncertainty surrounding this issue.[56]

In this respect, the aim is to limit undue risk from exposure reducing it everywhere in a cost-effective manner without posing additional burdens on the less polluted areas.

Secondly, Article 30 of the new Directive calls the Member States to introduce into their legal systems "effective, proportionate and dissuasive rules and penalties" applicable to the infringements of the national provisions adopted pursuant to this Directive.

Recalling what has been said in the previous paragraphs, this provision is very welcome, even if, due to the general lack of competence of the EC in imposing on Member States the compulsory use of criminal law, it is quite limited in its power and scope. It simply sets a general and broad obligation whose successful fulfilment relies on each and single Member State's will and capability of setting adequate penalties and ensuring their prompt and effective enforcement.

It is deeply disappointing that the new legislation misses the chance to formalise into legislative prescriptions some of the actions suggested in the Thematic Strategy on Air Pollution.[57] For instance, it does not require the integration of air quality concerns into relevant policy areas such as energy, transport and agriculture.[58]

Indeed, there is no trace of such an integration endeavour in the new directive, maybe because of the predictable difficulties of finding enough common ground of discussion for sectors usually in conflict, such as the environment, economy and transport.

Anyway, an 'integration-oriented' solution would have been more in line with the EC Treaty itself. Its Article 6 explicitly prescribes that environmental protection requirements 'must' be integrated into the definition and implementation of other Community policies with a view to promoting sustainable development.

---

56 *See id.*, arts. 12 *et seq.*

57 *See* COM (2005) 446.

58 *See* on the integration principle Jans, *supra* note 1, at 17 *et seq.*; Kramer, *supra* note 1, at 20 *et seq.*; Lee, *supra* note 37, at 43-46; N. Dhondt, Integration of Environmental Protection into Other EC Policies (2003). *See also* Advocate General Jacobs on 26 October 2000 in *Case C-379/98, PreussenElektra AG v. Schhleswag AG*, [2001] ECR I-2099, para. 231, and Judgment of 11 June 1991 in *Case C-300/89, Commission v. Council*, [1991] ECR I-2867, paras. 21-24 (on titanium dioxide).

Article 6 specific reference to the achievement of sustainable development has gained such prominence in the definition of the entire EC action, that its lack of any reference to the integration principle makes the new Directive appear to go against the tide.

Moreover, as said, the Thematic Strategy envisaged the inclusion of the integration principle in the revised directive, and more generally called for a much more effective and modern approach. These goals remain unfulfilled by the new Directive. Hence, one can question the real value of the EC Thematic Strategy itself in terms of its capability to promote the introduction of new principles and criteria likely to be furthered and consolidated by virtue of their translation into formal and mandatory legislative provisions.

Therefore, it seems that the new Directive on ambient air quality and cleaner air for Europe in theory raises great expectations about better regulation and integration but in practice fails to achieve them. It limits its objective, action and structure almost entirely to a mere redesigning and rephrasing of the current framework and daughter legislation.

This is clearly denying the promise of learning from past experience that should, allegedly, guide the EC action in the environmental field,[59] especially in those sectors subject to rapid changes due to progressive and dynamic scientific development.

[59] *See, inter alia,* the 3rd Recital in the Preamble of the new Directive (2008).

Arie Trouwborst

Modern Approaches to Enforcing Community Environmental Law:

A Special Focus on Direct Effect and Criminal Sanctions

The protection of the environment constitutes, as the European Court of Justice (ECJ) recently reaffirmed, "one of the essential objectives" of the European Community (EC).[1] This is mirrored by the development of EC environmental law, which has come to exercise a considerable and steadily growing impact on the national legal orders of the Member States of the European Union (EU). It does so in various ways. EC environmental directives have, for instance, played a major part in the introduction of the precautionary principle in the Dutch legal system, whether through transposition of relevant provisions into national law,[2] their direct effect,[3] or through interpretation of national legislation in accordance with the Community rules in question.[4]

[1] Case C-176/03, *Commission v. Council*, 2005 ECR I-7879, para. 41. *See also* Case 240/83, *ADBHU*, 1983 ECR 531, para. 13; Case 302/86, *Commission v. Denmark*, 1988 ECR 4607, para. 8; Case C-2123/96, *Outokumpu*, 1998 ECR I-1777, para. 32. *See also* Arts. 2, 6 and 174-176 of the EC Treaty.

[2] *E.g.*, the transposition of Art. 6 of Directive 92/43 of 21 May 1992 on the conservation of natural habitats and of wild fauna and flora, OJ 1992 L 206/7 (Habitats Directive), into the Nature Protection Act 1998 (Natuurbeschermingswet 1998).

[3] *E.g.*, the same Art. 6 of the Habitats Directive in cases like Council of State (Raad van State, or ABRvS) 22 December 2004, 200000690/1-A and 200101670/1-A, on cockle fisheries in the Wadden Sea.

[4] *E.g.*, *ABRvS 28 July 2004, 200301664* (with note by J. H. Jans), 31 Milieu en Recht 645 (2004), where Art. 4 of Directive 01/18/EC on genetically modified organisms was 'read into' Art. 26 of the Act on Environmentally Hazardous Substances (Wet Milieugevaarlijke Stoffen).

Harry H. G. Post (Ed.), The Protection of Ambient Air in International and European Law, 89-120.

As other contributions to this book make abundantly clear, EC legislation also occupies a dominant position in the field of ambient air protection in Europe today. By way of another Dutch example, over fifty spatial projects, involving zoning plans for housing and business parks and permits for industrial and infrastructural developments, have been appealed in the Netherlands because of the expected exceedance of air quality limit values since the first ambient air 'daughter directive'[5] was transposed into national law in 2001. Appeals were sustained by the Council of State, the highest court in these matters, in about one-third of all cases.[6]

New environmental rules continue to be agreed on by the European legislator and thus by, or on behalf of, the Member States. These rules are created to deal with problems that cannot be handled effectively at the national level. Air pollution, drifting on the winds from one country to the next, illustrates this like no other issue and has in fact figured prominently on intergovernmental agendas ever since international environmental law took shape with the classical *Trail Smelter* arbitration,[7] as set out by Phoebe Okowa in Chapter 3 of this book. In spite of this evident rationale of EC environmental law, "local, regional and national administrations in the [twenty-seven] Member States are not all convinced to the same extent that Community environmental standards are to be enforced, complied with and applied in practice," as Krämer put it perhaps a touch euphemistically.[8] Indeed, problems of implementation and enforcement of EC environmental law have reportedly been on the increase of late.[9]

The number and outcome of the many recent environmental infringement procedures initiated by the European Commission against Member States on the basis of Article 226 of the EC Treaty are some indicator of both the frequency of violations and the significance the Commission and the European Court of Justice attach to compliance with Community environmental standards. It is also telling that environmental and natural resource cases figure prominently among the scarce instances in which the Court has so far availed itself of the possibility afforded by Article 228 of the EC Treaty to

[5] Directive 99/30 relating to limit values for sulphur dioxide, nitrogen dioxide and oxides of nitrogen, particulate matter and lead in ambient air, OJ 1999 L 163/41.

[6] For an overview and discussion of cases until February 2005, *see* R. B. A. Koelemeijer *et al.*, *Consequenties van de EU-Luchtkwaliteitsrichtlijnen voor Ruimtelijke Ontwikkelingsplannen in Verschillende EU-Landen*, Milieu- en Natuurplanbureau (MNP) Report 500052001/2005 (2005).

[7] Trail Smelter Arbitral Tribunal, *Trail Smelter (United States v. Canada)*, 1938/1941, 3 RIAA 1905.

[8] L. Krämer, E.C. Environmental Law 282 (2000); *see also* J. H. Jans *et al.*, Europeanisation of Public Law 199-200 (2007).

[9] Krämer, *id.*, at 277-295; C. Demmke, *Trends in European Environmental Regulation: Issues of Implementation and Enforcement*, 3 YEEL 329 (2003); *see also* H. H. B. Vedder, *Recente Ontwikkelingen in het EG-Milieurecht*, 32 Milieu en Recht 262, at 263-264 (2005).

impose financial sanctions on disobedient Member States.[10] The EC Sixth Environmental Action Programme, covering the period 2002-2012, likewise lays great emphasis on implementation and enforcement in order to ensure that European environmental law is put into practice.[11]

The pursuit of greater effectiveness of EC environmental law and the (closely related) mounting effect of EC environmental law on the national legal orders of the Member States are the focus of this chapter. In Section 1 below a concise overview is presented of the various tools and mechanisms for promoting compliance with environmental law which are at the Community's disposal. Two conspicuous items from this toolbox, namely the *direct effect* of environmental EC directives in national legal systems and the influence of European environmental law on the use of *criminal penalties* by EU Member States, are singled out for more in-depth treatment in Sections 2 and 3 on account of their particular contemporary significance from both a practical and academic point of view. Concluding remarks are, finally, made in Section 4. The chapter's primary subject matter is thus of a generic nature, but nonetheless of obvious importance for the challenge of safeguarding ambient air quality in Europe. At any rate, where possible this generic subject matter is illustrated with examples from the air quality ambit.

1. Enforcing EC Environmental Law

1.1. Environmental Directives

The host of EC environmental legislation is in the form of directives. Over two hundred environmental directives are presently in force, covering anything from air quality to genetically modified organisms. As Article 249 of the EC Treaty stipulates, each directive is "*binding*, as to the *result* to be achieved, upon each *Member State* to which it is addressed, but shall leave to the national authorities the choice of form and methods."[12] Another provision of the EC Treaty that is crucial to any discussion of the implementation of European law, whether environmental or otherwise, is Article 10, which articulates the so-called principle of loyal co-operation[13] as follows:

---

[10] *E.g.*, Case C-387/97, *Commission v. Greece*, 2000 ECR I-5047 (waste); Case C-279/01, *Commission v. Spain*, 2003 ECR I-14141 (bathing water); Case C-304/02, *Commission v. France*, 2005 ECR I-6263 (fisheries). *See also* Vedder, *supra* note 9, at 264; Jans *et al.*, *supra* note 8, at 200.

[11] *See* Art. 3(2) of the Action Programme, as adopted by Decision 1600/2002, OJ 2002 L 242/1.

[12] Art. 249(3); emphasis added.

[13] Generally, *see* R. J. G. M. Widdershoven, *The Principle of Loyal Cooperation: Lawmaking by the European Court of Justice and the Dutch Courts*, *in* F. Stroink & E. van der Linden (Eds.), Judicial Lawmaking and Administrative Law 3 (2005).

> 1) Member States shall take all appropriate measures, whether general or particular, to ensure fulfilment of the obligations arising out of this Treaty or resulting from action taken by the institutions of the Community. They shall facilitate the achievement of the Community's tasks.
>
> 2) They shall abstain from any measure which could jeopardise the attainment of the objectives of this Treaty.

The two principal duties of Member States in respect of environmental directives are to incorporate the directives' provisions into national law (transposition) and to make sure these provisions are in fact abided by (application).[14] Transposition must take place in a timely manner, that is, before the deadline(s) indicated in the directive expire(s), and correctly. A correct transposition will, generally, require that the directive's provisions are converted into legally binding national measures, as opposed to voluntary schemes, so as to guarantee, in the words of the European Court, "full implementation of directives in law and not only in facts."[15] It follows from the text of Article 249 that word-for-word copying of directive provisions into national rules is normally not called for, although concrete bans and numerical values, including quality standards like the limit and target values from the ambient air directives, must be incorporated by the Member States literally.[16] Even though EC directives themselves generally have nothing to say on the subject of sanctions for non-observance of the rules they contain, providing for such penalties is requisite for a proper transposition by Member States.[17] In accordance with the principle of loyal co-operation, these penalties must be effective, proportionate and dissuasive, and correspond to sanctions imposed for violation of comparable provisions of domestic law.[18] Transposition is a formal legal act which is to be accompanied, as stated above, by the actual application of the Community provisions involved by the Member States.[19]

According to Article 249 of the EC Treaty, directives impose on Member States obligations of result. The case law of the European Court of Justice furthermore affirms that it is not enough for a Member State to make an *effort* to achieve the result called for in an environmental directive, but that it must actually *achieve* that result.[20] One of the cases in which the Court underscored

---

[14] Arts. 10, 175(4) and 211 of the EC Treaty. Generally, *see* J. H. Jans & A.-K. von der Heide, Europäisches Umweltrecht 187-193 (2003); and Krämer, *supra* note 8, at 278-282.

[15] Case C-131/88, *Commission v. Germany*, 1991 ECR I-825, para. 8; Krämer, *id.*, at 278-280.

[16] Krämer, *id.*, at 281.

[17] *Id.*; Jans *et al.*, *supra* note 8, at 206-213; Case C-68/88, *Commission v. Greece*, 1989 ECR 2965.

[18] *Id.*; Jans & Von der Heide, *supra* note 14, at 188-189.

[19] Case C-60/01, *Commission v. France*, of 18 June 2002; Jans & Von der Heide, *id.*, at 187-189; Krämer, *supra* note 8, at 281.

[20] Jans & Von der Heide, *id.*, at 189-193; J. H. Jans, *Europees Milieurecht*, *in* Ch. W. Backes *et al.* (Eds.), Milieurecht 76 (2006).

this concerned, in point of fact, an obligation from an air quality directive regarding the observance of limit values for certain pollutants by a given date.[21] As the 1991 judgement reads:

> It is necessary [...] to consider whether the provisions referred to by the Federal Republic of Germany *guarantee a correct implementation* of the directive.
>
> Article 3(1) of the directive requires the Member States to take appropriate measures *so that the concentrations* of sulphur dioxide and suspended particulates in the air *are not higher* than the limit values.
>
> There are [...] no general and mandatory rules under which the administrative authorities are required to adopt measures in all the cases where the limit values of the directive are likely to be exceeded.[22]

According to the Court this meant that Germany had violated its obligation under Article 3 of the directive.[23] Another ECJ decision, however, indicates that the mere fact that a situation on the ground apparently fails the standard set in an environmental directive does not always by itself justify the conclusion that the Member State has breached its obligations – especially if the standard is loosely phrased and lacks the precision of, to use the example just cited, an air quality limit value.[24]

It is clear from the foregoing that the effectiveness of EC environmental law is to a large extent a function of the quality of the transposition and application of directives by the EU Member States. Sometimes that quality is defied by the fact that EC directives must find their way into well established legal systems in which they are not necessarily welcomed wholeheartedly.[25] Besides, EC environmental directives face the common problems that tend to hamper the application of environmental law at all levels, whether international, European or national, such as the regular conflict between environmental and other interests.[26] In view of these factors, it is far from self-evident that European environmental law is uniformly and effectively put into practice in all EU Member States.

---

[21] Art. 3(1) of Directive 80/779 on air quality limit values and guide values for sulphur dioxide and suspended particulates, OJ 1980 L 229/30.

[22] Case C-361/88, *Commission v. Germany (TA Luft)*, 1991 ECR I-2567, excerpts from paras. 26, 28 and 29. Emphasis added.

[23] *Id.*, paras. 30, 32. *See also* Case C-42/89 of 5 July 1990, *Commission v. Belgium*, in which Belgium was convicted because the quality of the drinking water in the town of Verviers did *in fact* not comply with the standards in the directive concerned; *see* Jans, *supra* note 20, at 76.

[24] *See, e.g.,* Case C-365/97, *Commission v. Italy*, 1999 ECR I-7773; Jans & Von der Heide, *supra* note 14, at 192.

[25] Krämer, *supra* note 8, at 281; G. Winter, *Problems Associated with the Transposition of European Nature Protection Law into National Law, in* K. Lambers *et al.* (Eds.), Trilateral or European Protection of the Wadden Sea? 157, at 157-158 (2003).

[26] Krämer, *id.*, at 282.

1.2. The EC Environmental Law Enforcement Toolbox

The tools for promoting compliance with, and effectiveness of, EC environmental law may be roughly divided in two categories: those at the level of the Community and those at the (national) level of the Member States.

At the Community level, the European Commission is the body pre-eminently endowed with the responsibility to monitor the implementation of EC law by the Member States and is to take action in cases of suspected breach.[27] The latter charge, as briefly described below, is performed in association with the ECJ. The European Parliament, the Community Ombudsman and the European Environmental Agency play marginal and/or indirect roles at best.[28] The European Commission's supervision function covers not only the transposition but also the actual application of EC law by the Member States.[29] This task and the rather far reaching powers – certainly when compared to other international agreements – that go with it, have earned the Commission the title 'guardian of the EC Treaty'.[30] In the environmental field, the information enabling the Commission to perform its monitoring function emanates from two main sources. Firstly, under virtually each environmental directive Member States are required to issue reports on their own implementation of the directive every so often.[31] Secondly, and rather more importantly, information on potential breaches of Community environmental law is provided by "individuals, environmental or professional organisations, national, regional or European deputies, local administrations, political parties, ambassadors and occasionally even […] environment ministers of Member States"[32] availing themselves of the Commission's so-called complaint procedure.[33]

Having determined the existence of a probable violation of Community environmental law, various sanctions are available to the Commission (the threat of) which might force the Member State(s) in question into compliance. There is, for instance, the possibility of financial sanctions related to the EC Cohesion and Structural Funds.[34] Member State projects are only eligible for funding from these sources if they comply with EC law at large, including secondary environmental legislation. As Regulation 2081/93 sets out:

[27] Art. 211 EC Treaty; *see* Krämer, *id.*, at 284; Jans & Von der Heide, *supra* note 14, at 193.
[28] *See* Krämer, *id.*, at 285-286.
[29] Ch. W. Backes, *European Law for a European Sea? The Role of European Law in Nature Conservation*, *in* K. Lambers *et al.* (Eds.), Trilateral or European Protection of the Wadden Sea? 149, at 152 (2003).
[30] Krämer, *supra* note 8, at 284.
[31] *Id.*, at 282-284.
[32] *Id.*, at 286.
[33] Generally *see, e.g.*, H. E. Woldendorp, *The European Commission's Complaint Procedure*, *in* K. Lambers *et al.* (Eds.), Trilateral or European Protection of the Wadden Sea? 227 (2003); Krämer, *id.*, at 286-288.
[34] *See* Krämer, *id.*, at 292-293.

> Measures financed by the Structural Funds or receiving assistance from the EIB or from another existing financial instrument shall be in conformity with the provisions of the Treaties, with the instruments adopted pursuant thereto and with Community policies, including those concerning [...] environmental protection.[35]

The existence of this condition has mostly a preventive effect. Reportedly, the Commission has on several occasions threatened to withhold financial assistance because of a Member State's non-observance of EC environmental law.[36]

However, by far the most important enforcement machinery in the Commission's armoury is provided by Articles 226 and 228 of the EC Treaty.[37] An infringement procedure is often triggered by a complaint filed with the Commission by an environmental interest group or another of the many possible complainants enumerated earlier. The procedure of Article 226 itself consists of three stages.[38] The purpose of the first two, the formal notice of breach and the 'reasoned opinion' by the Commission, is to enable the Member State involved to bring its legislation and/or conduct in line with Community law, or present its arguments as to why in its opinion there is no violation of the law.[39] Nine out of ten procedures used to end here,[40] although recently the Commission has been proceeding to the third stage, that is, actually bringing the case before the ECJ, more quickly. To give an impression of what the final outcome of an infringement procedure typically looks like when the Commission's application is upheld by the Court, the operative part of a recent (2006) judgement is reproduced here:

> The Court hereby:
> 1) Declares that, by failing to forward to the Commission of the European Communities for 2001 all necessary information concerning the substances subject to Council Directive 1999/30/EC of 22 April 1999 relating to limit values for sulphur dioxide, nitrogen dioxide and oxides of nitrogen, particulate matter and lead in ambient air, as required under Article 11(1)(a)(i) and (ii) and (b) of Council Directive 96/62/EC of 27 September 1996 concerning ambient air quality assessment management, the Italian Republic has failed to fulfil its obligations under Article 11 of Directive 96/62 in conjunction with Article 4(1) of that directive and with Directive 1999/30 and Article 1 of Commission Decision 2001/839/EC of 8 November 2001 laying down a questionnaire to be used for annual reporting on ambient air quality assessment under Directives 96/62 and 1999/30;
> 2) Orders the Italian Republic to pay the costs.[41]

[35] Art. 7 of Regulation 2081/93, OJ 1993 L 193/5. Art. 8 of Regulation 1164/94, OJ 1994 L 130/1 has a similar stipulation in respect of the Cohesion Fund.

[36] Krämer, *supra* note 8, at 293.

[37] *Id.*, at 289; Jans & Von der Heide, *supra* note 14, at 193.

[38] *See* Krämer, *id.*, at 289-291; Jans & Von der Heide, *id.*, at 194-196.

[39] Krämer, *id.*, at 289-290.

[40] *Id.*, at 291.

[41] Case C-139/04, *Commission v. Italy*, OJ 2006 C 60/08. Emphasis added.

Whereas this particular passage has admittedly also been selected for its added value for the real EC ambient air quality law experts,[42] it illustrates above all the predominantly declaratory nature of a judgement under Article 226. The Court merely states that Italy has breached its obligations under various provisions from EC directives. Infringement decisions by the ECJ do not tend to prescribe particular measures to be taken by the noncompliant Member State or to annul, where these exist, and national measures at variance with EC law. It is thus normally up to the Member State to draw its conclusions from a judgement and take the necessary action to end the breach,[43] although recent jurisprudence might be heralding changes to this non-committal approach.[44]

The whole procedure under Article 226 arguably gets its muscle from another provision of the EC Treaty. If a Member State does not duly follow up a 'sentence' by the ECJ under Article 226, then Article 228 empowers the Commission, as part of a procedure similar to the one set out in the former provision, to ask the Court for a second declaratory judgment and for the imposition of a financial sanction in the form of a lump sum or a specific penalty payment for every further day of non-compliance. The very existence of this possibility has a deterrent and therefore preventive effect.[45] As indicated in paragraph 1 above, the Commission has had to resort to Article 228 relatively often in the environmental field. Even so, procedures seldom reach the stage of an actual ECJ judgement on account of the sudden diligence and haste of Member States to fulfil their EC obligations concerned which tends to be the result of a Commission decision to apply for a financial penalty.[46] All things considered, Member States against which an infringement procedure has been started are usually inclined, in the end, to comply.[47]

Be that as it may be, the "watchdog function of the European Commission and the European Court must not be overestimated" [48] either. From the point of view of the effectiveness of European environmental law the Community enforcement tools just discussed have a number of drawbacks.

---

[42] Other infringement cases of interest from the air quality perspective are Case C-361/88, *Commission v. Germany (TA Luft)* (treated above in section 2.1, *see supra* note 22); Case C-59/89, *Commission v. Germany (TA Luft)*; Case C-13/90, *Commission v. France*; Case C-14/90, *Commission v. France*; Case C-64/90, *Commission v. France*; Case C-146/04, *Commission v. Netherlands*; and Case C-63/05, *Commission v. Greece*.

[43] Art. 228(1) EC Treaty; Krämer, *supra* note 8, at 291; Jans & Von der Heide, *supra* note 14, at 196.

[44] *E.g.*, Case C-503/04, *Commission v. Germany*, Judgment of 18 July 2007 (pursuant to Art. 228 EC Treaty), in which the ECJ ruled that contracts awarded in violation of the public procurement rules from EC Directive 92/50 had to be rescinded; *see also* Case C-508/03, *Commission v. United Kingdom*, 2006 ECR I-3969.

[45] Krämer, *supra* note 8, at 291.

[46] *See, e.g.*, the overview in Krämer, *id.*, at 292.

[47] Backes, *supra* note 29, at 152.

[48] *Id.*

Firstly, the infringement procedure from the EC Treaty is subject to several more or less inherent limitations. The three-stage procedure of Article 226, not to mention 228, is a lengthy one and can easily take three or four years, whereas the complaint procedure often preceding it may take another year.[49] To be sure, Article 226 and, to an even larger degree, Article 228 have been primarily designed to deal with the worst excesses of non-implementation, rather than with day-to-day violations of Community (environmental) law.[50] Accordingly, even though it is employed by the European Commission increasingly often, the infringement procedure remains a last resort.[51]

Secondly, the approach to enforcement taken by the Commission in practice is, on the whole, fairly formalistic. Procedures initiated against Member States typically concern the failure to *transpose* a directive timely and/or correctly into national law (see the *TA Luft* case discussed above[52]) or the violation of reporting requirements (see the Italian case discussed above[53]) and not so much the law's material *application*[54] – whereas the latter, from the perspective of effective environmental protection, is of course what really matters at the end of the day. This relative lack of action on the part of the Commission against shortcomings of application has more than a single cause. The practice of reporting by the Member States on their own performance is, for one, unsatisfactory.[55] Contrary to the instructions in environmental directives, implementation reports are often not timely, or at all drawn up and submitted, as illustrated by the Italian infringement case quoted from above.[56] Those reports that are presented to the Commission paint a relatively reliable picture on the transposition of directives but fall short with regard to their application. They normally lack information on "difficulties of practical application or cases of non-compliance, lacunae and omissions on the side of local, regional or national administrations, inspections, sanctions, or on specific interpretations of individual provisions."[57] Some of the data which is lacking in the reports of the Member States reaches the Commission through its other main information source, the complaints procedure. Many of the complaints received by the Commission precisely concern local or regional environmental problems. The Commission, however, is located too

---

[49] Krämer, *supra* note 8, at 288 & 291; H. H. B. Vedder, *Direct Commission Enforcement of European Community Nature Conservation Law*, *in* K. Lambers *et al.* (Eds.), Trilateral or European Protection of the Wadden Sea? 181, at 182 (2003).

[50] Vedder, *id.*, at 181-182.

[51] Jans & Von der Heide, *supra* note 14, at 193.

[52] Case C-361/88; *see* Sec. 2.1 of this chapter.

[53] Case C-139/04.

[54] Vedder, *supra* note 9, at 264. There are, however, significant exceptions to this rule, e.g. Case C-494/01, *Commission v. Ireland*, 2005 ECR I-3331; *also* Jans, *supra* note 20, at 75-76.

[55] Krämer, *supra* note 8, at 282-284.

[56] Case C-139/04.

[57] Krämer, *supra* note 8, at 283.

far away and is not well enough equipped to carefully research the details of each case.[58] The dual dearth of legal power and manpower to verify on the spot in the Member State involved, whether European law is complied with is often noted in this regard.[59] As one author summarizes, the "close and overall control of the implementation of EC law in the Member States is not the task of the European Commission, nor are there enough European civil servants to fulfil such a task."[60]

Thirdly, the Commission has a broad margin of discretion in deciding whether to follow up on a citizen complaint. Private persons or organizations submitting a complaint against a Member State cannot force the Commission to act under Article 226 and no appeal is available against a decision not to do so.[61] This state of affairs is not conducive to the effectiveness of EC environmental law, all the more when considering that "not even the European Commission always seems to be fully resistant to the political pressure the Member States apply for economic reasons."[62] The "very strong influence"[63] economic interests reportedly exert on the decisions of the Commission in environmental matters is especially apparent in cases involving large infrastructural projects.[64] For these and other reasons, the overall chances of success of a complaint filed with the Commission against a Member State disregarding its European environmental duties are rather slim.[65]

The deficiencies of the Community level enforcement tools considered up to this point are, to some extent, compensated by the enforcement mechanisms applicable at the level of the individual Member States. The treatment of this national level toolset need not nearly be as elaborate here, given that its most important components are discussed at length in paragraphs 3 and 4 below. For present purposes it suffices to identify the main mechanisms and to place them in context. They are:

a) direct effect;
b) consistent interpretation ('indirect effect');
c) anticipatory effect ('*Inter-Environnement* doctrine');
d) state liability ('*Francovich* liability');
e) EC standards for (criminal) sanctions in the Member States.

The influence of the fourth, 'state liability', option appears relatively limited, although the possibility of individuals holding a Member State liable for

[58] Jans & Von der Heide, *supra* note 14, at 198.
[59] *Id.*, at 188; Krämer, *supra* note 8, at 284.
[60] Backes, *supra* note 29, at 152.
[61] Case 48/65, *Lütticke*, 1966 ECR 19; Krämer, *supra* note 8, at 287; Jans & Von der Heide, *supra* note 14, at 193.
[62] Backes, *supra* note 29, at 153.
[63] *Id.*
[64] Krämer, *supra* note 8, at 288.
[65] *Id.*

damages caused by failure to correctly transpose Community environmental directives into national law[66] may, through its preventive effect, contribute to compliance with EC environmental law. It presents citizens with a final resort when other options fail.[67] The other four 'tools' are considered in more detail below.[68]

By way of a general remark, it is probably fair to say that the watchdog function performed by the European Commission and the European Court at the Community level is performed by citizens (whether natural or legal persons) and national courts at the Member State level. Most experts would agree that the two most powerful instruments for ensuring compliance with EC environmental law are the infringement procedure of Article 226 – backed up by the silent threat of Article 228 – and the direct effect of provisions of Community law in the national legal orders of the Member States.[69]

2. Direct Effect

2.1. Leeway and Limits of Direct Effect as Enforcement Mechanism

The 45 year old doctrine of 'direct effect', which enables individuals,[70] under certain conditions, to rely directly on provisions of Community law before the national courts of the Member States, is the oldest instrument from the national level 'enforcement kit' concisely described above.[71] Many also regard it as the single most effective instrument across the board, surpassing the procedure of Article 226/228. "Millions of individuals and thousands of judges," as Vedder puts it, "will inevitably be able to keep a closer eye on the application and interpretation of European law than one institution that has a limited staff."[72]

Many academic publications on the legal ins and outs of direct effect have appeared over the years. Rather than attempting to comprehensively summarize this literature, the discussion here will focus chiefly on the role of direct effect in the context of compliance with EC environmental law.[73]

66 Joined Cases C-6/90 and C-9/90, *Francovich v. Italy*, 1991 ECR I-5357; Case C-48/93, *Factortame*, 1996 ECR I-1029.
67 Krämer, *id.*, at 292; Jans, *supra* note 14, at 243-247; J. H. Jans, *Rechtsbescherming in het Europees Milieurecht, in* J. H. Jans, H. G. Sevenster & H. H. B. Vedder (Eds.), Europees Milieurecht in Nederland 239, at 276-281 (2000); Jans *et al.*, *supra* note 8, at 321-361.
68 Direct effect in Secs. 2.1 and 2.2; consistent interpretation and anticipatory effect in Sec. 2.3; criminal sanctions in Sec. 3.
69 *E.g.*, Vedder, *supra* note 49, at 181.
70 Hereinafter, 'individual' is taken to include both natural and legal persons.
71 Case 26/62, *Van Gend & Loos*, 1963 ECR 1, is usually regarded as marking the doctrine's birth.
72 Vedder, *supra* note 49, at 185.
73 On direct effect generally, *see* S. Prechal, Directives in EC Law (2005); P. Craig &

After sketching the basics of direct effect, including its limits, the various ways in which these limits are being adjusted and circumvented to meet the enforcement needs of the Community will be discussed. As can be expected, the case law of the European Court of Justice will be a central part of this discussion. This jurisprudence, with its characteristic purposive interpretations of the EC Treaty, has been the driving force behind the birth of the direct effect doctrine and its dynamic development since.[74]

Stressing the autonomous nature of the Community legal order, the Court first launched the concept of direct effect of EC Treaty provisions, that is, the immediate enforceability of these provisions by individual citizens in national courts, in "probably the most famous of all of its rulings,"[75] *Van Gend & Loos*.[76] 'Direct' and 'immediate' in this context signify that the Community provisions take effect in the national legal orders of the Member States *of their own accord*, independently from domestic constitutions or other legislation.[77] This sets them apart from regular norms of public international law.

In 1974 the ECJ made clear, in *Van Duyn*,[78] that provisions from directives are also capable of having this direct effect:

> It would be incompatible with the *binding effect* attributed to a directive by Article [249][79] to exclude, in principle, the possibility that the obligation which it imposes may be invoked by those concerned. In particular, where the Community authorities have, by directive, imposed on Member States the obligation to pursue a particular course of conduct, the *useful effect* of such an act would be weakened if individuals were prevented from relying on it before their national courts and if the latter were prevented from taking it into consideration as an element of Community law. [...] It is necessary to examine, in every case, whether the nature, general scheme and wording of the provision in question are capable of having direct effects on the relations between Member States and individuals.[80]

The foremost implications for national judges confronted with directly effective provisions from directives which are not correctly implemented are that they must apply these EC provisions to the circumstances of the domestic cases before them. They must safeguard the legal rights these provisions afford to individuals and – as a consequence of the absolute supremacy of Community

G. de Búrca, EU Law: Text, Cases, and Materials 178-229 (2003); Jans *et al.*, *supra* note 8, at 63-96. On direct effect of environmental law *see* Jans & Von der Heide, *supra* note 14, at 203-242; Jans, *supra* note 67, at 241-291.

[74] Craig & De Búrca, *id.*, at 184.

[75] *Id.*, at 182.

[76] Case 26/62, *Van Gend & Loos*, 1963 ECR 1, at 12-13.

[77] *Id.*

[78] Case 41/74, *Van Duyn*, 1974 ECR 1337.

[79] Here and in all citations from ECJ jurisprudence below, old EC Treaty article numbers, like Art. 189 in this case, are replaced by the current ones.

[80] Para. 12; emphasis added.

law over national law[81] – render inapplicable any conflicting provisions of national law.[82] The concrete legal effects will vary along with the nature and subject matter of the national proceedings, and with the characteristics and content of the domestic legislation involved.[83] Prechal offers the following overview of different ways in which directly effective directive provisions may be deployed:

> On the one hand, there is the possible *application of the provisions of the directive to the facts of the case*. This application may often result in the creation of rights. On the other hand, there is the *review of legality* of national rules or individual decisions made under national law. Here the directive serves as a touchstone, as a standard in the light of which the legality of the measures at stake must be reviewed. In some cases the control of legality, often with the inapplicability of the contrary national rules as a sanction, thus by way of *exclusion*, may suffice to achieve the result the directive is aiming at. In other cases it may be necessary for the domestic court to apply the provisions of the directive *instead* of the national provisions, by way of *substitution*. This will be necessary in particular where the mere disapplication results in a lacuna or where there are no national legal provisions at all.[84]

The preliminary reference system founded on Article 234 of the EC Treaty is key to ensuring that domestic courts in the twenty-seven Member States apply Community law as uniformly as possible. Incidentally, most of the jurisprudence considered in the current chapter is the product of this system. However, from the perspective of direct effect as an enforcement tool the prejudicial procedure also has a hitch: it has become a victim of its own success.[85] A deluge of references by national judges is burdening the already overstrained Court of Justice and the regular time span consumed before a prejudicial decision is delivered, between one and two years, is arguably not far from "the point where it detracts from the effectiveness of the procedure."[86]

The principal conditions for and limitations on the direct effect of directive provisions are comprised, whether explicitly or implicitly, in the following excerpt from a representative ECJ judgement from 1994 on an environmental matter:

> The Court has consistently held that wherever the provisions of a directive appear, as far as their subject-matter is concerned, to be *unconditional* and *sufficiently precise*, those provisions may be relied upon by an individual *against the State* where the State *fails* to implement the directive in national law by the *period* prescribed or where it fails to implement the directive *correctly*.[87]

[81] Case 6/64, *Costa v. ENEL*, 1964 ECR 585.
[82] Case 107/77, *Simmenthal*, 1978 ECR 629.
[83] Prechal, *supra* note 73, at 232.
[84] *Id.*, at 234. Footnotes omitted; emphasis in original.
[85] Vedder, *supra* note 49, at 186.
[86] *Id.*
[87] Case C-236/92, *Comitato*, 1994 ECR I-483; emphasis added.

Firstly, the direct effect of a directive provision only comes into play when the directive involved is not (correctly) implemented and, quite understandably, after its transposition deadline has expired.[88] Already in the 1979 *Ratti* judgment, another constituent of the ECJ's extensive jurisprudence in the environmental field, it was held that such effect can exclusively arise "at the end of the prescribed period and in the event of the Member State's default."[89] Secondly, the provision in question must be *unconditional*, that is, "not subject, in its implementation or effects, to the taking of any measure either by the institutions of the Community or by the Member States,"[90] and *sufficiently precise*, which is the case "where the obligation it imposes is set out in unequivocal terms."[91] These two conditions essentially concern the provision's 'justiciability': it is unconditional and sufficiently precise when the national judge can apply it without taking on the role of legislator.[92] Thirdly, provisions meeting these criteria can only be invoked 'vertically', i.e., by citizens against a Member State. The possibility of 'horizontal' (citizen against citizen) and 'inverse vertical' (State against citizen) direct effect of directive provisions has been expressly ruled out by the European Court.[93] Both of these limitations are to be understood against the background of Article 249, according to which directives are binding only upon Member States.[94] Finally, it is frequently held that in order to have direct effect, directive provisions must confer rights on individuals.[95] The Court's jurisprudence on this matter does not seem to be entirely consistent and unequivocal and there is no agreement in the academic literature as to whether this is actually a (separate) condition for the direct effect of directive provisions.[96] This is one of the issues which will receive further attention below.

2.2. Stretching the Limits of Direct Effect: Effectiveness First

It is apparent from the *Van Duyn* passage quoted above as well as from other pertinent jurisprudence of the European Court of Justice, that the need for a full and uniform application of Community law, including directives, in all Member States is at the heart of the Court's reasoning relating to the doctrine

[88] Craig & De Búrca, *supra* note 73, at 205; Krämer, *supra* note 8, at 288.
[89] Case 148/78, *Ratti*, 1979 ECR 1629, para. 43.
[90] Case C-236/92, *Comitato*.
[91] *Id.*
[92] Prechal, *supra* note 73, at 243-244.
[93] Case 152/84, *Marshall I*, 1986 ECR 723 and Case C-91/92, *Faccini Dori*, 1994 ECR I-3325 (prohibition of horizontal direct effect); Case 80/86, *Kolpinghuis*, 1987 ECR 3969 and Case C-168/95, *Arcaro*, 1996 ECR I-4705 (prohibition of inverse vertical direct effect).
[94] The text of Art. 249(3) is reproduced above, at the beginning of section 2.1.
[95] *E.g.*, Krämer, *supra* note 8, at 289.
[96] For an overview of the discussion, *see* Prechal, *supra* note 73, at 231-241.

of direct effect.[97] As Craig and De Búrca submit, the Court in *Van Gend & Loos* "evidently considered a strong enforcement method was needed to ensure that Member States did in practice comply with the provisions to which they had agreed."[98] Similarly, the decision in *Van Duyn* was in all likelihood not entirely unconnected to the prospect of myriad citizens contributing as vigilant watchdogs to the practical operation of Community directives.[99] In legal terms it would probably be most correct to say that the ECJ's main argument in favor of the thesis of direct effect of Community law is based on the binding nature of directives as interpreted according to the interpretational rule of useful effect or *effet utile*. This interpretation assigns preference to the construction which gives a rule its fullest effect and maximum practical value and is, in turn, linked to the principle of loyal cooperation from Article 10 of the EC Treaty.[100] In brief: effectiveness first.

Additional considerations relate, *inter alia*, to legal integration and the protection of individuals' rights. Regarding the latter, it should be borne in mind that in many instances the protection of rights and the full effect of the law are two sides of the same coin. As the Court put it not too long ago, it is the responsibility of the national courts "to provide the legal protection which individuals derive from the rules of Community law *and* to ensure that those rules are fully effective."[101] In cases like *Ratti*, the ECJ made use of an auxiliary argument with a certain punitive quality, based on the notion of estoppel:[102]

> a Member State which has not adopted the implementing measures required by the directive in the prescribed periods *may not rely*, as against individuals, *on its own failure* to perform the obligations which the directive entails.
>
> It follows that a national court requested by a person who has complied with the provisions of a directive not to apply a national provision incompatible with the directive not incorporated into the internal legal order of a defaulting Member State, must uphold that request if the obligation in question is unconditional and sufficiently precise.[103]

The importance of this 'estoppel argument' should, however, not to be overrated, and it is certainly not the quintessential basis underlying the direct

[97] Jans & Von der Heide, *supra* note 14, at 203; Craig & De Búrca, *supra* note 73, at 185.
[98] Craig & De Búrca, *id.*
[99] Prechal, *supra* note 73, at 219.
[100] Prechal, *id.*, at 218-219; Jans & Von der Heide, *supra* note 14, at 203.
[101] Joined Cases C-397/01 through C-403/01, *Pfeiffer and others*, 2004 ECR I-08835.
[102] *See* Craig & De Búrca, *supra* note 73, at 204-206; Prechal, *supra* note 73, at 219-226.
[103] Case 148/78, *Ratti*, 1979 ECR 1629, paras. 22-23; emphasis added.

effect of directives.[104] Thereto, considerations of effectiveness are clearly a more convincing candidate.[105]

Against this background, it is hardly surprising that the jurisprudence of the European Court has embraced a broad concept of the State, in order to draw the boundaries of the permitted vertical direct effect as widely as possible.[106] According to jurisprudence from the late 1980s and early 1990s, the 'Member State' includes "all organs of the administration, including decentralized authorities such as municipalities"[107] as well as semi-public bodies such as nationalized industries.[108] This general rule was affirmed in the area of EC *environmental* law in 2004.[109] Needless to say, this is of substantial consequence for the enforcement options of European environmental law. It often involves appeals by non-governmental organizations (NGOs) against plans or permits drawn up and issued by decentralized governments.[110]

The possibility to invoke EC environmental directives before national courts has also been greatly enhanced by the ECJ's interpretation of the prerequisites of 'sufficiently clear' and 'unconditional', which must be met for a directive provision to have direct effect.[111] The common denominator of these two apparently strict conditions is the absence of discretion on the part of the Member States.[112] However, as the European Court has made clear, if a provision does leave the Member States a choice this does not automatically entail that it lacks direct effect. That is to say, if the provision sets out the outer limits within which that choice may be exercised, then national courts are mandated to examine whether the Member States have remained within these bounds, as long as the outer limits themselves are defined in a sufficiently unequivocal manner.[113] The case typically quoted in this connection, *Kraaijeveld*,[114] is an environmental one which revolved around a broadly drafted obligation from a directive on the performance of Environmental Impact Assessments (EIAs).[115] The judgement reiterates the *Van Duyn* statement reproduced above on the binding nature of directives and their useful effect being weakened

[104]Convincing arguments countering that thesis have been presented by Prechal, *supra* note 73, at 223-226.

[105]Craig & De Búrca, *supra* note 73, at 185; Jans & Von der Heide, *supra* note 14, at 203; Prechal, *id.*, at 219.

[106]*See* Craig & De Búrca, *id.*, at 208-211.

[107]Case 103/88, *Fratelli Costanzo*, 1989 ECR 1839, para. 31.

[108]Case C-188/89, *Foster*, 1990 ECR I-3313.

[109]Case C-201/02, *Wells*, 2004 ECR I-723, *see also* 2004 Milieu en Recht 11 (considered in more detail below) and Jans, *supra* note 20, at 80.

[110]Vedder, *supra* note 49, at 185.

[111]Jans, *supra* note 20, at 77.

[112]Prechal, *supra* note 73, at 247; Jans, *supra* note 67, at 241.

[113]Prechal, *id.*, at 236-237, 249-250; Jans, *id.*, at 248; Jans & Von der Heide, *supra* note 14, at 205; Craig & De Búrca, *supra* note 73, at 186.

[114]Case C-72/95, *Kraaijeveld*, 1996 ECR I-5403.

[115]Directive 85/337 of 27 June 1985, OJ 1985 L 175/40.

if individuals are prevented from relying on a directive provision before national courts. If the latter are prevented from applying it, the judgement adds that those courts can use such a directly effective provision "in order to rule whether the national legislature, in exercising the choice open to it as to the form and methods for implementation, has kept within the limits of its discretion set out in the directive."[116]

Two other determining factors for the possibilities of enforcing EC environmental law through the national courts are the prohibitions of inverse vertical effect and horizontal direct effect. The latter is generally perceived as the most important limitation on the direct effect of directives and a patent obstacle to the uniform application and useful effect of environmental directives.[117] The jurisprudence of the ECJ reflects the dilemma between the wording of Article 249 of the EC Treaty and the coveted *effet utile* of directives.[118] Both prohibitions come to the fore in the so-called triangular relationships that are a recurrent feature of environmental litigation.[119] Consider, for instance, environmental interest group X invoking a provision of an air quality directive which has not been properly transposed, in order to challenge the authorization granted by a government authority to polluting business Y, yet permitting it to expand its operations. Although this situation does not as such concern the invocation of a faulty implemented directive by a Member State against a private party (inverse vertical relationship), nor by one private party against another (horizontal relationship), the legal positions of the three parties involved are inextricably linked. In particular, the potential adverse legal consequences of NGO X's appeal for company Y are crystal clear. The chief question in such situations is what takes precedence under Community law: the rule that directives cannot of themselves create obligations for individuals as reflected in the two familiar prohibitions, or the need for the effective application of Community law?

A decisive preliminary judgment in this regard was handed down by the ECJ in 2004: *Wells*.[120] At issue was an appeal by Ms. Delena Wells against a license for mining operations which had been granted to Conygar Quarry by the UK Secretary of State for Transport, Local Government and the Regions. Specifically, Wells criticized the lack of a prior environmental impact assessment, directly invoking the EIA Directive that was also the subject of the *Kraaijeveld* case. The European Court answered the inevitable question put to it by the British judiciary as follows:

[116] *Kraaijeveld*, para. 56; *see also* Case C-435/97, *World Wildlife Fund*, 1999 ECR, I-5613/69.
[117] Prechal, *supra* note 73, at 255, 258.
[118] *Id.*, at 261.
[119] *Id.*, at 262-266; B. A. Beijen, *Driehoeksrelaties en de Toepassing van het Gemeenschapsrecht*, 2004 TO 150; H. F. M. W. van Rijswick & R. J. G. M. Widdershoven, *Rechtspraak: Rechtstreekse Werking van Richtlijnen in Driehoeksverhoudingen*, 2004 NTER 42.
[120] Case C-201/02, *Wells*, 2004 ECR I-723.

> an individual may not rely on a directive against a Member State where it is a matter of a State obligation directly linked to the performance of another obligation falling, pursuant to that directive, on a third party.
>
> On the other hand, *mere adverse repercussions on the rights of third parties*, even if the repercussions are certain, do not justify preventing an individual from invoking the provisions of a directive against the Member State concerned.[121]

In other words, the directive had direct effect and the fact that mining operations had to be halted during the proceedings and that the authorization might even be reversed, had to be taken for granted. Negative consequences, or 'horizontal side-effects' of this often occurring kind are thus no obstacle to the direct effect of environmental directives.[122] Another victory for the *effet utile*.

A final issue to be treated in the present context is the question whether a directive provision should create rights for individuals to qualify for direct effect, i.e., whether in order to invoke a provision an individual should fall under the provision's protective scope.[123] Again, this question is the subject of extensive debate which need not be reproduced here.[124] It will do to consider two ECJ judgments, *TA Luft* of 1991 and *Cockle Fisheries* of 2004. In the first, repeatedly addressed above already,[125] the Court determined that

> the obligation imposed on the Member States to prescribe limit values not to be exceeded [...] is imposed 'in order to protect human health in particular'.[126] It implies, therefore, that whenever the exceeding of the limit values could endanger human health, the persons concerned must be in a position to rely on mandatory rules in order to be able to assert their rights [and] where appropriate, rely on them before the national courts.

Such air quality limit values – and this goes for all comparable limit values in ambient air directives – thus have direct effect.[127] This has been affirmed by

---

[121] Paras. 56-57; emphasis added.

[122] For a more detailed discussion *see* Van Rijswick & Widdershoven, *supra* note 119. *See also* Beijen, *supra* note 119; Prechal, *supra* note 73, at 264; Vedder, *supra* note 9, at 264.

[123] *See above* at the end of section 3.1.

[124] Generally, *see* Prechal, *supra* note 73, at 231-241; R. Meijer, *De Schutznorm in het Gemeenschapsrecht: Over de Rol van Rechten van Particulieren bij Rechtstreekse Werking en Aansprakelijkheid*, 2005 TMA 189.

[125] Case C-361/88; *see* para. 2, *see supra* note 22, 42 and 51.

[126] Reference is made to Art. 1 of Directive 80/779 of 15 July 1980 on air quality limit values and guide values for sulphur dioxide and suspended particulates.

[127] *See also* M. Gasparinetti & D. van den Hout, *Revising the EU Air Quality Legislation: Experiences and Proposed Improvements*, 4 JEEPL 292, at 298 (2006); R. Klinger, *Exceedance of Limit Values for Fine Dust Particles: Violation of Community Law before German Courts*, 4 JEEPL 300 (2006); T. P. Streppel, *Rechtsschutzmöglichkeiten des Einzelnen im Luftqualitätsrecht*, 2006 EurUP 191, at 192.

the European[128] and national courts[129] alike. The protective scope of the duty relating to limit values was thus interpreted in a broad, contextual manner.

The last judgment to be considered in this section, *Cockle Fisheries*,[130] is a landmark decision from more than a single point of view, although its discussion here will be confined to direct effect.[131] In the Dutch proceedings leading to the prejudicial reference, two nature protection NGOs contested the lawfulness of licenses issued by the Secretary of State for Nature, Agriculture and Fisheries to the 'PO Kokkelvisserij', the producers' association of Netherlands cockle fisheries, for the mechanical fishing of cockles in the protected natural site Wadden Sea. This area had been designated as a Special Protection Area (SPA) under the Birds Directive,[132] so that activities potentially harmful to it were subject to the authorization scheme of Article 6 of the Habitats Directive,[133] which should have but had not yet been transposed into Dutch law. The NGOs invoked the Habitats Directive in court and contended that an 'appropriate assessment' should have been carried out in respect of mechanical cockle fisheries – alleged to cause serious and irreversible damage to the Wadden Sea ecosystem – in accordance with Article 6(3) of the Habitats Directive.[134] The European Court was asked by the Dutch Council of State, among other things, whether Article 6(3) of the Habitats Directive has direct effect.

By way of an affirmative answer, the judgment of the ECJ reiterates the *Van Duyn* formula, as extended in *Kraaijeveld*:

> As regards the right of an individual to rely on a directive and of the national court to take it into consideration, it would be incompatible with the binding effect attributed to a directive by Article 249 EC to exclude, in principle, the possibility that the obligation which it imposes may be relied on by those

[128]Case C-59/89, *Commission v. Germany (TA Luft)*; Cases C-13/90, C-14/90 and C-64/90, *Commission v. France*.

[129]*Bayerischer Verwaltungsgerichtshof* (highest administrative law court in Bavaria, Germany), 18 May 2006, Az 22 BV 05/2462.

[130]Case C-127/02, *Cockle Fisheries*, 2004 ECR I-07405, *also in* 2004 AB, 365 (with note by Ch. W. Backes).

[131]On other implications of the judgment, relating to substantive European nature conservation law and the application of the precautionary principle, *see* J. Verschuuren, *Shellfish for Fishermen or for Birds? Article 6 Habitats Directive and the Precautionary Principle*, 17 JEL 265 (2005); A. Trouwborst, *The Precautionary Principle in General International Law: Combating the Babylonian Confusion*, 16 RECIEL 185, at 192-193 (2007); H. H. G. Post, *Waddenzeebeleid: Nederland Teruggefloten door het EU Hof*, 2005 NJB 1194; J. E. Hoitink & M. P. E. du Manoir-Schutte, *Europees Hof Verduidelijkt Toetsingskader Artikel 6 Habitatrichtlijn*, 2004 TO 238.

[132]Directive 79/409 on the conservation of wild birds, OJ 1979 L 103/1.

[133]*See* Art. 7 of the 'Habitats' Directive, Directive 92/43/EEC on the conservation of natural habitats and of wild fauna and flora, OJ 1992 L 206/7.

[134]The first part of Art. 6(3) states: "Any plan or project not directly concerned with or necessary to the management of the site but likely to have a significant effect thereon, either individually or in combination with other plans or projects, shall be subject to appropriate assessment of its implications for the site in view of the site's conservation objectives."

> concerned. In particular, where the Community authorities have, by directive, imposed on Member States the obligation to pursue a particular course of conduct, the effectiveness of such an act would be weakened if individuals were prevented from relying on it before their national courts, and if the latter were prevented from taking it into consideration as an element of Community law in order to rule whether the national legislature, in exercising the choice open to it as to the form and methods for implementation, has kept within the limits of its discretion set by the directive (see *Kraaijeveld and Others*, paragraph 56). That also applies to ascertaining whether, failing transposition into national law of the relevant provision of the directive concerned, the national authority which has adopted the contested measure has kept within the limits of its discretion set by that provision.
>
> Consequently, the answer to the [...] question must be that where a national court is called on to ascertain the lawfulness of an authorisation for a plan or project within the meaning of Article 6(3) of the Habitats Directive, it can determine whether the limits on the discretion of the competent national authorities set by that provision have been complied with, even though it has not been transposed into the legal order of the Member State concerned despite the expiry of the time-limit laid down for that purpose.[135]

Cockle Fisheries is obviously of the *Kraaijeveld* type (direct effect of outer limits) and also of the *Wells* type (triangular relationship with horizontal 'side effects') and confirms the outcome of each.[136] It also reaffirms that legality review is not, contrary to what is sometimes held, necessarily confined to national implementing legislation but may concern any measure, in this case fishing permits granted in the absence of transposition legislation.[137] Most interesting, however, is the judgment's meaning for the question raised above on individual rights and protective scope.

If one accepts that the creation of subjective rights is a condition for the direct effect of directive provisions, then *TA Luft* already made clear that 'protective scope' is to be interpreted extensively.[138] The Court's ruling in *Cockle Fisheries*, however, makes it more difficult to defend the former position. After all, unlike EC rules on air or water quality, Article 6(3) of the Habitats Directive does *not* create subjective rights for individuals, but serves the exclusive interest of nature protection.[139] *Cockle Fisheries* is not at all about individual rights, and all about effectiveness. The judgment, therefore, seems to corroborate the position of those who believe that individual rights

[135]Case C-127/02, paras. 66 and 70.

[136]Paras. 148-150 of the Opinion of Advocate-General J. Kokott of 29 January 2004 contain reasoning similar to *Wells*, which is implicitly followed by the Court in its judgment.

[137]Prechal, *supra* note 73, at 237; Jans *et al.*, *supra* note 8, at 70.

[138]Jans, *supra* note 67, at 279.

[139]Opinion of A-G J. Kokott in Case C-127/02, 29 January 2004, para. 143; H. F. M. W. van Rijswick & R. J. G. M. Widdershoven, *Doorwerking van het EG-Recht, in het Bijzonder in het Waterbeheer*, 2005 TMA 50, at 55.

are not a decisive factor for determining direct effect.[140] Alternatively, the individual rights concept can be understood in a procedural sense, namely as the real possibility to invoke the directive provision involved – also when a real subjective right does not exist and when the individual relying on the provision clearly falls outside of its protective scope.[141] In this sense, direct effect, itself determined by the absence of discretion and the other criteria as discussed above, creates a right to invoke. According to yet another view, protective scope does play a role in determining whether a directive provision has direct effect, but the limits of this scope are simply stretched very widely when direct effect is considered necessary for realizing the full effect of the directive – a situation of which *Cockle Fisheries* would be a prime example.[142] Whichever theory may be the right one, the fact of the matter remains that the European Court has not allowed the issue of individual rights and protective scope to get in the way of the enforceability of environmental directives through the courts of the Member States.

2.3. Skirting the Limits of Direct Effect: Indirect and Anticipatory Effect

The limits of direct effect can only be stretched so far. Apart from optimizing enforcement possibilities *within* the established outer limits of direct effect as just discussed, the EC Treaty as interpreted by the European Court of Justice also provides ways to *bypass* these limits altogether. Below, two doctrines or approaches are discussed which offer alternative routes in cases where the proper direct effect of an environmental directive is blocked by the prohibition of horizontal direct effect, by the condition that the implementation period of the deadline must have expired, or by the criterion demanding that provisions must be 'unconditional' to have direct effect. Under certain circumstances these doctrines make it possible to achieve the same result, namely the full application of provisions of EC (environmental) law, even when relying on the direct effect of this law as such is out of the question.

The first of these two approaches is the doctrine referred to as consistent interpretation, directive-conform interpretation, or *'indirect effect'*, according to which the national legislation of Member States is to be interpreted in conformity with pertinent (but poorly implemented) directives: the judge

140 *E.g.*, Jans & Von der Heide, *supra* note 14, at 222; Jans, *supra* note 67, at 242 & 256; Prechal, *supra* note 73, at 240; Hoitink & Du Manoir-Schutte, *supra* note 131, at 241. If it is correct that individual rights are *not* a prerequisite for direct effect, then cases like *TA Luft* would of course still be relevant for the establishment of *Francovich* liability, where subjective rights do form a hard condition.

141 Jans & Von der Heide, *id.*

142 Meijer, *supra* note 124, at 190-191.

formally applies the national law, but still accomplishes the directive's result.[143] After setting out the basics of this doctrine in the *Von Colson* case,[144] these were further clarified by the European Court of Justice in *Marleasing*:[145]

> the Member States' obligation arising from a directive to achieve the result envisaged by the directive and their duty under Article [10] of the Treaty to take all appropriate measures, whether general or particular, to ensure the fulfillment of that obligation, is binding on all the authorities of Member States including, for matters within their jurisdiction, the courts. It follows that, in applying national law, whether the provisions in question were adopted before or after the directive, the national court called upon to interpret it is required to do so, as far as possible, in the light of the wording and purpose of the directive in order to achieve the result pursued by the latter and thereby comply with the third paragraph of Article [249] of the Treaty.[146]

Marleasing demonstrated that the doctrine of consistent interpretation applied to all national law – not only to legislation adopted to implement the directive involved – and seemed, implicitly, to indicate that the doctrine also applied in proceedings between individuals.[147] Although later jurisprudence of the Court shed some doubt on the latter premise,[148] all traces of such doubt were removed by yet another important ECJ prejudicial judgment from the, for present purposes, rich harvest (*Wells*, *Cockle Fisheries*) of the year 2004: *Pfeiffer*.[149] Indeed, in *Pfeiffer* the European Court stated that the principle of consistent interpretation demands that national judges do the utmost, within the limits of their competence, to ensure the effectiveness of directive provisions which are by their nature 'directly effective' but cannot be applied as such on account of the prohibition of horizontal direct effect.[150] The directive-conform interpretation of national law was thus presented by the Court, in so many words, as the ideal – and indeed, mandatory – solution for problems provoked by the ban on horizontal direct effect.[151]

In sum, the doctrine of consistent interpretation makes it possible for one individual to rely in court on a provision from a defectively transposed environmental directive against another private party, albeit *indirectly*, namely by invoking relevant national law as interpreted in light of the directive provision concerned. Like this, the application and effectiveness of directives

---

[143] Generally, *see* Craig & De Búrca, *supra* note 73, at 211-220; Jans *et al.*, *supra* note 8, at 99-112. On indirect effect of EC environmental law, *see* Jans & Von der Heide, *supra* note 14, at 234-238; Van Rijswick & Widdershoven, *supra* note 139, at 52-53. For a concrete example, *see supra* note 4.

[144] Case 14/83, *Von Colson*, 1984 ECR 1891, *see* para. 26.

[145] Case C-106/89, *Marleasing*, 1990 ECR I-4135.

[146] *Id.*, para. 8.

[147] Craig & De Búrca, *supra* note 73, at 211; Jans & Von der Heide, *supra* note 14, at 228 & 234.

[148] Case C-168/95, *Arcaro*, 1996 ECR I-4705.

[149] Joined Cases C-397/01 through C-403/01, *Pfeiffer*, 5 October 2004.

[150] *Id.*; Van Rijswick & Widdershoven, *supra* note 139, at 52.

[151] Van Rijswick & Widdershoven, *id.*

which have not been properly transposed is promoted notwithstanding the prohibition of horizontal direct effect of directives.[152] *Marleasing* and *Pfeiffer* did not concern environmental law, but it is evident that they have enhanced the possibilities for enforcement of environmental directives through civil law proceedings – for instance by an environmental NGO against a polluting factory – in the courts of the Member States.[153] To all intents and purposes, after *Wells*[154] and *Pfeiffer* the prohibition of horizontal direct effect does not seem to pose much of an obstacle any more to the effective application of EC environmental law.[155]

Turning now to the doctrine of *anticipatory effect*, as mentioned above directive provisions can only have direct effect after the applicable transposition period has come to pass. Put differently, individuals cannot in a national court invoke a provision from a directive prior to the implementation date indicated in that directive. After all, the Member State is only bound to accomplish the directive's result by the time this deadline expires. Similarly, directive provisions can only have direct effect if no further national or European implementation is required; they must be unconditional.

In its 1997 prejudicial judgment in the *Inter-Environnement* case,[156] the European Court of Justice pointed the way to a potential getaway route to escape the effect of these fundamental limitations of direct effect. In order to solve the national case before it, which involved an EC directive on hazardous wastes,[157] the Belgian Council of State had asked the ECJ to explain the obligations, if any, of the Member States *during* the prescribed implementation period, and in particular whether Member States were prevented by Community law from adopting measures contrary to a directive during this period.

The starting point for the ECJ's answer is similar to its reasoning with regard to indirect effect, namely that the duty of a Member State, including its courts, to take all the measures necessary to achieve the result prescribed by a directive is a binding obligation imposed by Article 249 and the directive itself.[158] From the moment of its notification, the Court argued, a directive has legal effect with respect to the Member States to which it is addressed.[159] The judgment concedes that the implementation period laid down in directives is specifically intended to give Member States sufficient time to take the necessary action.[160] Even so, "it is during the transposition period that the

[152]Craig & De Búrca, *supra* note 73, at 212.
[153]Van Rijswick & Widdershoven, *supra* note 139, at 52-53; Jans & Von der Heide, *supra* note 14, at 234-238.
[154]*See supra* section 3.2.
[155]*See also* Van Rijswick & Widdershoven, *supra* note 119, at 45.
[156]Case C-129/96, *Inter-Environnement*, 1997 ECR I-7411.
[157]Directive 75/442, as amended.
[158]Para. 40.
[159]Para. 41.
[160]Para. 43.

Member States must take the measures necessary to ensure that the result prescribed by the directive is achieved at the end of that period."[161] What is more:

> Although the Member States are not obliged to adopt those measures before the end of the period prescribed for transposition, it follows from [Article 10(2)] in conjunction with [Article 249] and from the directive itself that during that period they must *refrain from taking any measures liable seriously to compromise the result prescribed.*[162]

It is up to the national courts to assess whether this is the case.[163]

There is a clear resemblance between the Court's application of the principle of loyal co-operation – see especially the text of Article 10(2) of the EC Treaty reproduced above[164] – to the implementation period of directives, and the duty of States under the Vienna Convention on the Law of Treaties to abstain, in the period between signature and entry into force of a treaty, from acts which are contrary to the treaty's object and purpose.[165]

Meanwhile, national courts have in several environmental cases successfully traveled along the route laid out by the European Court in *Inter-Environnement* and subsequent jurisprudence,[166] also referred to as the doctrine of anticipatory effect.[167] One of these is the Dutch Council of State. In a 2001 case, a permit was challenged by an NGO on grounds of expected adverse effects for a natural site.[168] Although the area had *not* then been designated as a Site of Community Importance (SCI) under the Habitats Directive, the Council of State upheld the appeal and annulled the permit because the licensing authority had failed to consider whether the permit could seriously jeopardize the result of the Habitats Directive.[169] The German highest administrative court, the *Bundesverwaltungsgericht*, has applied a similar approach in cases involving planning decisions, ruling that such decisions ought to be reviewed in light of the obligation not to compromise the Habitats Directive's objectives.[170]

---

[161] Para. 44.

[162] Para. 45; emphasis added.

[163] Para. 46.

[164] At the outset of Sec. 2.1.

[165] Art. 18 of the Convention on the Law of Treaties (Vienna, 23 May 1969).

[166] *See* Cases C-157/02, *Rieser*, 2004 ECR I-1477; C-14/02, *ATRAL*, 2003 ECR I-4431; C-316/04, *Stichting Zuid-Hollandse Milieufederatie*, 2005 ECR I-9759; C-212/04, *Adeneler*, 2006 ECR I-6057; C-138/05, *Stichting Zuid-Hollandse Milieufederatie*, 2006 ECR I-8339; C-244/05, *Bund Naturschutz in Bayern*, 2006 ECR I-8445; and C-422/05, *Commission v. Belgium*, Judgment of 14 June 2007.

[167] *See, e.g.*, J. H. Jans, *Beyond Direct Effect: Some Observations on Article 6 of the Habitats Directive*, *in* K. Lambers *et al.* (Eds.), Trilateral or European Protection of the Wadden Sea? 143, at 145-147 (2003); Jans *et al.*, *supra* note 8, at 72-73; Winter, *supra* note 25, at 163.

[168] ABRvS 11 July 2001, *see also* 2001 Milieu en Recht 38 and Jans, *id.*, at 146.

[169] *Id.*

[170] BVerwGE 107 1, at 21, *A 20*, and BVerwGE 110 302, at 308, *Hildesheimer Ortsumgehung*; *see* Jans, *id.*

Recently, an environmental NGO successfully invoked the anticipatory effect of EC directive provisions on plant protection products and biocides before the Dutch Administrative Court for Trade and Industry.[171]

Individuals or environmental groups can thus bypass the conditions for direct effect which demand that the applicable implementation deadline must have expired and that provisions should be unconditional, by relying on the doctrine of anticipatory effect. As with the indirect effect doctrine discussed above, the *Inter-Environnement* approach makes it possible to achieve a direct-effect-like outcome, even if proper direct effect is precluded. The significance of anticipatory effect for the implementation and enforcement of EC environmental law is obvious. As Jans sums it up, it can be:

> a very useful weapon in the hands of NGOs, in particular in those areas of European law where the other instruments of legal action (direct effect, indirect effect and *Francovich* liability) fail to produce the desired result.[172]

3. Penalties Under Criminal Law

3.1. The EC and Criminal Penalties: A Shifting Frontier?

On 9 February 2007 the European Commission presented a Proposal for a Directive on the protection of the environment through criminal law.[173] The proposal is the latest effort in a drawn-out campaign by the Commission to improve the implementation of European environmental law. The topic of environmental protection through criminal penalties illustrates very well the ongoing pursuit of greater effectiveness for EC environmental law and the growing impact of European law on the domestic legal orders of the Member States. It also illustrates the tension between the Community and the Member States that is the, apparently, unavoidable by-product of the latter two phenomena.

Member States have traditionally been wary of relinquishing (part of) their sovereign powers in the realm of criminal law, a wariness which is reflected in the fact that the EC Treaty does not specifically attribute competence to the Community in the fields of criminal law and criminal procedure.[174] Also, as stated before, environmental directives hardly ever contain provisions on the sanctions to be imposed by Member States for non-compliance.[175] In the

[171] College van Beroep voor het Bedrijfsleven, *Stichting Zuid-Hollandse Milieufederatie v. College voor de Toelating van Bestrijdingsmiddelen*, BA4400, AWB 04/185, Judgment of 4 May 2007; *see also* Cases C-316/04 and 138/05, *supra* note 166.

[172] Jans, *supra* note 167, at 146-147.

[173] COM(2007)51.

[174] Krämer, *supra* note 8, at 281.

[175] *See* section 1.1.

rare instances where they do, the provisions involved tend to remain rather imprecise about the character and severity of the penalties required. They limit themselves to the statement that sanctions must be effective, proportionate and act as a deterrent[176] – thus merely reiterating the general standard already applicable to the implementation of any directive owing to Article 10 of the EC Treaty.[177] Even in respect of administrative sanctions under directives the Community has generally exercised self-restraint by avoiding detailed provisions.[178] Similar considerations apply to penalties under the, much less common, environmental regulations that have been adopted by the Community, even though Article 229 of the EC Treaty indicates that regulations could contain punitive sanctions.[179]

The European Commission, convinced that the existing penalties established by the Member States were not sufficient to achieve full compliance with EC environmental law let go of some of its own self-restraint when it issued a first proposal for a directive on environmental crime in 2001.[180] This attempt to push back the frontier between Community and Member States in the field of sanctions for environmental crime was met with a frosty response from the Council and, by implication, many a Member State. The ensuing institutional skirmishes between Council and Commission over proper legal bases, decision-making procedures and competences merit some consideration here as a prelude to the discussion of the currently pending 2007 Directive Proposal below.

Ignoring the Commission's original proposal for a directive, in 2003 the Council instead adopted a Framework Decision on the same subject matter, and with partly overlapping content, on the basis of Title VI of the Treaty on European Union (EU Treaty).[181] Such a Framework Decision had already been called for by Denmark in February 2000. The Commission, in turn, reacted to the Framework Decision through the prompt instigation of an action for its annulment before the European Court of Justice.[182] A comparison of the 2001 Commission proposal and the 2003 Framework Decision will clarify the stakes of the standoff. The legal basis for the proposed directive would be the *environment* title of the *EC* Treaty.[183] The legal basis for the Framework Decision was the *police and justice co-operation in criminal matters* title of

[176] *E.g.*, Art. 11 of Directive 99/32 on the sulphur content of certain fuels, OJ 1999 L 121/13.
[177] Case C-68/88, *Commission v. Greece*, 1989 ECR 2965; *see supra* section 1.1.
[178] Krämer, *supra* note 8, at 281.
[179] *Id.*
[180] Proposal for a Directive on the protection of the environment through criminal law, OJ 2001 C 180 E.
[181] Framework Decision 2003/80/JHA on the protection of the environment through criminal law, OJ 2003 L 29/55.
[182] Action brought on 15 April 2003, Case C-176/03.
[183] Art. 175(1) EC Treaty.

the *EU* Treaty.[184] In brief, the first pillar of the European Union was pitted against the third pillar. For decision-making the most important consequences of acting within the third pillar instead of the first one are that the Commission does not propose the instrument, that unanimity is required for its adoption, and that the role of the European Parliament is limited. For the implementation of an adopted instrument, it means that the Commission lacks monitoring competence and the European Court lacks powers of enforcement. Also, Framework Decisions lack direct effect.[185]

In the annulment procedure, in which the Commission was supported by the European Parliament, and the Council by eleven EU Member States,[186] it was up to the ECJ to cut the Gordian knot. It did so in September 2005.[187] In its judgment, the Court recognized that "[a]s a general rule, neither criminal law nor the rules of criminal procedure fall within the Community's competence."[188] However, the protection of the environment clearly does.[189] In this regard, the Court highlighted the prominent position of environmental protection amongst the objectives of the Community.[190] Consequently, the Court continued (in a pronouncement the significance of which extends well beyond the environmental sphere) that the lack of a general EC competence in criminal law affairs:

> does not prevent the Community legislature, when the application of effective, proportionate and dissuasive criminal penalties by the competent national authorities is an essential measure for combating serious environmental offences, from taking measures which relate to the criminal law of the Member States which it considers necessary in order to ensure that the rules which it lays down on environmental protection are fully effective.[191]

Therefore, given their environmental aim and content, the relevant provisions from the Framework Decision could – and should[192] – have been adopted on the basis of Article 175 of the EC Treaty.[193] Accordingly, the Court annulled the Framework Decision. With the latter instrument off the table, the European Commission went on to prepare another proposal for a directive, namely the one it presented in February 2007.

---

[184] Arts. 29, 31(3) and 34(2)(b) EU Treaty.

[185] Art. 34(2)(b) EU Treaty.

[186] Denmark, Finland, France, Germany, Greece, Ireland, the Netherlands, Portugal, Spain, Sweden, and the United Kingdom.

[187] Case C-176/03, *Commission v. Council*, 2005 ECR I-7879; *see also* Jans *et al.*, *supra* note 8, at 236-237.

[188] Case C-176/03, para. 47.

[189] Paras. 41-43.

[190] Para. 41.

[191] Para. 48.

[192] According to Art. 47 (and 29(1)) of the EU Treaty, nothing in the EU Treaty is to affect the EC Treaty.

[193] Para. 51 of the judgment.

3.2. The 2007 Directive Proposal

Before reviewing the substance of the most recent proposal, it is appropriate to dwell for a moment on the rationale of the Commission's efforts, as reflected in the following excerpts from the proposed directive's preamble:

> The Community is concerned at the rise in environmental offences and their effects, which are increasingly extending beyond the borders of the States in which the offences are committed. Such offences pose a threat to the environment and therefore call for an appropriate response.
>
> Experience has shown that the existing systems of sanctions have not been sufficient to achieve complete compliance with laws for the protection of the environment. Such compliance can and should be strengthened by the application of criminal sanctions, which demonstrate a social disapproval of a qualitatively different nature compared to administrative sanctions or a compensation mechanism under civil law.
>
> In order to achieve effective protection of the environment, there is a particular need for more dissuasive sanctions for environmentally harmful activities, which typically cause or are likely to cause substantial damage to the air, including the stratosphere, soil, water, animals or plants, including to the conservation of species.
>
> Environmentally harmful activities should be punishable by effective, proportionate and dissuasive criminal sanctions, which should also apply to legal persons throughout the Community, because environmental offences are committed, to a large extent, in the interest of legal persons or for their benefit.
>
> Furthermore, the significant differences in the level of sanctions in the Member States make it necessary to foresee, under certain circumstances, an approximation of those levels corresponding to the seriousness of the offence.[194]

As these paragraphs have been selected in part for their self-explanatory nature, it suffices to consider a few concrete examples and statistics that can be found in Commission documents to illustrate the various reasons behind the proposed EC rules.[195]

Organized environmental crime is allegedly booming. It turns out to be much cheaper, e.g., to dump noxious wastes illegally (in EU or third countries) than to dispose of them legally, as the recent *Probo Koala* incident exemplifies. In Italy alone the 'eco-mafia' is estimated to have a business potential of 22 billion euros. Besides, offences like illegal waste disposal, to stick to the example, have an adverse impact not only on the environment, but also on the economic viability of law-abiding businesses. Supposedly, about three-fourths

[194]Proposal for a Directive on the protection of the environment through criminal law of 9 February 2007, COM(2007)51, preambular paras. and 2, 3, 6, 10 and 12.

[195]These are mostly taken from a Commission staff working document (Impact assessment), SEC(2007)160, accompanying the Proposal.

of all organized environmental criminal operations in Europe have cross-border implications and the lives of those committing them is made easier by the considerable differences in sanctions that exist between the twenty-seven EU Member States. The maximum fine for illegally trading endangered species varies from 1,293 euros in Poland to 450,000 euros in the Netherlands. Maximum prison sentences for the same offence range from 6 months in Luxemburg to 8 years in the Czech Republic, Lithuania and Slovakia.[196] Upon presentation of the directive proposal, and as an ostensible part of the policy of 'naming, shaming and faming' announced by the Commission in 2001,[197] Justice Commissioner Franco Frattini told the press that overall the Czech Republic, Germany and Finland were amongst the best at environmental law enforcing, while Cyprus, Italy and Malta were amongst the worst.[198]

The aim of the 2007 proposal is straightforward. As the first substantive provision indicates, the proposed directive establishes measures relating to criminal law "in order to protect the environment more effectively."[199] The main obligations for Member States in the proposal are to qualify certain activities as criminal offences, and to make those offences punishable by maximum penalties, the minimum of which is specified in the directive.

Regarding the former, the proposal stipulates that the Member States are to ensure that the following acts constitute criminal offences, "when committed intentionally or with at least serious negligence." (a) the emission, whether lawful or unlawful, of materials into air, soil or water causing the death or serious injury of any person; (b) the emission of materials into air, soil or water, waste treatment, the operation of environmentally risky plants and acts concerning radioactive substances, insofar as these activities are unlawful and cause or are likely to cause death or serious injury to any person or "substantial damage to the quality of air, soil, water, animals or plants"; (c) illegal waste shipments; (d) unlawful acts involving wild fauna or flora; (e) the unlawful significant deterioration of protected habitat; and (f) unlawful trade in or use of ozone-depleting substances.[200] The instigation of and participation in any of these acts must also be qualified as criminal offences.[201] Member States must furthermore make sure that not only natural, but also legal persons may be held liable for the criminal offences just enumerated.[202] Incidentally, the reader will have noted the obvious relevance of the proposed directive to the topic of ambient air quality.

---

[196] *Id.*, at 15-16.
[197] *See* para. 2(1) of the Commission's Proposal for the Sixth Environmental Action Programme, COM(2001)31, OJ 2001 C 154 E/218; *also* Vedder, *supra* note 9, at 264.
[198] *E.g.*, A. Kroeger, *EU Gets Tough on 'Green Crimes*, BBC News, 9 February 2007, available at http://news.bbc.co.uk.
[199] Directive proposal, COM(2007)51, Art. 1.
[200] Art. 3.
[201] Art. 4.
[202] Art. 6.

These environmental criminal offences must be made punishable by "effective, proportionate and dissuasive" sanctions which, in the case of natural persons, are to be "criminal" and, in the case of legal persons, have got to include "criminal or non-criminal" fines.[203] The proposed directive lays down the ranges of the 'minimum maximum penalties' to be implemented by the Member States, in the form of prison sentences for individuals or fines for legal persons.[204] For all the qualified criminal offences the prescribed severity of these sanctions is determined by the mental state of the offender – serious negligence or intent – and the result of the offence – substantial damage to the environment or serious injury or death of people.[205] Because the provisions in question are fairly convoluted it is convenient to depict the 'minimum maximum' ranges schematically:

<table>
<tr><th></th><th>'minimum maximum'
for natural persons</th><th>'minimum maximum'
for legal persons</th></tr>
<tr><td>serious negligence & substantial environmental harm*</td><td>1 – 3 years in prison</td><td>€ 300,000 – 500,000</td></tr>
<tr><td>serious negligence & death or serious injury</td><td rowspan="2">2 – 5 years in prison</td><td rowspan="2">€ 500,000 – 750,000</td></tr>
<tr><td>intent & substantial environmental harm</td></tr>
<tr><td>intent & death or serious injury</td><td>5 – 10 years in prison</td><td>€ 750,000 – 1,000,000</td></tr>
</table>

The various penalties may, according to the proposed directive, be accompanied by other sanctions or measures, such as publication of the conviction or an obligation to reinstate the environment.[206]

Whichever way, it is clear that the proposed directive, which is now subject to the cogs and wheels of the EC co-decision procedure, does not please everyone. "It's a significant transfer of power to the Commission," the leader of the British Conservatives in the European Parliament was quoted as saying, while adding that decisions on the criminalization of offences in

[203] Arts. 5(1) and 7(1).

[204] Arts. 5(2)-(4) and 7(2).

[205] To give an impression, Art. 5(2) determines that "Member States shall ensure that the commission of the offences referred to in Article 3(b) to (h) is punishable by a maximum of at least between one and three years imprisonment where the offence is committed with serious negligence and causes substantial damage to air, soil, water, animals and plants."

* The term actually employed in the proposed directive is "substantial damage to the quality of air, soil, water, animals or plants."

[206] Arts. 5(5) and 7(4).

Britain should be a matter for the United Kingdom and not the EU.[207] "We all support penalties against environmental vandals but this sets an alarming precedent."[208]

The last chapter in the story – for now, that is – came in the form of an October 2007 ECJ ruling on the (non-)validity of a Framework Decision containing rules to improve the criminal-law regime relating to ship-source contamination, which had been adopted by the Council in the aftermath of the *Prestige* oil pollution episode.[209] In this case, as in the 2005 one, the Commission had challenged the Framework Decision contending that its subject matter should be dealt with in the 'first pillar'. The Court recalled its earlier jurisprudence and determined that:

> when the application of effective, proportionate and dissuasive criminal penalties by the competent national authorities is an essential measure for combating serious environmental offences, the Community legislature may require the Member States to introduce such penalties in order to ensure that the rules which it lays down in that field are fully effective.[210]

Overall, however, the judgment proved a setback for the Commission's efforts. The 2007 procedure boiled down to the specific question whether the EC is also empowered to prescribe the imposition of 'minimum maximum penalties'. The answer by the Court was categorically in the negative: "the determination of the *type and level* of the criminal penalties to be applied does *not* fall within the Community's sphere of competence."[211] The ECJ thus gives and takes away. As a result of the clear line drawn by it here, the minimum maximum penalties outlined above will have to be removed from the proposed directive on environmental protection through criminal law.

The new ambient air quality directive that has been finally adopted on 14th April 2008 by the Council and Parliament, in any case, obliges the Member States to "lay down the rules on penalties applicable to infringements" of the national implementation provisions, to "take all measures necessary to ensure that they are implemented," and to ensure that the penalties provided for are "effective, proportionate and dissuasive."[212]

To be continued …

---

207 Timothy Kirkhope, quoted by Kroeger, *supra* note 198.

208 *Id.*

209 Case C-440/05, *Commission v. Council*, Judgment of 23 October 2007; Framework Decision 2005/667/JHA of 12 July 2005 to strengthen the criminal-law framework for the enforcement of the law against ship-source pollution, OJ 2005 L 255/264.

210 Case C-440/05, para. 66.

211 Para. 70; emphasis added.

212 Directive 2008/50/EC on ambient air quality and cleaner air in Europe (OJ 2008 L152/1), Appendix, *infra*; *see also* para. 26 of the preamble.

4. Conclusion

The spotlight of this chapter has been on the quest for greater effectiveness of European environmental law and the related growing impact of this law on the national legal orders of the EU Member States, orders which are gradually being 'Europeanised'.[213] The relatively frequent resort to Articles 226 and 228 of the EC Treaty in environmental cases and the 2007 directive proposal on environmental protection through criminal law are some indication of the European Commission's determination to ensure better compliance with EC environmental legislation by the EU Member States. Likewise, the ECJ jurisprudence on direct effect in environmental cases and the recent judgments on criminal penalties leave little room for doubt about the stance of the European Court. The reasoning in this case law consistently emphasises the need for an effective application of European environmental law.

It remains to be seen whether the push for a more effective application of Community environmental law will actually result in a better protection of the environment. Regardless of the answer, however, an increased impact of this body of European law on the domestic legal orders of the Member States seems to be guaranteed.

[213] *See* (the title of) Jans *et al.*, *supra* note 8.

Part III

The Future

MARCO GASPARINETTI

Air Quality: A Breathtaking Directive?

In 2005 the Commission proposed a Directive on ambient air quality[1] to replace the existing air quality 'framework' Directive[2] and three of its 'daughter directives'.[3] The implementation of these Directives at the national and local level has attracted very significant public interest and media coverage. Therefore revising them was not an easy task for the EU Institutions who share the power to pass legislation. In fact, the existing Directives have been (and still are) the main driver for a number of measures taken (or currently considered) at the local level such as: the introduction of traffic bans, low emission zones, congestion charges, or emissions reduction programmes. As a consequence, they probably are one of the few examples where EU legislation has a visible, tangible meaning for the man in the street, and probably one of the most sensitive.

The sensitivity of the topic is due, on the one hand, to the increasing scientific evidence and public awareness of the consequences of air pollution on human health and, on the other, to the changing patterns of its causes. A related difficulty is striking the right balance between competing interests: unlike in the early stages of the industrial revolution, the causes of air pollution are much more diffuse. The culprits are not only the usual suspects (large combustion plants and other stationary sources, which are easier to control, in theory at least) but a wide range of mobile sources, including commercial lorries and individual cars.

---

1 Thematic strategy on air pollution: COM(2005) 446 of 21 September 2005; Proposal for a Directive on ambient air quality and cleaner air for Europe: COM(2005) 447 of 21 September 2005. Both documents are available at: http://ec.europa.eu/environment/air/cafe/index.htm.

2 Directive 96/62, OJ 1996 L296/55.

3 Directives 99/30 and 2000/69 (laying down limit values for lead, PM_{10}, SO_2, NO_2 and nitrogen oxides, carbon monoxide and benzene) and Directive 2002/3 (target values for ozone). For the full reference of these Directives, *see infra* note 5.

HARRY H. G. POST (ED.), The Protection of Ambient Air in International and European Law, 123-133.

The new Directive was approved by the European Parliament in 2nd reading on 11 December 2007 in a version which is very close to the 'common position' earlier reached by the Council, which is in turn fairly close to the text proposed by the Commission in 2005. The Institutions were therefore able to close the gap which had emerged in 1st reading. This being when the EP had advocated more ambitious limit values for $PM_{2.5}$ combined with longer time extensions for compliance with the existing limit values and the weakening of the daily limit value for PM_{10} (by increasing from 35 to 55 days the number of exceedances allowed over a calendar year).[4]

The following pages aim at summarising the main changes introduced by the new Directive, compared to the existing body of EU legislation. However, its focus is limited to the key provisions and does not encompass a number of technical issues; this would deserve a more comprehensive coverage.

1. The Existing Directives and the Challenge of Compliance

The framework Directive, adopted in 1996, lays down the general rules applying to all pollutants, such as the obligations to:

- assess ambient air quality throughout the territory of all Member States with regard to the regulated pollutants (Article 6), and to
- ensure compliance with the limit values (Article 7, paragraph 1);
- the obligation to establish action plans wherever there is a risk of the limit values being exceeded (Article 7, paragraph 3) and to
- prepare programmes aimed at ensuring future compliance, where the margins of tolerance have already been exceeded (Article 8, paragraph 3).

Finally, the framework Directive regulates the reporting obligations of the Member States (Article 11) and the 'committee' procedures under which the Commission can adopt implementing measures (Article 12, which should be read in conjunction with the relevant provisions of the 'daughter' Directives).

The framework Directive also sets out a list of 13 pollutants to be dealt with, and all of them were subsequently regulated by the 'daughter' directives.[5] The

[4] Directive 2008/50/EC on ambient air quality and cleaner air in Europe (OJ 2008 L152/1), Appendix, *infra*. *See*, R. Görgen & U. Lambrecht, *Feinstaubbelastung. Aktuelle Diskussion über den PM_{10} Tagesmittelwert*, 2007 Immissionsschutz 4; M. Gasparinetti & D. van den Hout, *Revising the EU Air Quality Legislation: Experiences and Proposed Improvements*, 2006 Journal for European Environmental & Planning Law 292; M. Doppelhammer & N. Notaro, *Environmental Law 2004-2005*, 25 Yearbook of European Law 616 (2006).

[5] 'First daughter': Directive 99/30 of 22 April 1999 relating to limit values for sulphur dioxide, nitrogen dioxide and oxides of nitrogen, particulate matter and lead in ambient air (OJ 1999

'daughter Directives', between 1999 and 2004 laid down the limit or target values[6] for a wide range of pollutants, and established specific rules on public information (see, for instance, Article 10 of Directive 99/30, and Article 6 of Directive 2002/3).

The implementation of these Directives has triggered (and is still triggering) a number of far reaching changes which in turn can play a key role in limiting the emissions of greenhouse gases. In fact, although the regulated pollutants are not the same, the emission sources very often coincide (heating and traffic, for instance) and the air quality limit values have been the main driver for bold decisions such as the introduction of traffic bans, low emission zones, congestion charges. Early in 2008, these kind of measures were in place in major cities such as London, Berlin, Milan and Stockholm, while only few years ago they would have been unthinkable.

In terms of compliance, air quality legislation has been a success story as regards benzene and SO_2 concentrations (apart from isolated cases of exceedance which still persist in some areas).[7] The most problematic pollutants proved to be PM_{10} and ozone. The consequences of the ozone peaks experienced in 2003 are still being assessed, but estimated to have caused some 60,000 premature deaths in the EU. For both pollutants, concentration levels are stable, compared to the very significant decrease achieved with regard to SO_2. For PM_{10} in particular, the situation was such that in 2005, only one Member State was able to comply with the binding limit values[8] throughout its territory. With a view to the 2010 deadline for compliance with NO_2 limit values, similar problems of compliance are anticipated for this pollutant.

L 163/41); 'second daughter': Directive 2000/69 of 16 November 2000 relating to limit values for benzene and carbon monoxide in ambient air (OJ 2000 L 313/12); 'third daughter': Directive 2002/3 of 12 February 2002 relating to ozone in ambient air (OJ 2002 L 67/14); 'fourth daughter': Directive 2004/107 of 15 December 2004 relating to arsenic, cadmium, mercury, nickel and polycyclic aromatic hydrocarbons in ambient air (OJ 2005 L 23/3).

6 On limit values, target values and the other air pollution 'standards', *see* Sec. 3.

7 In October 2007, the Commission started infringement procedures against France, Italy, Spain, Slovenia and the UK for exceeding EU limits on ambient air concentrations of sulphur dioxide in some specific areas (Sardinia in particular, as regards Italy). On the same occasion, the Commission also requested almost all Member States to provide information on the measures that were taken to reduce the levels of PM_{10} to meet the existing limit values.

8 Annual limit value: 40 $\mu g/m^3$; daily limit value: 50 $\mu g/m^3$ (with an allowed tolerance of 35 days per calendar year). The latter was exceeded in almost all agglomerations in Italy and Germany (agglomerations, for the purpose of the air quality Directives, are all cities with more than 250,000 inhabitants) . Similar problems were anticipated in the UK, with regard to the NO_2 limit value (which will only enter into force on 1 January 2010).

2. The Reasons for Changes

The reasons for amending and recasting this important body of legislation were twofold:

First, strongly supported by the World Health Organisation (WHO),[9] the new Directive aims at bridging the gap between existing legislation and scientific evidence as regards $PM_{2.5}$: *i.e.* the most hazardous fraction of particulate matter, which is still unregulated in the EU, while in the US and Japan it has already been the subject of strict limit values for the past few years.[10] Secondly, as part of the EU 'better regulation' policy, the Directive aims at streamlining the existing provisions and repealing the obsolete ones. It addresses a number of interpretative issues and (although not explicitly) it alleviates the widespread problems of compliance which emerged with regard to the PM_{10} limit values (compulsory since 1 January 2005) and the similar compliance problems which are expected for the NO_2 limit values (compulsory as from 1 January 2010).

The very first air quality Directives, adopted in the early eighties, had established limit values for 'suspended particulate', which was only a very rough indicator in terms of human health. At the time of drafting the first daughter directive, the evidence on health effects due to particulate matter related mainly to PM_{10}, *i.e.* fine particles with an aerodynamic diameter up to 10 micron (1 micron = millionth of a metre). At that time, however, there were still uncertainties as to which component of PM_{10} was most significant in terms of health effects. PM_{10} consists of a wide variety of chemical and physical components, with different toxicological characteristics and originating from many different sources. Also because data on other fractions of particulate matter were scarce, PM_{10} was chosen to be representative of particulate matter pollution, and limit values were laid down only for that fraction.

However, Article 5(2) of Directive 99/30/EC introduced the obligation to measure, although in a more limited number of sampling points, the concentrations of $PM_{2.5}$ and to report them to the Commission. Moreover, the 'review clause' (Article 10 of the same Directive) stipulated that, when reviewing the Directive, "the Commission will give particular attention to setting limit values for $PM_{2.5}$ or different fractions of particulate matter, as appropriate."

Based on the growing body of scientific evidence on health risks of particulate matter, the WHO concluded in its 2003 review[11] that $PM_{2.5}$ is

---

[9] World Health Organisation, *Air Quality Guidelines Global Update 2005*, and *Health Aspects of Air Pollution. Results from the WHO Systematic Review of Health Aspects of Air Pollution in Europe*, June 2004.

[10] 15 $\mu g/m^3$ in the US, compared to 25 $\mu g/m^3$ in the EU, once the new Directive enters into force.

[11] Health aspects of air pollution with particulate matter, ozone and nitrogen dioxide. Report

strongly associated with mortality and with cardiovascular and lung diseases. It also stated that there is strong evidence to conclude that $PM_{2.5}$ is more hazardous than larger particulates, though this does not imply that the coarse fraction of PM_{10} is innocuous. On the basis of information from WHO and integrated assessment studies carried out in the framework of CAFE (Clean Air for Europe)[12] it is estimated that air pollution by particulate matter in the EU causes some 350,000 premature deaths each year. Health costs are also huge due to increased hospital admissions, extra medication, and hundreds of millions of lost working days. Particulate matter has therefore become the first priority in the Thematic Strategy on Air Pollution.[13]

The proposed Directive, apart from some changes in the definitions, does not alter the list of regulated pollutants as such. As regards $PM_{2.5}$, however, it does introduce a binding limit value of 25 $\mu g/m^3$ combined with a non binding 'exposure reduction target' which aims at ensuring further improvements even in the less polluted areas (see section 4).

3. Limit Values, Target Values and Environmental Objectives in the Existing Directives

The existing Air Quality Directives establish a range of ambient air quality standards which differ in terms of legal consequences and binding nature. The distinction has important legal consequences, which can be summarised as follows.

a) *Limit values.* The limit values must be complied with as from a certain date set in the directives and can not be exceeded thereafter. Member States are under the obligation to ensure that limit values are not exceeded, and that obligation is unconditional. Current legislation includes limit values for the protection of vegetation and ecosystems on the one hand, and limit values for the protection of human health, on the other. The limit values for human health, according to the European Court of Justice, create individual rights and can be enforced by national Courts.[14]
b) *Margins of tolerance.* The margin of tolerance is an annually decreasing addition to the limit value which reaches zero when the limit value must be complied with. It was introduced because air quality cannot be improved overnight. As a consequence, the relevant Directives lay down a date for

on a WHO working group. Copenhagen, WHO Regional Office for Europe, 2003 (document EUR/03/5042688).

[12] Available at: http://ec.europa.eu/environment/air/cafe/pdf/ia_report_en050921_final.pdf.

[13] COM(2005) 446 (*see supra* note 1).

[14] Cases C-361/88 and C-59/89, *Commission v. Germany* (with regard to the 'old' limit values laid down by Directives 80/779 and 82/884) confirmed in cases C-13/90, C-14/90 and C-64/90, *Commission v. France*.

each pollutant by which the limit value is to be met (this is normally not the first year of implementation of the directive). The limit value is combined with a margin of tolerance that already applies from the entry into force of the Directive, and represents a kind of 'road map' towards compliance. In fact, when exceeded, the margin of tolerance, 'triggers' the obligation to adopt plans and programmes "for attaining the limit value within the specific time limit" (Article 8, paragraph 3 of Directive 96/62).

c) *Target values.* Because of the strong transboundary component of ozone, many Member States have only very limited control of their ozone levels. Therefore the ozone directive does not set a limit value, but a target value for ozone, which shall be attained 'where possible'. Legally speaking, this notion is very open to interpretation, and harder to enforce compared to that of 'limit values'. While the first and second 'daughter Directives' introduced limit values, the 3rd and the 4th focus on target values. As a matter of fact, experience shows that ozone concentrations have not declined in the past few years. This is partly due to the fact that, unlike limit values (which create an obligation of results) target values only trigger an obligation of means.
d) *Long-term objective.* The long-term objective for ozone is the level below which direct adverse effects are unlikely, as recommended by the World Health Organization. According to Directive 2002/3/EC, such objective is to be attained "save where not achievable through proportionate measures."
e) *Alert and information threshold.* For SO_2, NO_2 and ozone, alert thresholds have been defined which when exceeded or likely to be exceeded, determine the obligation to inform the population immediately. For ozone, Member States must also take short-term measures if effective. For ozone also an information threshold lower than the alert threshold is defined, with the requirement of informing the public if it is exceeded.
f) *Assessment Threshold.* For all pollutants assessment thresholds have been defined which, when exceeded, trigger certain minimum monitoring requirements (Article 6 of Directive 96/62, which lays down the assessment regime in terms of measurement, modelling and 'objective estimation techniques').

4. The New Directive: Limit Values, Critical Loads, Exposure Reduction Targets

The new Directive does not amend the existing air quality standards in terms of ambition level: in particular, all the existing limit values for the protection of human health are confirmed. This is a major achievement of the EU Institutions, which were confronted with very significant lobbying. In resisting the calls for weakening certain limit values, the EU Institutions proved that they put human health on top of other (although legitimate, and very powerful) interests. However, the new Directive does introduce the following substantial changes:

a) As regards the protection of vegetation, the concept of 'limit value' is replaced by the new definition of '*critical load*', and the relevant provision stipulates that critical loads only need to be met at certain locations. Contrarily as regards the protection of human health, the proposal confirms that limit values apply everywhere. Although concentrations do not need to be assessed at certain locations (this is the subject of a specific Annex), Member States must ensure that limit values are complied with 'throughout their territory'. The underlying reasoning is that, unlike trees, human beings are mobile and their exposure to air pollution can not be excluded except from a very limited number of places.
b) as regards $PM_{2.5}$, the Commission had proposed a twofold approach:
   - An 'exposure reduction target' that would require Member States to measure the levels of $PM_{2.5}$ in their cities to bring down the average of these levels over a ten year period between 2010 and 2020 (Article 15, paragraphs 1-3). According to the Commission proposal the exposure reduction target should have been 20%. However, the exposure reduction target was combined with:
   - a 'concentration cap' aimed at 'capping the risk', which would apply everywhere and, should have been legally binding as from 1 January 2010.

The final text of the Directive confirms the introduction of the exposure reduction target, although the target will no longer be the same for all Member States. The Council and Parliament considered that a bigger effort would be required for those countries where air quality is very poor, whilst room for improvement is smaller in those countries where air quality is already good. Therefore a sliding scale is introduced based on different starting points (called exposure reduction indicators).

As regards the concentration cap (which is significantly lower than the one recommended by the WHO), since the difference with limit values was the ambition level rather than its legal effects, the Council and Parliament decided to replace the word 'concentration cap' by 'limit value'. They agreed that the limit value would only enter into force as from 1 January 2015. From 2010 till 2015 the concentration cap proposed by the Commission would be a mere target value (for the difference between target value and limit value, see section 3).

5. Time Extensions, Derogations and Exceptions

Under the existing Directives, limit values must be complied with as from a given date. This obligation is unconditional and does not allow any time for extensions or derogations. The only exception is the benzene limit value, for which Article 3, paragraph 2 of Directive 2000/69 stipulates that: "Where the limit value [...] is difficult to achieve because of site-specific dispersion characteristics or relevant climatic conditions [...], and if the application of the measures were to result in severe socio-economic problems, a Member State may ask the Commission for a time-limited extension." Such time-extension cannot exceed five years, it must be limited to designated zones or agglomerations and is subject to strict conditions. In particular, the Member State must demonstrate "that all reasonable measures have been taken," and ensure that during the time-extension the benzene concentrations do not exceed a given margin of tolerance.

Building on the above precedent, the new Directive will introduce time extensions for PM_{10} and NO_2 as well. This issue unsurprisingly has proved to be the most controversial. However, this was not because the Commission had gone too far, in its proposal, but because according to many circles it had not gone far enough. The lack or delay of Community measures to reduce emissions at source (such as the long awaited Regulation on EURO5 for cars, and the delayed adoption of more stringent standards for heavy duty vehicles) was invoked by many as a compelling reason for allowing Member States much longer time extensions. Moreover, when the European Parliament voted on its amendments in 1st reading, this was even invoked as a reason for changing the PM_{10} daily limit values (which currently allow only 35 days of exceedance per year) so that the 50µg/m^3 could be exceeded up to 55 days per calendar year.

In fact, the EU Institutions had to strike a balance between the conflicting interests and this was not an easy task. On the one hand, in establishing limit values for the protection of human health the existing Directives created individual rights on which citizens can and do rely. This has been constantly held by the European Court[15] and recently reaffirmed by German Courts.[16] However, on the other hand, the existing limit values have created serious compliance problems in several Member States. Because such problems are partly due to transboundary pollution they cannot be solved unless all Member States make a simultaneous effort. The existence of several infringement procedures, initiated by the Commission in 2004 with regard to the failure to establish air quality plans and programs under Article 8(3) of the framework Directive, points to the fact that not all Member States took measures at an

[15] *Id.*

[16] Judgement of 18 May 2006 of the BayVGH (Bayerischer Verwaltungsgerichtshof, i.e. the highest Bavarian administrative court) Az 22 BV 05.2462.

early stage when compliance with the deadlines was still possible. However, it is also true that the Treaty provisions on free movement of goods make it impossible (or very difficult) for Member States to take regulatory action aimed at reducing the emissions of mobile sources.[17] This was shown by the recent case brought (and lost) by the Netherlands against the Commission on the possibility of earlier introduction of EURO5 standards for passenger cars. Although an appeal is currently pending, this case clearly proved that any attempt to introduce stricter standards at a national level, as regards cars, is a legal minefield.[18]

In the end, the EU Institutions agreed that 3 years for the entry into force of the Directive should suffice, i.e. until mid 2008. This was also based on a *Declaration* in which the Commission "recognises the need to reduce the emissions of harmful air pollutants" and makes a list of the measures which are being adopted or are in the process of being proposed in order to tackle pollution at source.[19]

In its final version, Article 22 of the new Directive allows Member States to request a time extension (no longer than 3 years from the entry into force of the Directive) for those zones or agglomerations where "conformity with the limit values for PM_{10} cannot be achieved because of site-specific dispersion characteristics, adverse climatic conditions or transboundary contributions." In addition, and irrespective of the above precondition, a time extension of up to 5 years can also be requested for NO_2 (resulting in shifting the deadline for compliance from 1 January 2010 to 1 January 2015). In both cases, the time extension can only be granted where an 'air pollution abatement programme' is established and demonstrates how conformity with the limit values will be achieved before the new deadline for each of the zones or agglomerations concerned. The abatement programmes will have to be communicated to the Commission, which will be empowered to raise objections and/or require adjustments. In terms of compliance, the programmes will have to meet certain criteria laid down in the Annexes of the Directive and will therefore be checked against those criteria.

Moreover, to 'cap' the health risks implied by the above postponement of the attainment deadlines Article 22(3) stipulates that the pollution levels, for

[17] While the emissions of stationary sources are regulated under Art. 175 of the EC Treaty, which allows stricter rules at the national level, mobile sources are regulated under Art. 95 of the Treaty, which aims at full harmonisation and leaves only very small room for manoeuvre for the Member States, even when the pollution levels would require stricter measures.

[18] The Appeals judgement of 6 November 2008 went in favour of The Netherlands; *see* OJ 2008 C 327/5.

[19] In particular, new legislation limiting the emissions of heavy duty vehicles, and the revision of Directive 96/61, which should already be made public by the time this book is published.

the period of the time-extension, shall not exceed the margins of tolerance laid down in the Annexes.[20]

While the other provisions of the Directive will need to be transposed by Member States within a given deadline, Article 22 is an 'enabling provision' which applies immediately since the new Directive entered into force (in May 2008).

As regards natural sources,[21] the Directive stipulates that Member States may designate zones and agglomerations where the exceedance of limit values is attributable to natural sources. In that event, the exceedance will not be considered as such for the purposes of the Directive, *i.e.* in terms of compliance with the limit values.

6. Conclusion

Whereas deterioration of water quality in the past, or the perception thereof, had seen the emergence of the mineral water business, no substitute for the air we breathe is available on the shelves. Even assuming that ambient air could be bottled and marketed, it will be a sad day when people pay even for the air they breathe. Although one may argue that air quality already has a price, testified by the real estate market in the most polluted cities. As a matter of fact, the highest prices for properties tend to be found in the less polluted areas.

The final result of the 'co-decision' procedure, thanks to the agreement between the Council and the European Parliament, is a compromise between the need of alleviating the compliance problems experienced by national and local authorities and the health imperative represented by the need of protecting human health against the most hazardous fraction of particulate matter ($PM_{2.5}$). Thereby the other pollutants which also have a very significant impact on human health are not neglected.

Compared to the Commission's proposal, the overall balance between the two objectives is broadly respected. However, regarding PM_{10}, the Commission had proposed that time extensions should not go beyond the year 2009 while the final text allows up to "three years after the entry into force" of the new Directive, which means until 2011. As regards the limit value for $PM_{2.5}$ (which will only be mandatory as from 1 January 2015) the Commission's proposal was to introduce it from 1 January 2010. In other words, the Commission's proposal was such that by 1 January 2010, all time extensions would cease

[20] This provision is modelled on the precedent of 'benzene', already referred to at the beginning of this section.

[21] Such as desert sand, which plays a significant role in PM concentrations recorded in some Mediterranean countries, or sea sprays in the coastal areas. Contributions from natural sources are defined in Art. 2(15) of the new Directive as all emissions of pollutants not caused directly or indirectly by human activities.

for PM_{10} and the binding requirement would enter into force for $PM_{2.5}$. The final text agreed by the Council and Parliament allows some more time for compliance with both limit values.

This delay was the price paid for reasserting a peculiar feature of the EU Directive, which reflects a crucial difference between US and EU clean air legislation. Whilst the former allows exceptions for the so called hot spots (the most densely populated areas), EU limit values apply everywhere. This is strongly linked to the idea that having clean air represents a fundamental right of every individual, as stated by the European Court of Justice.

At a time where almost all Member States were experiencing serious difficulties with the existing limit values, the political dilemma was whether to allow them more time or to introduce spatial exemptions to the binding nature of the limit values. The latter option, which was advocated on several occasions during the co-decision procedure, would probably have been much worse, in terms of discrimination and in terms of its permanent character (time extensions are, by definition, temporary).

All in all, the new Directive represents a significant step forward. It succeeds in introducing binding and enforceable limit values for $PM_{2.5}$. As for the other pollutants it confirms strict but credible objectives, which should not require further time-extensions in the future. At the same time, it does allow some flexibility where local conditions make it impossible to meet the original deadlines. This does exclude any free lunch for the laggards by introducing objective criteria against which the time extensions will be granted or refused by the Commission, and by maintaining strict margins of tolerance that are legally construed as a concentration cap. Concentration caps shall not be exceeded for the duration of the time extension.

The real challenge now, as is the case for most Directives, will be its enforcement. It is to be hoped that the successful accomplishment of this task will allow everybody to take a deep breath of clean(er) air at the end of the process. The sooner the better, and the earlier the healthier!

Harry Post

The Future of Ambient Air Management: Concluding Remarks

In 2008, in North-East China, in the area around Beijing, in particular, the quality of the air happened to be so poor that even the Chinese authorities could not hide it. They could not prevent that along with the Olympic Games, the whole world could very well see it on their television screens. In Beijing the appalling air pollution was very visible as 'smog'. A lot of the air pollution, often even more detrimental to human health is not visible at all, it is hardly perceptible, but it certainly is a 'stealth killer'. It can be measured by modern scientific methods and that is done in large parts of the world and systematically in Europe and North America. Large studies by the World Health Organisation, but also by the EU (and the US Environmental Protection Agency) have brought the results together and published them in order to inform authorities and the public. These results serve as the basis for decision making on air pollution policy.

In Northern Italy the quality of the ambient air (the air we breath) is low, in particular in respect to NO_x, low level ozone and particulate matter. Together with North-East China and the Ruhr (including the West of The Netherlands) it is among the three regions in the world competing for first place in respect to having the worst air quality. In this book the state of air pollution in Northern Italy and what has been done about it was used as the basic example and illustration for an assessment and explanation of European and International Law on the Protection of Ambient Air. Beyond that, this book has taken a serious look at the future as the European Union in 2008 has enacted a comprehensive new Directive to fight air pollution replacing (most) of the existing legislation regarding the protection of ambient air.

Although this new European instrument, indeed, means an overhaul of existing legislation at the European level and subsequently also nationally, that

Harry H. G. Post (Ed.), The Protection of Ambient Air in International and European Law, 135-145.

is not to say that the existing legislation has been inadequate. Its achievements certainly can be seen in the first two Parts of this book. However, modern problems of preserving and improving air quality to quite some extent demand new and different approaches in addition to – and partially replacing – those used so far: a more comprehensive, more integrated policy and law seem to be required. The European Union is generally considered a fore-runner in the world regarding the fight against air pollution, but in terms of results even in Europe, as is amply demonstrated above, air pollution appears to be a complicated phenomenon with no easy solutions. It has many different causes for which a diversity of remedies have to be developed.

Its scientific and management aspects need a thorough introduction before being comprehensible for lawyers (and other non-scientists). That has been covered above, in Chapter 1 by *Vittorio Boraldi* and *Luisa Guerra* who over a long period have been involved in measuring and monotoring air pollution and advising on its state in the Region of Emilia Romagna. In this contribution they have firstly explained the fundamental difference between primary pollutants of the air which are directly emitted in the environment and secondary ones which are the result of chemical reactions and physical processes of those primary pollutants with each other and other substances.

After explaining the nature and effects of what by now may be called the 'classic' primary substances that pollute the air, CO_2 and SO_2, and the equally classic secondary pollutant NO_x, they move to the two substances that have been defined as the most detrimental for human health: tropospheric ozone and particulate matter. They have also become the focus of modern anti-air pollution policy.

Tropospheric ozone is a completely secondary pollutant responsible, e.g., for the phenomenon of 'smog' in urban areas. It is generated from reactions of $N0_x$ and non-methane hydrocarbons favoured by radiation of the sun. These 'precursor gases' are produced during the combustion of fossile fuels, primarily in transport and industry.

Particulate matter (PM) consists of a mixture of organic and anorganic substances. They are classified (certainly in legal documents) primarily according to size. The most important distinction for our purposes is between coarse fractions with an aerodynamic diameter bigger than 2,5 μm and fine fractions smaller than 2,5 μm ($PM_{2,5}$). Although in Europe most legislation including EU law, addresses coarse fractions or PM_{10}, there is now general agreement that smaller particulate matter is particularly dangerous for human health. The most remarkable innovation in the substantive sense of the new 2008 EU Directive is that it addresses $PM_{2,5}$ very explicitly. $PM_{2,5}$ is principally generated by secondary particles and primary particles produced by combustion reactions. *Boraldi* and *Guerra* provide detailed insight in their morphology and chemical composition. The size of the particulate matter is also decisive for their physical behaviour in the atmosphere. $PM_{2,5}$ particles can move for days or even weeks in the atmosphere before they eventually are removed by deposition or precipitation. Modern air quality assessment therefore uses not only measuring but also other methods like emission inventories and modelling techniques and applies them not only to urban areas as was hitherto the case, but to larger 'Zones and Agglomerations' in order to manage the much more complicated secondary pollutants.

Boraldi & Guerra also briefly describe the development of legislation in Italy up to the 1996 EC Framework Directive. The Framework Directive was transposed in the 1999 Italian Framework Law (D.Lgs. 4/08/1999, n. 351) and subsequently further elaborated. This is the legislation that in practice has been applied with considerable success in (North) Italy. Similar achievements were recorded elsewhere in Europe, also as a result of the transposition of the commitments under the Protocols to the 1979 Geneva Convention on Long-Range Transboundary Air Pollution as analysed in *Phoebe Okowa*'s contribution in Part II. However, in the last decade of the 20th century success was foremost obtained with primary pollutants. Their emission sources were relatively easy to identify and they are characterised by low reactivity in the atmosphere. Secondary pollutants are involved in processes of a much larger scale that take place in a large area (like in the case of North Italy in the whole Po valley). Therefore the measures to be taken need to have a wider scope and require adequate co-ordination.

On the basis of their experiences with the pre-2008 legislation, the three authors from the world of practical application and implementation of air pollution laws in this book seem all to agree on the necessity of a more integrated and co-ordinated approach in order to effectively obtain the cleaner air objectives aimed for.

These contributions in Part I show how difficult and problematic decision-making in this area often is. The effects of measures are typically long term and in addition they are not very obvious or easily perceptible. Still considerable inconveniences and even sacrifices are often asked particularly in the area of transportation. The benefit for citizens of the measures needed are not so easy to convey as, say, the advantages of cleaning up a river or a lake.

Giovanni Franco Orlando does not hide that this is not an attractive area of policy-making, primarily because the measures and rules to be implemented often are controversial. They may restrict movement, or they are diffuse, i.e., rather diverse in nature. It is not simple to explain them as effectively solving specific air pollution problems. In addition, he and *Vanni Bulgarelli* also, emphasise the often considerable levels of ignorance and stubbornness in respect to air pollution policies. It seems that even important policy makers like *Orlando* and *Lino Zanicchelli* in fact would not mind more explicit guidance (an 'integrated' approach) from higher levels on precisely what to do and in what order. In the seventies and eighties the legislative response to air pollution at the EC level, according to *Massimiliano Montini* (in Chapter 4), was characterised by incoherent and dispersed actions. In that sense it corresponded to the ways the phenomenon had entered international law thirty years earlier. In Chapter 3, opening Part II, *Phoebe Okowa* describes the somewhat curious beginnings of the relationship between international law and air pollution. Its basic principles, notably the notorious 'no harm' principle, were after all identified in the 1941 Arbitral award in a rather extraordinary case between the United States and Canada, the *Trail Smelter* case. Although it stated some basic principles of international law in its application to (transboundary) air pollution, the *Trail Smelter* case also identified some of the problems which have been resonating ever since in international approaches to air polution, in particular the requirement of scientific certainty. *Dr Okowa* emphasises how difficult any criterion of scientific certainty can become in the much more 'cumulative' modern context of several forms of air pollution together in a multilateral regional setting: the States involved are in a complex relationship of being both receptors and generators of air pollution. This was one of the issues that had to be faced when the 1979 Geneva Convention was negotiated. The result is what *Okowa* rightly but carefully calls "perhaps the most comprehensive treaty directly regulating transboundary air pollution." The Geneva Convention is a typical 'Convention' in the 'Convention-Protocol' approach as it has been coined in social science.[1] The real substance of the Geneva Convention is to be found in its 8 additional Protocols on air polluting substances and ways and mechanisms to address them, that have successively been agreed upon in the thirty years since its creation. Looking back after her detailed examination of the Convention and its Protocols, she evaluates that they have had a "decisive positive effect on the reduction of transboundary air pollutants." However with the most recent 'multi-pollutant and multi-effect' 1999 Gothenburg Protocol as the promising innovative exception, the Geneva mechanism cannot be said to represent an integrated and comprehensive policy to fight air pollution. In that sense the Geneva Convention-Protocol approach chosen in this (slightly) wider geographical context than the EU, suffers from some of the same problems as the comparable EU 'Framework-Daughter' directives.

Massimiliano Montini introduces and explains the state of Community law primarily as it has taken shape as a result of the enactment of the EC Framework Directive in 1996 followed by the subsequent addition of its four 'daughter' directives. Together they form the basis for the systematic legislative approach in the Member States distinctly differing from the previous rather incoherent and reactive policy. This new phase of EC legislation was initiated in 1992 in the Fifth Action Programme on the Environment. The Fifth Action programme looked further ahead than the 'incoherent and dispersed' actions

[1] *See* L. Susskind & C. Ozawa, *Negotiating More Effective International Environmental Agreements*, *in* A. Hurrell & B. Kingsbury (Eds.), The International Politics of the Environment 144 ff (1992).

of the previous period by defining long term objectives. However it did not yet manage a coherent and co-ordinated approach to attain them notwithstanding the undoubtedly innovative and flexible 'Framework-Daughters' approach.

Montini explains the specific approaches in the four daughter directives enacted between 1999 and 2004: the system of limit values, target values and alert thresholds, with their differences due to the characteristics of the substances covered. He expresses satisfaction with the results obtained but also notes some serious shortcomings, in particular, in view of the most modern manifestations of air pollution, the secondary pollutants. He points at the lack of specificity in the annexes to the daughter directives which is where the actual limit values and alert thresholds are stipulated. These EC duties really require practical measures from the Member States. They leave too much room for effectively reversing the negative trend in air degradation, specifically in respect to $PM_{2,5}$ (not systematically addressed) and ozone, he argues. *Dr Montini*, furthermore, considers the absence of any reference to the precautionary principle as a missed opportunity. He also notes that founding these instruments explicitly on the integration principle, well-established in Community law, would have facilitated effective measures in respect to the essential sectors of transport, energy and industry.

In Chapter 5 *Arie Trouwborst* discusses enforcement of the Community's environmental law. He explains in detail, and criticically assesses, the whole scala of mechanisms available under EC law, from the infraction procedure of articles 226-228 of the EC Treaty – so well known in Italy – to the two mechanisms he focuses on: direct effect and criminal sanctions.

Even provisions of directives can have direct effect within the Member States although they impose obligations of result and leave discretion about the actual form of transposing them into binding national measures. Direct effect provides citizens with an opportunity to enforce their rights under Community law. At the same time *Trouwborst* emphasises: "... the protection of rights and the full effect of the law are two sides of the same coin" as it is the responsibility of national courts to provide legal protection to individuals but also to ensure that the rules of Community law are fully effective. In the general international law spectrum the ample opportunity provided for provisions to have direct effect is a unique characteristic of EC law. *Trouwborst* shows the development of Community law in the variety of ways in which the prerequisites set for direct effect by the European Court of Justice have become ever more relaxed. In recent times environmental law in particular has become an area where the EC institutions have emphasised the possibility of direct effect of often crucial provisions of directives. In the early nineties the European Court of Justice had already set the pace in respect to instruments on air pollution in the German *TA Luft* cases by stating that air quality limit values have direct effect. This has later been interpreted "in a broad and contextual manner" as *Trouwborst* concludes from his extensive review of relevant EC (and national) jurisprudence.

His discussion of 'criminal penalties' addresses part of one of *Montini*'s major points of criticism of the EC's air pollution instruments: the apparent lack of effective sanctions in the Framework-Daughter legislation. *Trouwborst* discusses the specific issue of criminal penalties. As a general rule criminal law does not fall within the EC's competence. However the protection of the environment does, the ECJ has stated, and on that basis EC legislation can make environmentally harmful activities punishable by criminal sanctions. This is the approach the European Commission has henceforth chosen in its 2007 Proposal for a Directive on the protection of the environment through criminal law, which still has a long way to go through the co-decision procedure. But it has done the same in the 2008 EC Directive on ambient Air quality and cleaner air in Europe. This new, core EC instrument to fight air pollution obliges the Member States to "lay down the rules on penalties applicable to infringements" of the national implementation provisions and to ensure that the penalties provided for are "effective, proportionate and dissuasive." Although *Montini* welcomes this provision in the new Directive he is not overly impressed. Due to its quite limited power and scope its success will largely depend on each Member State's will and capability to set adequate penalties and to ensure their prompt and effective enforcement.

More in general his first critical look at the new 'comprehensive and integrated' Directive does not make him very hopeful for its adequacy and success. He finds that the new instrument mainly consists of a re-statement of the objectives already contained in the predecessor EC legislation, although with the notable exception of the foreseen measures with regard to $PM_{2,5}$. This initial criticism is indeed warranted if the first 'grounds' mentioned in the *Explanatory Memorandum* for the 2005 Proposal for the Directive are considered. The Directive should be seen in the context of the EC Commission's 2000 'Better Regulation' initiative. The Proposal aims

> … to merge the provisions of five separate legal instruments into a single directive with the intention of simplifying, streamlining and reducing the volume of existing legislation.

However, the *Memorandum* continues by explaining that simplifying and streamlining are not the only purposes: "In addition the proposal aims to revise substantially the existing provisions so as to incorporate the latest health and scientific developments and the experience of the Member States."[2]

[2] *Explanatory Memorandum* to the Proposal for a Directive of the European Parliament and of the Council on ambient air quality and cleaner air for Europe of 21 September 2005, SEC(2005)1133.

Marco Gasparinetti who for a long time has been involved in the negotiating process of the 2008 Directive, sees the new instrument in a more positive light than Montini. He also argues that the previous legislation was a partial success. The levels of PM_{10}, ozone and NO_x remain (highly) problematic and appear not simple to lower. But in particular the highly improved insight in the health risks involved in high levels of $PM_{2,5}$ are a huge new challenge. Addressing these is the most important substantial innovation in the new 2008 instrument. On the basis of research carried out by the World Health Organisation (WHO) and in the framework of CAFE, the EU's own Cleaner Air for Europe programme, it is estimated that air pollution due to particulate matter causes around 350.000 premature deaths each year. Accepting this finding has made reducing PM levels the first priority in European air pollution policy. Whereas for the other air pollutants the 2008 Directive only brings some minor modifications not essentially altering the existing air quality standards, EC legislation now, for the first time, has also set binding limit values for $PM_{2,5}$.

In his detailed account of the negotiating process *Gasparinetti* considers it, from one point of view, to be quite a positive achievement that the existing air quality standards were not amended. The EU institutions were under considerable pressure to do just that. In the end extensive lobbying focused with some success on 'time extensions' and 'time derogations' for compliance with limit values. The existing directives were (virtually) unconditional as limit values simply had to be complied with at a given date. The 2008 Directive, however, provides Member States with the possibility of asking for a time extension for PM_{10} of three years and for NO_2 of five years. This in addition to the already existing five years extension possibility for benzene.[3]

With regard to $PM_{2,5}$ *Dr Gasparinetti* states that the European Commission had proposed binding limits which are to be imposed from January 2010 on. For the 2008 Directive, however, Council and Parliament decided that the $PM_{2,5}$ limit value will not be binding law untill January 2015. From 2010 till 2015 a 'mere' target value will apply.

This decision is certainly remarkable but also highly inoppertune if not shocking in light of the huge number of almost 350.000 premature deaths per year caused by the current high levels of $PM_{2,5}$.

How is this delay of effective action for another five years to be explained and/or justified? After all no less than 100.000's (!) of additional premature death will be the price to be paid according to the preparatory documentation. It may be worthwhile taking a somewhat closer look at the objectives in respect to $PM_{2,5}$ of the new EC legislation.

In the first paragraph of its Preamble the new Directive right away puts an emphasis on human health. Referring to the Sixth EC Environment Action Programme adopted in 2002, it states the need

3 *See* Chapter 6 of this book, *above*, at 130.

> … to reduce [air]pollution to levels which minimise harmful effects on human health, paying particular attention to sensitive populations, and the environment as a whole, …[4]

After extensive research in the CAFE programme, in 2005 the European Commission has adopted the Thematic Strategy on Air Pollution. The Thematic Strategy on Air Pollution was the first of seven thematic environmental strategies defined in the Sixth Environment Action Programme to be agreed upon.

As already said we are not talking minor matters here. The CAFE research has reported that the number of premature deaths in 2000 as a result of deteriorated air quality in the EU amounted to 370,000, about 20,000 caused by low-level (tropospheric) ozone or 'smog' and no less than 348,000 as a result of high levels of particulate matter, primarily $PM_{2.5}$.[5]

Apart from the human loss, poor air quality (in particular high levels of nitrogen) also has a very considerably negative effect in forest areas and on surface fresh water due to excessive acid deposition, and in ecosystems as they are exposed to eutrophication.[6]

In view of all these consequences the European Union has set ambitious goals to improve the quality of ambient air, reflecting the seriousness of the problem. The 2005 Thematic Strategy on Air Pollution states that the EU has chosen

> … health and environmental objectives and emission reduction targets for the main pollutants. These objectives will be delivered in stages, and will make it possible to protect EU citizens from exposure to particulate matter and ozone in air, and protect European ecosystems more effectively from acid rain, excess nutrient nitrogen, and ozone.

By 2020, compared to the situation in 2000, the Strategy sets out in particular to achieve a reduction of 47% of the loss of life expectancy as a result of particulate matter and a 10% reduction in acute mortalities from exposure to ozone. To realise these objectives (and to fight acidification and eutrophication) by 2020, SO_2 emissions will need to decrease by 82%, NO_x emissions by

---

[4] Directive 2008/50/EC on ambient air quality and cleaner air for Europe, OJ 2008 L 152/1, as analysed and explained in the previous chapter by Marco Gasparinetti. Its predecessor, the 1996 Framework Directive 62/96/EC says in its second preamble less specifically: "Whereas, in order to protect the environment as a whole and human health, concentrations of harmful air pollutants should be avoided, prevented or reduced …"

[5] Not to mention possible other harmful effects, *see, e.g.*, the American Lung Association 2005 Research Highlights: Health Effects of Particulate Matter and Ozone Air Pollution, January 2006, reporting on studies conducted in 9 Californian Counties and in 22 European cities.

[6] Eutrophication is defined as excess nutrient nitrogen (in the form of ammonia and nitrogen oxides) which disrupts plant communities, and leaches into fresh waters, leading in each case to a loss of biodiversity, in COM(2005)446, Communication of 21 September 2005 from the Commission to the Council and the European Parliament – Thematic Strategy on Air Pollution.

60%, volatile organic compounds (VOCs) by 51%, ammonia by 27%, and primary $PM_{2.5}$, i.e. particles emitted directly into the air, by 59%. The greatest challenge is undoubtedly the reduction of $PM_{2.5}$ concentrations which have not been covered by the legislation previous to the new 2008 Directive. But as the figures show $PM_{2.5}$ is also – by far – the most serious threat to human health. Obtaining all these reductions demands costs of up to €7.1 billion per year. This is in addition to the spending on existing measures. These costs although huge are nevertheless easily offset by the savings to be made as a result of the Strategy: an estimated €42 billion per year. Seen in that financial light it may be somewhat surprising to read that the 2005 Thematic Strategy does not aim at all to remove all these very serious dangers. The Strategy does not argue that such a result would be impossible to obtain but states somewhat vaguely that

> … it was impossible to determine a level of exposure to particulate matter and tropospheric ozone that does not constitute a danger to human beings. However, a significant reduction in these substances will have beneficial effects in terms of public health, and will also generate benefits for ecosystems.[7]

The 2008 Directive repeats this argument as follows for $PM_{2,5}$:

> (11) Fine particulate matter ($PM_{2,5}$) is responsible for significant negative impacts on human health. Further, there is as yet no identifiable threshold below which $PM_{2,5}$ would not pose a risk.

However measures can nevertheless be taken, only in a different way than for other pollutants. In preamble (11) the new Directive says:

> As such, this pollutant should not be regulated in the same way as other air pollutants. The approach should aim at a general reduction of concentrations in the urban background to ensure that large sections of the population benefit from improved air quality.[8]

According to the Thematic Strategy (the Directive does not provide such figures in its objectives) the result of this general reduction of concentrations is to be that

> … the number of premature deaths should fall from 370 000 in 2000 to 230 000 in 2020 (compared with 293 000 in 2020 without the Strategy).

So the Thematic Strategy's implementation results in an extra reduction of premature deaths by 2020 of 63.000.

It seems that for this new episode in EU policy on air pollution in particular in respect to $PM_{2,5}$ – but perhaps also in respect to tropospheric ozone[9] – some important moral and ethical choices in favour of more limited measures than

---

[7] *Id.*

[8] 2008 Directive, *supra* note 4, Preamble (11).

[9] The measures will lead to an expected reduction of about 10% of premature deaths due to ozone by 2020.

were actually possible have been made. It is of course not at all unusual to see (considerably) more limited objectives in policies than can be realised or are imaginable in an ideal world. Financial grounds are the most common reasons for such restraint. However in this case the choices made are difficult to explain by financial considerations, at least not by 'over all' financial reasons. In fact according to the Thematic Strategy investing in cleaner air saves very considerable sums of money. Why then has the threshold of a reduction to 'only' 230,000 premature deaths been chosen? Why not aim at a reduction to 200,000, 100,000, or even 0 premature deaths by 2020? For answers to such rather delicate questions the documents here quoted do not offer much help. The statement both in the Thematic Strategy and in the new Directive that there is as yet no identifiable threshold below which $PM_{2,5}$ would not pose a risk, does not bring us any further. If anything it only seems to emphasise the urgency of the matter. No doubt implementing the reductions in $PM_{2,5}$ as well as in the other pollutants covered – as was reported already in the previous chapters regarding the existing legislation – imply considerable incursions in the daily life of citizens most notably in urban areas. Transport is the most sensitive of fields in this respect in particular where it includes the use of private cars. Politically, decision-makers tend to be very reluctant to impose limitations in that area. Implementing often controversial measures in respect to transport and mobility in general is quite a challenge for politicians and other decision-makers; the process does not usually increase their popularity. Perhaps the real costs EC decision makers were anticipating and reluctant to face were more of a 'political' than financial kind or did they come from sources unknown?

Some consolation for those who are unhappy with the rather less than effective route set out in respect to $PM_{2,5}$ (and ozone) may be found in the results envisaged by 2020 for the environment at large. After warning that "[w]here the environment is concerned, there is no agreed way to assign a monetary value to ecosystem damage or the likely benefits resulting from the Strategy," the Thematic Strategy continues: "However, there should be a favourable impact as a result of reducing acid rain and nutrient nitrogen inputs, resulting among other things in better protection for biodiversity."[10] The reduction, mentioned above, in such substances as SO_2, NO_x, and amonia in particular, will have a considerable positive effect on acidification and eutrophication. It is expected that there will be a 74% reduction in acid deposition in forest areas and a 39% reduction regarding surface fresh water. The areas subject to eutrophication will be reduced by 43%.

Of course, whether this and the decrease in $PM_{2,5}$ will all take place as envisioned depends also on whether the Member States adequately and speedily implement the new EC legislation on air pollution in their national law and, most importantly, effectively enforce it. Here the alertness and awareness of

[10] *See* COM (2005)446, *supra* note 6.

the public, of NGO's and other groups of citizens is particularly important. They, as well as the public authorities at all levels bear a great responsibility. The stakes are high.

Directive 2008/50/EC of the European Parliament and of the Council of 21 May 2008 on ambient air quality and cleaner air for Europe*

THE EUROPEAN PARLIAMENT AND THE COUNCIL OF THE EUROPEAN UNION,

Having regard to the Treaty establishing the European Community, and in particular Article 175 thereof,

Having regard to the proposal from the Commission,

Having regard to the opinion of the European Economic and Social Committee[1],

Having regard to the opinion of the Committee of the Regions[2],

Acting in accordance with the procedure laid down in Article 251 of the Treaty[3],

Whereas:

(1) The Sixth Community Environment Action Programme adopted by Decision No 1600/2002/EC of the European Parliament and of the Council of 22 July 2002[4] establishes the need to reduce pollution to levels which minimise harmful effects on human health, paying particular attention to sensitive populations, and the environment as a whole, to improve the monitoring and assessment of air quality including the deposition of pollutants and to provide information to the public.

(2) In order to protect human health and the environment as a whole, it is particularly important to combat emissions of pollutants at source and to identify and implement the most effective emission reduction measures at local, national and Community level. Therefore, emissions of harmful air pollutants should be avoided, prevented

* http://eur-lex.europa.eu/JOHtml.

1 OJ C 195, 18.8.2006, p. 84.

2 OJ C 206, 29.8.2006, p. 1.

3 Opinion of the European Parliament of 26 September 2006 (OJ C 306 E, 15.12.2006, p. 103), Council Common Position of 25 June 2007 (OJ C 236 E, 6.11.2007, p. 1) and Position of the European Parliament of 11 December 2007. Council Decision of 14 April 2008.

4 OJ L 242, 10.9.2002, p. 1.

Harry H. G. Post (Ed.), The Protection of Ambient Air in International and European Law, 147-188.

or reduced and appropriate objectives set for ambient air quality taking into account relevant World Health Organisation standards, guidelines and programmes.

(3) Council Directive 96/62/EC of 27 September 1996 on ambient air quality assessment and management[1], Council Directive 1999/30/EC of 22 April 1999 relating to limit values for sulphur dioxide, nitrogen dioxide and oxides of nitrogen, particulate matter and lead in ambient air[2], Directive 2000/69/EC of the European Parliament and of the Council of 16 November 2000 relating to limit values for benzene and carbon monoxide in ambient air[3], Directive 2002/3/EC of the European Parliament and of the Council of 12 February 2002 relating to ozone in ambient air[4] and Council Decision 97/101/EC of 27 January 1997 establishing a reciprocal exchange of information and data from networks and individual stations measuring ambient air pollution within the Member States[5] need to be substantially revised in order to incorporate the latest health and scientific developments and the experience of the Member States. In the interests of clarity, simplification and administrative efficiency it is therefore appropriate that those five acts be replaced by a single Directive and, where appropriate, by implementing measures.

(4) Once sufficient experience has been gained in relation to the implementation of Directive 2004/107/EC of the European Parliament and of the Council of 15 December 2004 relating to arsenic, cadmium, mercury, nickel and polycyclic aromatic hydrocarbons in ambient air[6] consideration may be given to the possibility of merging its provisions with those of this Directive.

(5) A common approach to the assessment of ambient air quality should be followed according to common assessment criteria. When assessing ambient air quality, account should be taken of the size of populations and ecosystems exposed to air pollution. It is therefore appropriate to classify the territory of each Member State into zones or agglomerations reflecting the population density.

(6) Where possible modelling techniques should be applied to enable point data to be interpreted in terms of geographical distribution of concentration. This could serve as a basis for calculating the collective exposure of the population living in the area.

(7) In order to ensure that the information collected on air pollution is sufficiently representative and comparable across the Community, it is important that standardised measurement techniques and common criteria for the number and location of measuring stations are used for the assessment of ambient air quality. Techniques other than measurements can be used to assess ambient air quality and it is therefore necessary to define criteria for the use and required accuracy of such techniques.

(8) Detailed measurements of fine particulate matter at rural background locations should be made in order to understand better the impacts of this pollutant and to

---

[1] OJ L 296, 21.11.1996, p. 55. Directive as amended by Regulation (EC) No 1882/2003of the European Parliament and of the Council (OJ L 284, 31.10.2003, p. 1).

[2] OJ L 163, 29.6.1999, p. 41. Directive as amended by Commission Decision 2001/744/EC (OJ L 278, 23.10.2001, p. 35).

[3] OJ L 313, 13.12.2000, p. 12.

[4] OJ L 67, 9.3.2002, p. 14.

[5] OJ L 35, 5.2.1997, p. 14. Decision as amended by Commission Decision 2001/752/EC (OJ L 282, 26.10.2001, p. 69).

[6] OJ L 23, 26.1.2005, p. 3.

develop appropriate policies. Such measurements should be made in a manner consistent with those of the cooperative programme for monitoring and evaluation of the long range transmission of air pollutants in Europe (EMEP) set up under the 1979 Convention on Long-range Transboundary Air Pollution approved by Council Decision 81/462/EEC of 11 June 1981[1].

(9) Air quality status should be maintained where it is already good, or improved. Where the objectives for ambient air quality laid down in this Directive are not met, Member States should take action in order to comply with the limit values and critical levels, and where possible, to attain the target values and long-term objectives.

(10) The risk posed by air pollution to vegetation and natural ecosystems is most important in places away from urban areas. The assessment of such risks and the compliance with critical levels for the protection of vegetation should therefore focus on places away from built-up areas.

(11) Fine particulate matter ($PM_{2,5}$) is responsible for significant negative impacts on human health. Further, there is as yet no identifiable threshold below which $PM_{2,5}$ would not pose a risk. As such, this pollutant should not be regulated in the same way as other air pollutants. The approach should aim at a general reduction of concentrations in the urban background to ensure that large sections of the population benefit from improved air quality. However, to ensure a minimum degree of health protection everywhere, that approach should be combined with a limit value, which is to be preceded in a first stage by a target value.

(12) The existing target values and long-term objectives of ensuring effective protection against harmful effects on human health and vegetation and ecosystems from exposure to ozone should remain unchanged. An alert threshold and an information threshold for ozone should be set for the protection of the general population and sensitive sections, respectively, from brief exposures to elevated ozone concentrations. Those thresholds should trigger the dissemination of information to the public on the risks of exposure and the implementation, if appropriate, of short-term measures to reduce ozone levels where the alert threshold is exceeded.

(13) Ozone is a transboundary pollutant formed in the atmosphere from the emission of primary pollutants addressed by Directive 2001/81/EC of the European Parliament and of the Council of 23 October 2001 on national emission ceilings for certain atmospheric pollutants[2]. Progress towards the air quality targets and long term objectives for ozone set in this Directive should be determined by the targets and emission ceilings provided for in Directive 2001/81/EC and, if appropriate, by implementing air quality plans as provided for in this Directive.

(14) Fixed measurements should be mandatory in zones and agglomerations where the long-term objectives for ozone or the assessment thresholds for other pollutants are exceeded. Information from fixed measurements may be supplemented by modelling techniques and/or indicative measurements to enable point data to be interpreted in terms of geographical distribution of concentrations. The use of

[1] OJ L 171, 27.6.1981, p. 11.

[2] OJ L 309, 27.11.2001, p. 22. Directive as last amended by Council Directive 2006/105/EC (OJ L 363, 20.12.2006, p. 368).

supplementary techniques of assessment should also allow for reduction of the required minimum number of fixed sampling points.

(15) Contributions from natural sources can be assessed but cannot be controlled. Therefore, where natural contributions to pollutants in ambient air can be determined with sufficient certainty, and where exceedances are due in whole or in part to these natural contributions, these may, under the conditions laid down in this Directive, be subtracted when assessing compliance with air quality limit values. Contributions to exceedances of particulate matter PM_{10} limit values attributable to winter-sanding or -salting of roads may also be subtracted when assessing compliance with air quality limit values provided that reasonable measures have been taken to lower concentrations.

(16) For zones and agglomerations where conditions are particularly difficult, it should be possible to postpone the deadline for compliance with the air quality limit values in cases where, notwithstanding the implementation of appropriate pollution abatement measures, acute compliance problems exist in specific zones and agglomerations. Any postponement for a given zone or agglomeration should be accompanied by a comprehensive plan to be assessed by the Commission to ensure compliance by the revised deadline. The availability of necessary Community measures reflecting the chosen ambition level in the Thematic Strategy on air pollution to reduce emissions at source will be important for an effective emission reduction by the timeframe established in this Directive for compliance with the limit values and should be taken into account when assessing requests to postpone deadlines for compliance.

(17) The necessary Community measures to reduce emissions at source, in particular measures to improve the effectiveness of Community legislation on industrial emissions, to limit the exhaust emissions of engines installed in heavy duty vehicles, to further reduce the Member States' permitted national emissions of key pollutants and the emissions associated with refuelling of petrol cars at service stations, and to address the sulphur content of fuels including marine fuels should be duly examined as a priority by all institutions involved.

(18) Air quality plans should be developed for zones and agglomerations within which concentrations of pollutants in ambient air exceed the relevant air quality target values or limit values, plus any temporary margins of tolerance, where applicable. Air pollutants are emitted from many different sources and activities. To ensure coherence between different policies, such air quality plans should where feasible be consistent, and integrated with plans and programmes prepared pursuant to Directive 2001/80/EC of the European Parliament and of the Council of 23 October 2001 on the limitation of emissions of certain pollutants into the air from large combustion plants[1], Directive 2001/81/EC, and Directive 2002/49/EC of the European Parliament and of the Council of 25 June 2002 relating to the assessment and management of environmental noise[2]. Full account will also be taken of the ambient air quality objectives provided for in this Directive, where permits are granted for industrial activities pursuant to Directive 2008/1/EC of the

[1] OJ L 309, 27.11.2001, p. 1. Directive as last amended by Directive 2006/105/EC.

[2] OJ L 189, 18.7.2002, p. 12.

European Parliament and of the Council of 15 January 2008 concerning integrated pollution prevention and control[1].

(19) Action plans should be drawn up indicating the measures to be taken in the short term where there is a risk of an exceedance of one or more alert thresholds in order to reduce that risk and to limit its duration. When the risk applies to one or more limit values or target values, Member States may, where appropriate, draw up such short-term action plans. In respect of ozone, such short-term action plans should take into account the provisions of Commission Decision 2004/279/EC of 19 March 2004 concerning guidance for implementation of Directive 2002/3/EC of the European Parliament and of the Council relating to ozone in ambient air[2].

(20) Member States should consult with one another if, following significant pollution originating in another Member State, the level of a pollutant exceeds, or is likely to exceed, the relevant air quality objectives plus the margin of tolerance where applicable or, as the case may be, the alert threshold. The transboundary nature of specific pollutants, such as ozone and particulate matter, may require coordination between neighbouring Member States in drawing up and implementing air quality plans and short-term action plans and in informing the public. Where appropriate, Member States should pursue cooperation with third countries, with particular emphasis on the early involvement of candidate countries.

(21) It is necessary for the Member States and the Commission to collect, exchange and disseminate air quality information in order to understand better the impacts of air pollution and develop appropriate policies. Up-to-date information on concentrations of all regulated pollutants in ambient air should also be readily available to the public.

(22) In order to facilitate the handling and comparison of air quality information, data should be made available to the Commission in a standardised form.

(23) It is necessary to adapt procedures for data provision, assessment and reporting of air quality to enable electronic means and the Internet to be used as the main tools to make information available, and so that such procedures are compatible with Directive 2007/2/EC of the European Parliament and the Council of 14 March 2007 establishing an infrastructure for spatial information in the European Community (INSPIRE)[3].

(24) It is appropriate to provide for the possibility of adapting the criteria and techniques used for the assessment of the ambient air quality to scientific and technical progress and adapting thereto the information to be provided.

(25) Since the objectives of this Directive cannot be sufficiently achieved by the Member States by reason of the transboundary nature of air pollutants and can therefore be better achieved at Community level, the Community may adopt measures, in accordance with the principle of subsidiarity as set out in Article 5 of the Treaty. In accordance with the principle of proportionality, as set out in that Article, this Directive does not go beyond what is necessary in order to achieve those objectives.

(26) Member States should lay down rules on penalties applicable to infringements

---

[1] OJ L 24, 29.1.2008, p. 8.
[2] OJ L 87, 25.3.2004, p. 50.
[3] OJ L 108, 25.4.2007, p. 1.

of the provisions of this Directive and ensure that they are implemented. The penalties should be effective, proportionate and dissuasive.

(27) Certain provisions of the acts repealed by this Directive should remain in force in order to ensure the continuance of existing air quality limits for nitrogen dioxide until they are replaced from 1 January 2010, the continuance of air quality reporting provisions until new implementing measures are adopted, and the continuance of obligations relating to the preliminary assessments of air quality required under Directive 2004/107/EC.

(28) The obligation to transpose this Directive into national law should be confined to those provisions which represent a substantive change as compared with the earlier Directives.

(29) In accordance with point 34 of the Interinstitutional Agreement on better lawmaking[1], Member States are encouraged to draw up, for themselves and in the interest of the Community, their own tables illustrating, as far as possible, the correlation between the Directive and the transposition measures, and to make them public.

(30) This Directive respects the fundamental rights and observes the principles recognised in particular by the Charter of Fundamental Rights of the European Union. In particular, this Directive seeks to promote the integration into the policies of the Union of a high level of environmental protection and the improvement of the quality of the environment in accordance with the principle of sustainable development as laid down in Article 37 of the Charter of Fundamental Rights of the European Union.

(31) The measures necessary for the implementation of this Directive should be adopted in accordance with Council Decision 1999/468/EC of 28 June 1999 laying down the procedures for the exercise of implementing powers conferred on the Commission[2].

(32) The Commission should be empowered to amend Annexes I to VI, Annexes VIII to X and Annex XV. Since those measures are of general scope and are designed to amend non-essential elements of this Directive, they must be adopted in accordance with the regulatory procedure with scrutiny provided for in Article 5a of Decision 1999/468/EC.

(33) The transposition clause requires Member States to ensure that the necessary urban background measurements are in place well in time to define the Average Exposure Indicator, in order to guarantee that the requirements related to the assessment of the National Exposure Reduction Target and to the calculation of the Average Exposure Indicator are met,

HAVE ADOPTED THIS DIRECTIVE:

[1] OJ C 321, 31.12.2003, p. 1.

[2] OJ L 184, 17.7.1999, p. 23. Decision as amended by Decision 2006/512/EC (OJ L 200, 22.7.2006, p. 11).

CHAPTER I
GENERAL PROVISIONS

Article 1

Subject matter

This Directive lays down measures aimed at the following:
1. defining and establishing objectives for ambient air quality designed to avoid, prevent or reduce harmful effects on human health and the environment as a whole;
2. assessing the ambient air quality in Member States on the basis of common methods and criteria;
3. obtaining information on ambient air quality in order to help combat air pollution and nuisance and to monitor long-term trends and improvements resulting from national and Community measures;
4. ensuring that such information on ambient air quality is made available to the public;
5. maintaining air quality where it is good and improving it in other cases;
6. promoting increased cooperation between the Member States in reducing air pollution.

Article 2

Definitions

For the purposes of this Directive:
1. 'ambient air' shall mean outdoor air in the troposphere, excluding workplaces as defined by Directive 89/654/EEC[1] where provisions concerning health and safety at work apply and to which members of the public do not have regular access;
2. 'pollutant' shall mean any substance present in ambient air and likely to have harmful effects on human health and/or the environment as a whole;
3. 'level' shall mean the concentration of a pollutant in ambient air or the deposition thereof on surfaces in a given time;
4. 'assessment' shall mean any method used to measure, calculate, predict or estimate levels;
5. 'limit value' shall mean a level fixed on the basis of scientific knowledge, with the aim of avoiding, preventing or reducing harmful effects on human health and/or the environment as a whole, to be attained within a given period and not to be exceeded once attained;
6. 'critical level' shall mean a level fixed on the basis of scientific knowledge, above which direct adverse effects may occur on some receptors, such as trees, other plants or natural ecosystems but not on humans;
7. 'margin of tolerance' shall mean the percentage of the limit value by which that value may be exceeded subject to the conditions laid down in this Directive;

[1] Council Directive 89/654/EEC of 30 November 1989 concerning the minimum safety and health requirements for the workplace (OJ L 393, 30.12.1989, p. 1). Directive as amended by Directive 2007/30/EC of the European Parliament and of the Council (OJ L 165, 27.6.2007, p. 21).

8. 'air quality plans' shall mean plans that set out measures in order to attain the limit values or target values;
9. 'target value' shall mean a level fixed with the aim of avoiding, preventing or reducing harmful effects on human health and/or the environment as a whole, to be attained where possible over a given period;
10. 'alert threshold' shall mean a level beyond which there is a risk to human health from brief exposure for the population as a whole and at which immediate steps are to be taken by the Member States;
11. 'information threshold' shall mean a level beyond which there is a risk to human health from brief exposure for particularly sensitive sections of the population and for which immediate and appropriate information is necessary;
12. 'upper assessment threshold' shall mean a level below which a combination of fixed measurements and modelling techniques and/or indicative measurements may be used to assess ambient air quality;
13. 'lower assessment threshold' shall mean a level below which modelling or objective-estimation techniques alone may be used to assess ambient air quality;
14. 'long-term objective' shall mean a level to be attained in the long term, save where not achievable through proportionate measures, with the aim of providing effective protection of human health and the environment;
15. 'contributions from natural sources' shall mean emissions of pollutants not caused directly or indirectly by human activities, including natural events such as volcanic eruptions, seismic activities, geothermal activities, wild-land fires, high-wind events, sea sprays or the atmospheric re-suspension or transport of natural particles from dry regions;
16. 'zone' shall mean part of the territory of a Member State, as delimited by that Member State for the purposes of air quality assessment and management;
17. 'agglomeration' shall mean a zone that is a conurbation with a population in excess of 250000 inhabitants or, where the population is 250000 inhabitants or less, with a given population density per km2 to be established by the Member States;
18. 'PM_{10}' shall mean particulate matter which passes through a size-selective inlet as defined in the reference method for the sampling and measurement of PM_{10}, EN 12341, with a 50 % efficiency cut-off at 10 μm aerodynamic diameter;
19. '$PM_{2,5}$' shall mean particulate matter which passes through a size-selective inlet as defined in the reference method for the sampling and measurement of $PM_{2,5}$, EN 14907, with a 50 % efficiency cut-off at 2,5 μm aerodynamic diameter;
20. 'average exposure indicator' shall mean an average level determined on the basis of measurements at urban background locations throughout the territory of a Member State and which reflects population exposure. It is used to calculate the national exposure reduction target and the exposure concentration obligation;
21. 'exposure concentration obligation' shall mean a level fixed on the basis of the average exposure indicator with the aim of reducing harmful effects on human health, to be attained over a given period;
22. 'national exposure reduction target' shall mean a percentage reduction of the average exposure of the population of a Member State set for the reference year with the aim of reducing harmful effects on human health, to be attained where possible over a given period;
23. 'urban background locations' shall mean places in urban areas where levels are representative of the exposure of the general urban population;

24. 'oxides of nitrogen' shall mean the sum of the volume mixing ratio (ppbv) of nitrogen monoxide (nitric oxide) and nitrogen dioxide expressed in units of mass concentration of nitrogen dioxide ($\mu g/m^3$);
25. 'fixed measurements' shall mean measurements taken at fixed sites, either continuously or by random sampling, to determine the levels in accordance with the relevant data quality objectives;
26. 'indicative measurements' shall mean measurements which meet data quality objectives that are less strict than those required for fixed measurements;
27. 'volatile organic compounds' (VOC) shall mean organic compounds from anthropogenic and biogenic sources, other than methane, that are capable of producing photochemical oxidants by reactions with nitrogen oxides in the presence of sunlight;
28. 'ozone precursor substances' means substances which contribute to the formation of ground-level ozone, some of which are listed in Annex X.

Article 3

Responsibilities

Member States shall designate at the appropriate levels the competent authorities and bodies responsible for the following:

(a) assessment of ambient air quality;
(b) approval of measurement systems (methods, equipment, networks and laboratories);
(c) ensuring the accuracy of measurements;
(d) analysis of assessment methods;
(e) coordination on their territory if Community-wide quality assurance programmes are being organised by the Commission;
(f) cooperation with the other Member States and the Commission.

Where relevant, the competent authorities and bodies shall comply with Section C of Annex I.

Article 4

Establishment of zones and agglomerations

Member States shall establish zones and agglomerations throughout their territory. Air quality assessment and air quality management shall be carried out in all zones and agglomerations.

CHAPTER II

ASSESSMENT OF AMBIENT AIR QUALITY

SECTION 1

Assessment of ambient air quality in relation to sulphur dioxide, nitrogen dioxide and oxides of nitrogen, particulate matter, lead, benzene and carbon monoxide

Article 5

Assessment regime

1. The upper and lower assessment thresholds specified in Section A of Annex II shall apply to sulphur dioxide, nitrogen dioxide and oxides of nitrogen, particulate matter (PM_{10} and $PM_{2,5}$), lead, benzene and carbon monoxide.

   Each zone and agglomeration shall be classified in relation to those assessment thresholds.
2. The classification referred to in paragraph 1 shall be reviewed at least every five years in accordance with the procedure laid down in Section B of Annex II.

   However, classifications shall be reviewed more frequently in the event of significant changes in activities relevant to the ambient concentrations of sulphur dioxide, nitrogen dioxide or, where relevant, oxides of nitrogen, particulate matter (PM_{10}, $PM_{2,5}$), lead, benzene or carbon monoxide.

Article 6

Assessment criteria

1. Member States shall assess ambient air quality with respect to the pollutants referred to in Article 5 in all their zones and agglomerations, in accordance with the criteria laid down in paragraphs 2, 3 and 4 of this Article and in accordance with the criteria laid down in Annex III.
2. In all zones and agglomerations where the level of pollutants referred to in paragraph 1 exceeds the upper assessment threshold established for those pollutants, fixed measurements shall be used to assess the ambient air quality. Those fixed measurements may be supplemented by modelling techniques and/or indicative measurements to provide adequate information on the spatial distribution of the ambient air quality.
3. In all zones and agglomerations where the level of pollutants referred to in paragraph 1 is below the upper assessment threshold established for those pollutants, a combination of fixed measurements and modelling techniques and/or indicative measurements may be used to assess the ambient air quality.
4. In all zones and agglomerations where the level of pollutants referred to in paragraph 1 is below the lower assessment threshold established for those pollutants, modelling techniques or objective-estimation techniques or both shall be sufficient for the assessment of the ambient air quality.
5. In addition to the assessments referred to in paragraphs 2, 3 and 4, measurements shall be made, at rural background locations away from significant sources of air

pollution, for the purposes of providing, as a minimum, information on the total mass concentration and the chemical speciation concentrations of fine particulate matter ($PM_{2,5}$) on an annual average basis and shall be conducted using the following criteria:

(a) one sampling point shall be installed every 100000 km^2;

(b) each Member State shall set up at least one measuring station or may, by agreement with adjoining Member States, set up one or several common measuring stations, covering the relevant neighbouring zones, to achieve the necessary spatial resolution;

(c) where appropriate, monitoring shall be coordinated with the monitoring strategy and measurement programme of the Cooperative Programme for Monitoring and Evaluation of the Long-range Transmission of Air Pollutants in Europe (EMEP);

(d) Sections A and C of Annex I shall apply in relation to the data quality objectives for mass concentration measurements of particulate matter and Annex IV shall apply in its entirety.

Member States shall inform the Commission of the measurement methods used in the measurement of the chemical composition of fine particulate matter ($PM_{2,5}$).

Article 7

Sampling points

1. The location of sampling points for the measurement of sulphur dioxide, nitrogen dioxide and oxides of nitrogen, particulate matter (PM_{10}, $PM_{2,5}$), lead, benzene and carbon monoxide in ambient air shall be determined using the criteria listed in Annex III.
2. In each zone or agglomeration where fixed measurements are the sole source of information for assessing air quality, the number of sampling points for each relevant pollutant shall not be less than the minimum number of sampling points specified in Section A of Annex V.
3. For zones and agglomerations within which information from fixed measurement sampling points is supplemented by information from modelling and/or indicative measurement, the total number of sampling points specified in Section A of Annex V may be reduced by up to 50 %, provided that the following conditions are met:
   (a) the supplementary methods provide sufficient information for the assessment of air quality with regard to limit values or alert thresholds, as well as adequate information for the public;
   (b) the number of sampling points to be installed and the spatial resolution of other techniques are sufficient for the concentration of the relevant pollutant to be established in accordance with the data quality objectives specified in Section A of Annex I and enable assessment results to meet the criteria specified in Section B of Annex I.

   The results of modelling and/or indicative measurement shall be taken into account for the assessment of air quality with respect to the limit values.
4. The application in Member States of the criteria for selecting sampling points shall be monitored by the Commission so as to facilitate the harmonised application of those criteria throughout the European Union.

Article 8

Reference measurement methods

1. Member States shall apply the reference measurement methods and criteria specified in Section A and Section C of Annex VI.
2. Other measurement methods may be used subject to the conditions set out in Section B of Annex VI.

SECTION 2

Assessment of ambient air quality in relation to ozone

Article 9

Assessment criteria

1. Where, in a zone or agglomeration, concentrations of ozone have exceeded the long-term objectives specified in Section C of Annex VII during any of the previous five years of measurement, fixed measurements shall be taken.
2. Where fewer than five years' data are available, Member States may, for the purposes of determining whether the long-term objectives referred to in paragraph 1 have been exceeded during those five years, combine the results from measurement campaigns of short duration carried out when and where levels are likely to be at their highest, with the results obtained from emission inventories and modelling.

Article 10

Sampling points

1. The siting of sampling points for the measurement of ozone shall be determined using the criteria set out in Annex VIII.
2. The sampling points for fixed measurements of ozone in each zone or agglomeration within which measurement is the sole source of information for assessing air quality shall not be less than the minimum number of sampling points specified in Section A of Annex IX.
3. For zones and agglomerations within which information from sampling points for fixed measurements is supplemented by information from modelling and/or indicative measurements, the number of sampling points specified in Section A of Annex IX may be reduced provided that the following conditions are met:
   (a) the supplementary methods provide sufficient information for the assessment of air quality with regard to target values, long-term objectives, information and alert thresholds;
   (b) the number of sampling points to be installed and the spatial resolution of other techniques are sufficient for the concentration of ozone to be established in accordance with the data quality objectives specified in Section A of Annex I and enable assessment results to meet the criteria specified in Section B of Annex I;
   (c) the number of sampling points in each zone or agglomeration amounts to at least one sampling point per two million inhabitants or one sampling point per 50000 km^2, whichever produces the greater number of sampling points, but must not be less than one sampling point in each zone or agglomeration;

(d) nitrogen dioxide is measured at all remaining sampling points except at rural background stations as referred to in Section A of Annex VIII.

The results of modelling and/or indicative measurement shall be taken into account for the assessment of air quality with respect to the target values.

4. Nitrogen dioxide shall be measured at a minimum of 50 % of the ozone sampling points required under Section A of Annex IX. That measurement shall be continuous except at rural background stations, as referred to in Section A of Annex VIII, where other measurement methods may be used.
5. In zones and agglomerations where, during each of the previous five years of measurement, concentrations are below the long-term objectives, the number of sampling points for fixed measurements shall be determined in accordance with Section B of Annex IX.
6. Each Member State shall ensure that at least one sampling point is installed and operated in its territory to supply data on concentrations of the ozone precursor substances listed in Annex X. Each Member State shall choose the number and siting of the stations at which ozone precursor substances are to be measured, taking into account the objectives and methods laid down in Annex X.

Article 11

Reference measurement methods

1. Member States shall apply the reference method for measurement of ozone, set out in point 8 of Section A of Annex VI. Other measuring methods may be used subject to the conditions set out in Section B of Annex VI.
2. Each Member State shall inform the Commission of the methods it uses to sample and measure VOC, as listed in Annex X.

CHAPTER III

AMBIENT AIR QUALITY MANAGEMENT

Article 12

Requirements where levels are lower than the limit values

In zones and agglomerations where the levels of sulphur dioxide, nitrogen dioxide, PM_{10}, $PM_{2,5}$, lead, benzene and carbon monoxide in ambient air are below the respective limit values specified in Annexes XI and XIV, Member States shall maintain the levels of those pollutants below the limit values and shall endeavour to preserve the best ambient air quality, compatible with sustainable development.

Article 13

Limit values and alert thresholds for the protection of human health

1. Member States shall ensure that, throughout their zones and agglomerations, levels of sulphur dioxide, PM_{10}, lead, and carbon monoxide in ambient air do not exceed the limit values laid down in Annex XI.

   In respect of nitrogen dioxide and benzene, the limit values specified in Annex XI may not be exceeded from the dates specified therein.

Compliance with these requirements shall be assessed in accordance with Annex III.

The margins of tolerance laid down in Annex XI shall apply in accordance with Article 22(3) and Article 23(1).

2. The alert thresholds for concentrations of sulphur dioxide and nitrogen dioxide in ambient air shall be those laid down in Section A of Annex XII.

Article 14

Critical levels

1. Member States shall ensure compliance with the critical levels specified in Annex XIII as assessed in accordance with Section A of Annex III.
2. Where fixed measurements are the sole source of information for assessing air quality, the number of sampling points shall not be less than the minimum number specified in Section C of Annex V. Where that information is supplemented by indicative measurements or modelling, the minimum number of sampling points may be reduced by up to 50 % so long as the assessed concentrations of the relevant pollutant can be established in accordance with the data quality objectives specified in Section A of Annex I.

Article 15

National $PM_{2,5}$ exposure reduction target for the protection of human health

1. Member States shall take all necessary measures not entailing disproportionate costs to reduce exposure to $PM_{2,5}$ with a view to attaining the national exposure reduction target laid down in Section B of Annex XIV by the year specified therein.
2. Member States shall ensure that the average exposure indicator for the year 2015 established in accordance with Section A of Annex XIV does not exceed the exposure concentration obligation laid down in Section C of that Annex.
3. The average exposure indicator for $PM_{2,5}$ shall be assessed in accordance with Section A of Annex XIV.
4. Each Member State shall, in accordance with Annex III, ensure that the distribution and the number of sampling points on which the average exposure indicator for $PM_{2,5}$ is based reflect the general population exposure adequately. The number of sampling points shall be no less than that determined by application of Section B of Annex V.

Article 16

$PM_{2,5}$ target value and limit value for the protection of human health

1. Member States shall take all necessary measures not entailing disproportionate costs to ensure that concentrations of $PM_{2,5}$ in ambient air do not exceed the target value laid down in Section D of Annex XIV as from the date specified therein.
2. Member States shall ensure that concentrations of $PM_{2,5}$ in ambient air do not exceed the limit value laid down in Section E of Annex XIV throughout their zones and agglomerations as from the date specified therein. Compliance with this requirement shall be assessed in accordance with Annex III.
3. The margin of tolerance laid down in Section E of Annex XIV shall apply in accordance with Article 23(1).

Article 17

Requirements in zones and agglomerations where ozone concentrations exceed the target values and long-term objectives

1. Member States shall take all necessary measures not entailing disproportionate costs to ensure that the target values and long-term objectives are attained.
2. For zones and agglomerations in which a target value is exceeded, Member States shall ensure that the programme prepared pursuant to Article 6 of Directive 2001/81/EC and, if appropriate, an air quality plan is implemented in order to attain the target values, save where not achievable through measures not entailing disproportionate costs, as from the date specified in Section B of Annex VII to this Directive.
3. For zones and agglomerations in which the levels of ozone in ambient air are higher than the long-term objectives but below, or equal to, the target values, Member States shall prepare and implement cost-effective measures with the aim of achieving the long-term objectives. Those measures shall, at least, be consistent with all the air quality plans and the programme referred to in paragraph 2.

Article 18

Requirements in zones and agglomerations where ozone concentrations meet the long-term objectives

In zones and agglomerations in which ozone levels meet the long-term objectives, Member States shall, in so far as factors including the transboundary nature of ozone pollution and meteorological conditions permit, maintain those levels below the long-term objectives and shall preserve through proportionate measures the best ambient air quality compatible with sustainable development and a high level of environmental and human health protection.

Article 19

Measures required in the event of information or alert thresholds being exceeded

Where the information threshold specified in Annex XII or any of the alert thresholds laid down therein is exceeded, Member States shall take the necessary steps to inform the public by means of radio, television, newspapers or the Internet.

Member States shall also forward to the Commission, on a provisional basis, information concerning the levels recorded and the duration of the periods during which the alert threshold or information threshold was exceeded.

Article 20

Contributions from natural sources

1. Member States shall transmit to the Commission, for a given year, lists of zones and agglomerations where exceedances of limit values for a given pollutant are attributable to natural sources. Member States shall provide information on concentrations and sources and the evidence demonstrating that the exceedances are attributable to natural sources.
2. Where the Commission has been informed of an exceedance attributable to natural sources in accordance with paragraph 1, that exceedance shall not be considered as an exceedance for the purposes of this Directive.

3. The Commission shall by 11 June 2010 publish guidelines for demonstration and subtraction of exceedances attributable to natural sources.

Article 21

Exceedances attributable to winter-sanding or -salting of roads

1. Member States may designate zones or agglomerations within which limit values for PM_{10} are exceeded in ambient air due to the re-suspension of particulates following winter-sanding or -salting of roads.
2. Member States shall send the Commission lists of any such zones or agglomerations together with information on concentrations and sources of PM_{10} therein.
3. When informing the Commission in accordance with Article 27, Member States shall provide the necessary evidence to demonstrate that any exceedances are due to re-suspended particulates and that reasonable measures have been taken to lower the concentrations.
4. Without prejudice to Article 20, in the case of zones and agglomerations referred to in paragraph 1 of this Article, Member States need to establish the air quality plan provided for in Article 23 only in so far as exceedances are attributable to PM_{10} sources other than winter-sanding or -salting of roads.
5. The Commission shall by 11 June 2010 publish guidelines for determination of contributions from the re-suspension of particulates following winter-sanding or -salting of roads.

Article 22

Postponement of attainment deadlines and exemption from the obligation to apply certain limit values

1. Where, in a given zone or agglomeration, conformity with the limit values for nitrogen dioxide or benzene cannot be achieved by the deadlines specified in Annex XI, a Member State may postpone those deadlines by a maximum of five years for that particular zone or agglomeration, on condition that an air quality plan is established in accordance with Article 23 for the zone or agglomeration to which the postponement would apply; such air quality plan shall be supplemented by the information listed in Section B of Annex XV related to the pollutants concerned and shall demonstrate how conformity will be achieved with the limit values before the new deadline.
2. Where, in a given zone or agglomeration, conformity with the limit values for PM_{10} as specified in Annex XI cannot be achieved because of site-specific dispersion characteristics, adverse climatic conditions or transboundary contributions, a Member State shall be exempt from the obligation to apply those limit values until 11 June 2011 provided that the conditions laid down in paragraph 1 are fulfilled and that the Member State shows that all appropriate measures have been taken at national, regional and local level to meet the deadlines.
3. Where a Member State applies paragraphs 1 or 2, it shall ensure that the limit value for each pollutant is not exceeded by more than the maximum margin of tolerance specified in Annex XI for each of the pollutants concerned.
4. Member States shall notify the Commission where, in their view, paragraphs 1 or 2 are applicable, and shall communicate the air quality plan referred to in paragraph 1 including all relevant information necessary for the Commission to assess whether

or not the relevant conditions are satisfied. In its assessment, the Commission shall take into account estimated effects on ambient air quality in the Member States, at present and in the future, of measures that have been taken by the Member States as well as estimated effects on ambient air quality of current Community measures and planned Community measures to be proposed by the Commission.

Where the Commission has raised no objections within nine months of receipt of that notification, the relevant conditions for the application of paragraphs 1 or 2 shall be deemed to be satisfied.

If objections are raised, the Commission may require Member States to adjust or provide new air quality plans.

CHAPTER IV
PLANS

Article 23

Air quality plans

1. Where, in given zones or agglomerations, the levels of pollutants in ambient air exceed any limit value or target value, plus any relevant margin of tolerance in each case, Member States shall ensure that air quality plans are established for those zones and agglomerations in order to achieve the related limit value or target value specified in Annexes XI and XIV.

   In the event of exceedances of those limit values for which the attainment deadline is already expired, the air quality plans shall set out appropriate measures, so that the exceedance period can be kept as short as possible. The air quality plans may additionally include specific measures aiming at the protection of sensitive population groups, including children.

   Those air quality plans shall incorporate at least the information listed in Section A of Annex XV and may include measures pursuant to Article 24. Those plans shall be communicated to the Commission without delay, but no later than two years after the end of the year the first exceedance was observed.

   Where air quality plans must be prepared or implemented in respect of several pollutants, Member States shall, where appropriate, prepare and implement integrated air quality plans covering all pollutants concerned.
2. Member States shall, to the extent feasible, ensure consistency with other plans required under Directive 2001/80/EC, Directive 2001/81/EC or Directive 2002/49/EC in order to achieve the relevant environmental objectives.

Article 24

Short-term action plans

1. Where, in a given zone or agglomeration, there is a risk that the levels of pollutants will exceed one or more of the alert thresholds specified in Annex XII, Member States shall draw up action plans indicating the measures to be taken in the short term in order to reduce the risk or duration of such an exceedance. Where this risk applies to one or more limit values or target values specified in Annexes VII, XI

and XIV, Member States may, where appropriate, draw up such short-term action plans.

However, where there is a risk that the alert threshold for ozone specified in Section B of Annex XII will be exceeded, Member States shall only draw up such short-term action plans when in their opinion there is a significant potential, taking into account national geographical, meteorological and economic conditions, to reduce the risk, duration or severity of such an exceedance. When drawing up such a short-term action plan Member States shall take account of Decision 2004/279/EC.

2. The short-term action plans referred to in paragraph 1 may, depending on the individual case, provide for effective measures to control and, where necessary, suspend activities which contribute to the risk of the respective limit values or target values or alert threshold being exceeded. Those action plans may include measures in relation to motor-vehicle traffic, construction works, ships at berth, and the use of industrial plants or products and domestic heating. Specific actions aiming at the protection of sensitive population groups, including children, may also be considered in the framework of those plans.
3. When Member States have drawn up a short-term action plan, they shall make available to the public and to appropriate organisations such as environmental organisations, consumer organisations, organisations representing the interests of sensitive population groups, other relevant health-care bodies and the relevant industrial federations both the results of their investigations on the feasibility and the content of specific short-term action plans as well as information on the implementation of these plans.
4. For the first time before 11 June 2010 and at regular intervals thereafter, the Commission shall publish examples of best practices for the drawing-up of short-term action plans, including examples of best practices for the protection of sensitive population groups, including children.

Article 25

Transboundary air pollution

1. Where any alert threshold, limit value or target value plus any relevant margin of tolerance or long-term objective is exceeded due to significant transboundary transport of air pollutants or their precursors, the Member States concerned shall cooperate and, where appropriate, draw up joint activities, such as the preparation of joint or coordinated air quality plans pursuant to Article 23 in order to remove such exceedances through the application of appropriate but proportionate measures.
2. The Commission shall be invited to be present and to assist in any cooperation referred to in paragraph 1. Where appropriate, the Commission shall, taking into account the reports established pursuant to Article 9 of Directive 2001/81/EC, consider whether further action should be taken at Community level in order to reduce precursor emissions responsible for transboundary pollution.
3. Member States shall, if appropriate pursuant to Article 24, prepare and implement joint short-term action plans covering neighbouring zones in other Member States. Member States shall ensure that neighbouring zones in other Member States which have developed short-term action plans receive all appropriate information.

4. Where the information threshold or alert thresholds are exceeded in zones or agglomerations close to national borders, information shall be provided as soon as possible to the competent authorities in the neighbouring Member States concerned. That information shall also be made available to the public.
5. In drawing up plans as provided for in paragraphs 1 and 3 and in informing the public as referred to in paragraph 4, Member States shall, where appropriate, endeavour to pursue cooperation with third countries, and in particular with candidate countries.

CHAPTER V
INFORMATION AND REPORTING

Article 26

Public information

1. Member States shall ensure that the public as well as appropriate organisations such as environmental organisations, consumer organisations, organisations representing the interests of sensitive populations, other relevant health-care bodies and the relevant industrial federations are informed, adequately and in good time, of the following:
   (a) ambient air quality in accordance with Annex XVI;
   (b) any postponement decisions pursuant to Article 22(1);
   (c) any exemptions pursuant to Article 22(2);
   (d) air quality plans as provided for in Article 22(1) and Article 23 and programmes referred to in Article 17(2).

   The information shall be made available free of charge by means of any easily accessible media including the Internet or any other appropriate means of telecommunication, and shall take into account the provisions laid down in Directive 2007/2/EC.
2. Member States shall make available to the public annual reports for all pollutants covered by this Directive.

   Those reports shall summarise the levels exceeding limit values, target values, long-term objectives, information thresholds and alert thresholds, for the relevant averaging periods. That information shall be combined with a summary assessment of the effects of those exceedances. The reports may include, where appropriate, further information and assessments on forest protection as well as information on other pollutants for which monitoring provisions are specified in this Directive, such as, inter alia, selected non-regulated ozone precursor substances as listed in Section B of Annex X.
3. Member States shall inform the public of the competent authority or body designated in relation to the tasks referred to in Article 3.

Article 27

Transmission of information and reporting

1. Member States shall ensure that information on ambient air quality is made

available to the Commission within the required timescale as determined by the implementing measures referred to in Article 28(2).

2. In any event, for the specific purpose of assessing compliance with the limit values and critical levels and the attainment of target values, such information shall be made available to the Commission no later than nine months after the end of each year and shall include:
   (a) the changes made in that year to the list and delimitation of zones and agglomerations established under Article 4;
   (b) the list of zones and agglomerations in which the levels of one or more pollutants are higher than the limit values plus the margin of tolerance where applicable or higher than target values or critical levels; and for these zones and agglomerations:
      (i) levels assessed and, if relevant, the dates and periods when such levels were observed;
      (ii) if appropriate, an assessment on contributions from natural sources and from re-suspension of particulates following winter-sanding or -salting of roads to the levels assessed, as declared to the Commission under Articles 20 and 21.
3. Paragraphs 1 and 2 shall apply to information collected as from the beginning of the second calendar year after the entry into force of the implementing measures referred to in Article 28(2).

Article 28

Implementing measures

1. Measures designed to amend the non-essential elements of this Directive, namely Annexes I to VI, Annexes VIII to X and Annex XV, shall be adopted in accordance with the regulatory procedure with scrutiny referred to in Article 29(3).

   However, the amendments may not have the effect of directly or indirectly modifying either of the following:
   (a) the limit values, exposure reduction targets, critical levels, target values, information or alert thresholds or long-term objectives specified in Annex VII and Annexes XI to XIV;
   (b) the dates for compliance with any of the parameters referred to in point (a).
2. The Commission shall, in accordance with the regulatory procedure referred to in Article 29(2), determine the additional information to be made available by Member States pursuant to Article 27 as well as the timescales in which such information is to be communicated.

   The Commission shall also identify ways of streamlining the way data are reported and the reciprocal exchange of information and data from networks and individual stations measuring ambient air pollution within the Member States, in accordance with the regulatory procedure referred to in Article 29(2).
3. The Commission shall draw up guidelines for the agreements on setting up common measuring stations as referred to in Article 6(5).
4. The Commission shall publish guidance on the demonstration of equivalence referred to in Section B of Annex VI.

CHAPTER VI
COMMITTEE, TRANSITIONAL AND FINAL PROVISIONS

Article 29

Committee

1. The Commission shall be assisted by a committee, 'the Ambient Air Quality Committee'.
2. Where reference is made to this paragraph, Articles 5 and 7 of Decision 1999/468/EC shall apply, having regard to the provisions of Article 8 thereof.
   The period laid down in Article 5(6) of Decision 1999/468/EC shall be set at three months.
3. Where reference is made to this paragraph, Article 5a(1) to (4) and Article 7 of Decision 1999/468/EC shall apply, having regard to the provisions of Article 8 thereof.

Article 30

Penalties

Member States shall lay down the rules on penalties applicable to infringements of the national provisions adopted pursuant to this Directive and shall take all measures necessary to ensure that they are implemented. The penalties provided for must be effective, proportionate and dissuasive.

Article 31

Repeal and transitional provisions

1. Directives 96/62/EC, 1999/30/EC, 2000/69/EC and 2002/3/EC shall be repealed as from 11 June 2010, without prejudice to the obligations on the Member States relating to time-limits for transposition or application of those Directives.
   However, from 11 June 2008, the following shall apply:
   (a) in Directive 96/62/EC, paragraph 1 of Article 12 shall be replaced by the following:
   '1. The detailed arrangements for forwarding the information to be provided under Article 11 shall be adopted in accordance with the procedure referred to in paragraph 3.';
   (b) in Directive 1999/30/EC, Article 7(7), footnote 1 in point I of Annex VIII and point VI of Annex IX shall be deleted;
   (c) in Directive 2000/69/EC, Article 5(7) and point III in Annex VII shall be deleted;
   (d) in Directive 2002/3/EC, Article 9(5) and point II of Annex VIII shall be deleted.
2. Notwithstanding the first subparagraph of paragraph 1, the following Articles shall remain in force:
   (a) Article 5 of Directive 96/62/EC until 31 December 2010;
   (b) Article 11(1) of Directive 96/62/EC and Article 10(1), (2) and (3) of Directive 2002/3/EC until the end of the second calendar year following the entry

into force of the implementing measures referred to in Article 28(2) of this Directive;

(c) Article 9(3) and (4) of Directive 1999/30/EC until 31 December 2009.

3. References made to the repealed Directives shall be construed as being made to this Directive and should be read in accordance with the correlation table in Annex XVII.

4. Decision 97/101/EC shall be repealed with effect from the end of the second calendar year following the entry into force of the implementing measures referred to in Article 28(2) of this Directive.

However, the third, fourth and fifth indents of Article 7 of Decision 97/101/EC shall be deleted with effect from 11 June 2008.

Article 32

Review

1. In 2013 the Commission shall review the provisions related to $PM_{2,5}$ and, as appropriate, other pollutants, and shall present a proposal to the European Parliament and the Council.

As regards $PM_{2,5}$, the review shall be undertaken with a view to establishing a legally binding national exposure reduction obligation in order to replace the national exposure reduction target and to review the exposure concentration obligation laid down in Article 15, taking into account, inter alia, the following elements:

- latest scientific information from WHO and other relevant organisations,
- air quality situations and reduction potentials in the Member States,
- the revision of Directive 2001/81/EC,
- progress made in implementing Community reduction measures for air pollutants,

2. The Commission shall take into account the feasibility of adopting a more ambitious limit value for $PM_{2,5}$, shall review the indicative limit value of the second stage for $PM_{2,5}$ and consider confirming or altering that value.

3. As part of the review, the Commission shall also prepare a report on the experience and on the necessity of monitoring of PM_{10} and $PM_{2,5}$, taking into account technical progress in automatic measuring techniques. If appropriate, new reference methods for the measurement of PM_{10} and $PM_{2,5}$ shall be proposed.

Article 33

Transposition

1. Member States shall bring into force the laws, regulations and administrative provisions necessary to comply with this Directive before 11 June 2010. They shall forthwith communicate to the Commission the text of those measures.

When Member States adopt these measures, they shall contain a reference to this Directive or shall be accompanied by such reference on the occasion of their official publication. The methods of making such reference shall be laid down by Member States.

2. However, Member States shall ensure that a sufficient number of urban background measurement stations of $PM_{2,5}$ necessary for the calculation of the Average Exposure Indicator, in accordance with Section B of Annex V, is established at the

latest by 1 January 2009, in order to comply with the timeframe and the conditions indicated in Section A of Annex XIV.

3. Member States shall communicate to the Commission the text of the main provisions of national law which they adopt in the field covered by this Directive.

Article 34

Entry into force

This Directive shall enter into force on the day of its publication in the Official Journal of the European Union.

Article 35

Addressees

This Directive is addressed to the Member States.

Done at Strasbourg, 21 May 2008.

For the European Parliament	For the Council
The President	The President
H.-G. Pöttering	J. Lenarčič

ANNEX I

Data quality objectives

A. Data quality objectives for ambient air quality assessment

	Sulphur dioxide, nitrogen dioxide and oxides of nitrogen and carbon monoxide	Benzene	Particulate matter (PM_{10}/$PM_{2,5}$) and lead	Ozone and related NO and NO_2
Fixed measurements[1]		2		
Uncertainty	15 %	5 %	25 %	15 %
Minimum data capture	90 %	90 %	90 %	90 % during summer 75 % during winter
Minimum time coverage:				
–urban background and traffic	–	35 %[2]	–	–
–industrial sites	–	90 %	–	–
Indicative measurements				
Uncertainty	25 %	30 %	50 %	30 %
Minimum data capture	90 %	90 %	90 %	90 %
Minimum time coverage	14 %[4]	14 %[3]	14 %[4]	> 10 % during summer

Modelling uncertainty: Hourly Eight-hour averages Daily averages Annual averages	 50 % 50 % 50 % 30 %	 – – – 50 %	 – – not yet defined 50 %	 50 % 50 % – –
Objective estimation Uncertainty	75 %	100 %	100 %	75 %

(1) Member States may apply random measurements instead of continuous measurements for benzene, lead and particulate matter if they can demonstrate to the Commission that the uncertainty, including the uncertainty due to random sampling, meets the quality objective of 25 % and the time coverage is still larger than the minimum time coverage for indicative measurements. Random sampling must be evenly distributed over the year in order to avoid skewing of results. The uncertainty due to random sampling may be determined by the procedure laid down in ISO 11222 (2002) 'Air Quality – Determination of the Uncertainty of the Time Average of Air Quality Measurements'. If random measurements are used to assess the requirements of the PM_{10} limit value, the 90,4 percentile (to be lower than or equal to 50 $\mu g/m^3$) should be evaluated instead of the number of exceedances, which is highly influenced by data coverage.
(2) Distributed over the year to be representative of various conditions for climate and traffic.
(3) One day's measurement a week at random, evenly distributed over the year, or eight weeks evenly distributed over the year.
(4) One measurement a week at random, evenly distributed over the year, or eight weeks evenly distributed over the year.

The uncertainty (expressed at a 95 % confidence level) of the assessment methods will be evaluated in accordance with the principles of the CEN Guide to the Expression of Uncertainty in Measurement (ENV 13005-1999), the methodology of ISO 5725:1994 and the guidance provided in the CEN report 'Air Quality – Approach to Uncertainty Estimation for Ambient Air Reference Measurement Methods' (CR 14377:2002E). The percentages for uncertainty in the above table are given for individual measurements averaged over the period considered by the limit value (or target value in the case of ozone), for a 95 % confidence interval. The uncertainty for the fixed measurements shall be interpreted as being applicable in the region of the appropriate limit value (or target value in the case of ozone).

The uncertainty for modelling is defined as the maximum deviation of the measured and calculated concentration levels for 90 % of individual monitoring points, over the period considered, by the limit value (or target value in the case of ozone), without taking into account the timing of the events. The uncertainty for modelling shall be interpreted as being applicable in the region of the appropriate limit value (or target value in the case of ozone). The fixed measurements that have to be selected for comparison with modelling results shall be representative of the scale covered by the model.

The uncertainty for objective estimation is defined as the maximum deviation of the measured and calculated concentration levels, over the period considered, by the limit value (or target value in the case of ozone), without taking into account the timing of the events.

The requirements for minimum data capture and time coverage do not include losses of data due to the regular calibration or the normal maintenance of the instrumentation.

B. Results of air quality assessment

The following information shall be compiled for zones or agglomerations within which sources other than measurement are employed to supplement information from measurement or as the sole means of air quality assessment:

– a description of assessment activities carried out,
– the specific methods used, with references to descriptions of the method,
– the sources of data and information,
– a description of results, including uncertainties and, in particular, the extent of any area or, if relevant, the length of road within the zone or agglomeration over which concentrations exceed any limit value, target value or long-term objective plus margin of tolerance, if applicable, and of any area within which concentrations exceed the upper assessment threshold or the lower assessment threshold,
– the population potentially exposed to levels in excess of any limit value for protection of human health.

C. Quality assurance for ambient air quality assessment: data validation

1. To ensure accuracy of measurements and compliance with the data quality objectives laid down in Section A, the appropriate competent authorities and bodies designated pursuant to Article 3 shall ensure the following:
   – that all measurements undertaken in relation to the assessment of ambient air quality pursuant to Articles 6 and 9 are traceable in accordance with the requirements set out in Section 5.6.2.2 of the ISO/IEC 17025:2005,
   – that institutions operating networks and individual stations have an established quality assurance and quality control system which provides for regular maintenance to assure the accuracy of measuring devices,
   – that a quality assurance/quality control process is established for the process of data collection and reporting and that institutions appointed for this task actively participate in the related Community-wide quality assurance programmes,
   – that the national laboratories, when appointed by the appropriate competent authority or body designated pursuant to Article 3, that are taking part in Community-wide intercomparisons covering pollutants regulated in this Directive, are accredited according to EN/ISO 17025 by 2010 for the reference methods referred to in Annex VI. These laboratories shall be involved in the coordination on Member States territory of the Community wide quality assurance programmes to be organised by the Commission and shall also coordinate, on the national level, the appropriate realisation of reference methods and the demonstration of equivalence of non-reference methods.
2. All reported data under Article 27 shall be deemed to be valid except data flagged as provisional.

ANNEX II

Determination of requirements for assessment of concentrations of sulphur dioxide, nitrogen dioxide and oxides of nitrogen, particulate matter (PM_{10} and $PM_{2,5}$), lead, benzene and carbon monoxide in ambient air within a zone or agglomeration

A. Upper and lower assessment thresholds

The following upper and lower assessment thresholds will apply:

1. Sulphur dioxide

	Health protection	Vegetation protection
Upper assessment threshold	60 % of 24-hour limit value (75 µg/m^3, not to be exceeded more than 3 times in any calendar year)	60 % of winter critical level (12 µg/m^3)
Lower assessment threshold	40 % of 24-hour limit value (50 µg/m^3, not to be exceeded more than three times in any calendar year)	40 % of winter critical level (8 µg/m^3)

2. Nitrogen dioxide and oxides of nitrogen

	Hourly limit value for the protection of human health (NO_2)	Annual limit value for the protection of human health (NO_2)	Annual critical level for the protection of vegetation and natural ecosystems (NO_x)
Upper assessment threshold	70 % of limit value (140 µg/m^3, not to be exceeded more than 18 times in any calendar year)	80 % of limit value (32 µg/m^3)	80 % of critical level (24 µg/m^3)
Lower assessment threshold	50 % of limit value (100 µg/m^3, not to be exceeded more than 18 times in any calendar year)	65 % of limit value (26 µg/m^3)	65 % of critical level (19,5 µg/m^3)

3. Particulate matter (PM_{10}/$PM_{2,5}$)

	24-hour average PM_{10}	Annual average PM_{10}	Annual average $PM_{2,5}$ (1)
Upper assessment threshold	70 % of limit value (35 µg/m^3, not to be exceeded more than 35 times in any calendar year)	70 % of limit value (28 µg/m^3)	70 % of limit value (17 µg/m^3)
Lower assessment threshold	50 % of limit value (25 µg/m^3, not to be exceeded more than 35 times in any calendar year)	50 % of limit value (20 µg/m^3)	50 % of limit value (12 µg/m^3)

(1) The upper assessment threshold and the lower assessment threshold for $PM_{2,5}$ do not apply to the measurements to assess compliance with the $PM_{2,5}$ exposure reduction target for the protection of human health.

4. Lead

	Annual average
Upper assessment threshold	70 % of limit value (0,35 μg/m^3)
Lower assessment threshold	50 % of limit value (0,25 μg/m^3)

5 Benzene

	Annual average
Upper assessment threshold	70 % of limit value (3,5 μg/m^3)
Lower assessment threshold	40 % of limit value (2 μg/m^3)

6. Carbon monoxide

	Eight-hour average
Upper assessment threshold	70 % of limit value (7 mg/m^3)
Lower assessment threshold	50 % of limit value (5 mg/m^3)

B. Determination of exceedances of upper and lower assessment thresholds

Exceedances of upper and lower assessment thresholds shall be determined on the basis of concentrations during the previous five years where sufficient data are available. An assessment threshold shall be deemed to have been exceeded if it has been exceeded during at least three separate years out of those previous five years.

Where fewer than five years' data are available, Member States may combine measurement campaigns of short duration during the period of the year and at locations likely to be typical of the highest pollution levels with results obtained from information from emission inventories and modelling to determine exceedances of the upper and lower assessment thresholds.

ANNEX III

Assessment of ambient air quality and location of sampling points for the measurement of sulphur dioxide, nitrogen dioxide and oxides of nitrogen, particulate matter (PM_{10} and $PM_{2,5}$), lead, benzene and carbon monoxide in ambient air

A. General

Ambient air quality shall be assessed in all zones and agglomerations in accordance with the following criteria:

1. Ambient air quality shall be assessed at all locations except those listed in paragraph 2, in accordance with the criteria established by Sections B and C for the location of sampling points for fixed measurement. The principles established by Sections B and C shall also apply in so far as they are relevant in identifying the specific locations in which concentration of the relevant pollutants are established where ambient air quality is assessed by indicative measurement or modelling.

2. Compliance with the limit values directed at the protection of human health shall not be assessed at the following locations:
   (a) any locations situated within areas where members of the public do not have access and there is no fixed habitation;
   (b) in accordance with Article 2(1), on factory premises or at industrial installations to which all relevant provisions concerning health and safety at work apply;
   (c) on the carriageway of roads; and on the central reservations of roads except where there is normally pedestrian access to the central reservation.

B. Macroscale siting of sampling points

1. Protection of human health
   (a) Sampling points directed at the protection of human health shall be sited in such a way as to provide data on the following:
      – the areas within zones and agglomerations where the highest concentrations occur to which the population is likely to be directly or indirectly exposed for a period which is significant in relation to the averaging period of the limit value(s),
      – levels in other areas within the zones and agglomerations which are representative of the exposure of the general population,
   (b) Sampling points shall in general be sited in such a way as to avoid measuring very small micro-environments in their immediate vicinity, which means that a sampling point must be sited in such a way that the air sampled is representative of air quality for a street segment no less than 100 m length at traffic-orientated sites and at least 250 m × 250 m at industrial sites, where feasible;
   (c) Urban background locations shall be located so that their pollution level is influenced by the integrated contribution from all sources upwind of the station. The pollution level should not be dominated by a single source unless such a situation is typical for a larger urban area. Those sampling points shall, as a general rule, be representative for several square kilometres;
   (d) Where the objective is to assess rural background levels, the sampling point shall not be influenced by agglomerations or industrial sites in its vicinity, i.e. sites closer than five kilometres;
   (e) Where contributions from industrial sources are to be assessed, at least one sampling point shall be installed downwind of the source in the nearest residential area. Where the background concentration is not known, an additional sampling point shall be situated within the main wind direction;
   (f) Sampling points shall, where possible, also be representative of similar locations not in their immediate vicinity;
   (g) Account shall be taken of the need to locate sampling points on islands where that is necessary for the protection of human health.
2. Protection of vegetation and natural ecosystems

   Sampling points targeted at the protection of vegetation and natural ecosystems shall be sited more than 20 km away from agglomerations or more than 5 km away from other built-up areas, industrial installations or motorways or major roads with traffic counts of more than 50000 vehicles per day, which means that a sampling point must be sited in such a way that the air sampled is representative of air quality in a surrounding area of at least 1000 km^2. A Member State may provide for a sampling point to be sited at a lesser distance or to be representative of air quality in a less extended area, taking account of geographical conditions or of the opportunities to protect particularly vulnerable areas.

Account shall be taken of the need to assess air quality on islands.

C. Microscale siting of sampling points

In so far as is practicable, the following shall apply:

– the flow around the inlet sampling probe shall be unrestricted (free in an arc of at least 270°) without any obstructions affecting the airflow in the vicinity of the sampler (normally some metres away from buildings, balconies, trees and other obstacles and at least 0,5 m from the nearest building in the case of sampling points representing air quality at the building line),
– in general, the inlet sampling point shall be between 1,5 m (the breathing zone) and 4 m above the ground. Higher positions (up to 8 m) may be necessary in some circumstances. Higher siting may also be appropriate if the station is representative of a large area,
– the inlet probe shall not be positioned in the immediate vicinity of sources in order to avoid the direct intake of emissions unmixed with ambient air,
– the sampler's exhaust outlet shall be positioned so that recirculation of exhaust air to the sampler inlet is avoided,
– for all pollutants, traffic-orientated sampling probes shall be at least 25 m from the edge of major junctions and no more than 10 m from the kerbside.,

The following factors may also be taken into account:

– interfering sources,
– security,
– access,
– availability of electrical power and telephone communications,
– visibility of the site in relation to its surroundings,
– safety of the public and operators,
– the desirability of co-locating sampling points for different pollutants,
– planning requirements.,

D. Documentation and review of site selection

The site-selection procedures shall be fully documented at the classification stage by such means as compass-point photographs of the surrounding area and a detailed map. Sites shall be reviewed at regular intervals with repeated documentation to ensure that selection criteria remain valid over time.

ANNEX IV

Measurements at rural background locations irrespective of concentration

[not reproduced]

ANNEX V

Criteria for determining minimum numbers of sampling points for fixed measurement of concentrations of sulphur dioxide, nitrogen dioxide and oxides of nitrogen, particulate matter (PM_{10}, $PM_{2,5}$), lead, benzene and carbon monoxide in ambient air

A. Minimum number of sampling points for fixed measurement to assess compliance with limit values for the protection of human health and alert thresholds in zones and agglomerations where fixed measurement is the sole source of information

1. Diffuse sources

Population of agglomeration or zone (thousands)	If maximum concentrations exceed the upper assessment threshold(1)		If maximum concentrations are between the upper and lower assessment thresholds	
	Pollutants except PM	PM(2) (sum of PM_{10} and $PM_{2,5}$)	Pollutants except PM	PM(2) (sum of PM_{10} and $PM_{2,5}$)
0-249	1	2	1	1
250-499	2	3	1	2
500-749	2	3	1	2
750-999	3	4	1	2
1000-1499	4	6	2	3
1500-1999	5	7	2	3
2000-2749	6	8	3	4
2750-3749	7	10	3	4
3750-4749	8	11	3	6
4750-5999	9	13	4	6
$\geq$ 6000	10	15	4	7

(1) For nitrogen dioxide, particulate matter, benzene and carbon monoxide: to include at least one urban background monitoring station and one traffic-orientated station provided this does not increase the number of sampling points. For these pollutants, the total number of urban-background stations and the total number of traffic oriented stations in a Member State required under Section A(1) shall not differ by more than a factor of 2. Sampling points with exceedances of the limit value for PM_{10} within the last three years shall be maintained, unless a relocation is necessary owing to special circumstances, in particular spatial development.
(2) Where $PM_{2,5}$ and PM_{10} are measured in accordance with Article 8 at the same monitoring station, these shall count as two separate sampling points. The total number of $PM_{2,5}$ and PM_{10} sampling points in a Member State required under Section A(1) shall not differ by more than a factor of 2, and the number of $PM_{2,5}$ sampling points in the urban background of agglomerations and urban areas shall meet the requirements under Section B of Annex V.

2. Point sources

For the assessment of pollution in the vicinity of point sources, the number of sampling points for fixed measurement shall be calculated taking into account emission densities, the likely distribution patterns of ambient-air pollution and the potential exposure of the population.

B. Minimum number of sampling points for fixed measurement to assess compliance with the $PM_{2,5}$ exposure reduction target for the protection of human health

One sampling point per million inhabitants summed over agglomerations and additional urban areas in excess of 100000 inhabitants shall be operated for this purpose. Those sampling points may coincide with sampling points under Section A.

C. Minimum number of sampling points for fixed measurements to assess compliance with critical levels for the protection of vegetation in zones other than agglomerations

If maximum concentrations exceed the upper assessment threshold	If maximum concentrations are between upper and lower assessment threshold
1 station every 20000 km^2	1 station every 40000 km^2

In island zones the number of sampling points for fixed measurement should be calculated taking into account the likely distribution patterns of ambient-air pollution and the potential exposure of vegetation.

ANNEX VI

Reference methods for assessment of concentrations of sulphur dioxide, nitrogen dioxide and oxides of nitrogen, particulate matter (PM_{10} and $PM_{2,5}$), lead, benzene, carbon monoxide, and ozone

[not reproduced]

ANNEX VII

Ozone target values and long-term objectives

A. Definitions and criteria

1. Definitions

AOT40 (expressed in ($\mu g/m^3$) · hours) means the sum of the difference between hourly concentrations greater than 80 $\mu g/m^3$ (= 40 parts per billion) and 80 $\mu g/m^3$ over a given period using only the one-hour values measured between 8.00 and 20.00 Central European Time (CET) each day.

2. Criteria

The following criteria shall be used for checking validity when aggregating data and calculating statistical parameters:

Parameter	Required proportion of valid data
One hour values	75 % (i.e. 45 minutes)
Eight hours values	75 % of values (i.e. six hours)

Maximum daily 8 hours mean from hourly running 8 hours	75 % of the hourly running eight hours averages (i.e. 18 eight-hourly averages per day)
AOT40	90 % of the one hour values over the time period defined for calculating the AOT40 value(1)
Annual mean	75 % of the one hour values over summer (April to September) and 75 % over winter (January to March, October to December) seasons separately
Number of exceedances and maximum values per month	90 % of the daily maximum eight hours mean values (27 available daily values per month) 90 % of the one hour values between 8.00 and 20.00 CET
Number of exceedances and maximum values per year	five out of six months over the summer season (April to September)

(1) In cases where all possible measured data are not available, the following factor shall be used to calculate AOT40 values:

$$AOT40_{estimate} = AOT40_{measured} \times \frac{\text{total possible number of hours}^{(*)}}{\text{number of measured hourly values}}$$

(*) being the number of hours within the time period of AOT40 definition, (i.e. 08:00 to 20:00 CET from 1 May to 31 July each year, for vegetation protection and from 1 April to 30 September each year for forest protection).

B. Target values

Objective	Averaging period	Target value	Date by which target value should be met(1)
Protection of human health	Maximum daily eight-hour mean(2)	120 µg/m³ not to be exceeded on more than 25 days per calendar year averaged over three years(3)	1.1.2010
Protection of vegetation	May to July	AOT40 (calculated from 1 h values) 18000 µg/m³ · h averaged over five years(3)	1.1.2010

(1) Compliance with target values will be assessed as of this date. That is, 2010 will be the first year the data for which is used in calculating compliance over the following three or five years, as appropriate.
(2) The maximum daily eight-hour mean concentration shall be selected by examining eight-hour running averages, calculated from hourly data and updated each hour. Each eight -hour average so calculated shall be assigned to the day on which it ends. i.e. the first calculation period for any one day will be the period from 17:00 on the previous day to 01:00 on that day; the last calculation period for any one day will be the period from 16:00 to 24:00 on the day.
(3) If the three or five year averages cannot be determined on the basis of a full and consecutive set of annual data, the minimum annual data required for checking compliance with the target values will be as follows:
- for the target value for the protection of human health: valid data for one year,
- for the target value for the protection of vegetation: valid data for three years.

C. Long-term objectives

Objective	Averaging period	Longterm objective	Date by which the longterm objective should be met
Protection of human health	Maximum daily eight-hour mean within a calendar year	120 μg/m^3	not defined
Protection of vegetation	May to July	AOT40 (calculated from 1 h values) 6000 μg/m^3 · h	not defined

ANNEX VIII

Criteria for classifying and locating sampling points for assessments of ozone concentrations

[not reproduced]

ANNEX IX

Criteria for determining the minimum number of sampling points for fixed measurement of concentrations of ozone

[not reproduced]

ANNEX X

Measurements of ozone precursor substances

[not reproduced]

ANNEX XI

Limit values for the protection of human health

A. Criteria

Without prejudice to Annex I, the following criteria shall be used for checking validity when aggregating data and calculating statistical parameters:

Parameter	Required proportion of valid data
One hour values	75 % (i.e. 45 minutes)
Eight hours values	75 % of values (i.e. 6 hours)
Maximum daily 8-hour mean	75 % of the hourly running eight hour averages (i.e. 18 eight hour averages per day)
24-hour values	75 % of the hourly averages (i.e. at least 18 hour values)
Annual mean	90 %(1) of the one hour values or (if not available) 24-hour values over the year

(1) The requirements for the calculation of annual mean do not include losses of data due to the regular calibration or the normal maintenance of the instrumentation.

B. Limit values

Averaging Period	Limit value	Margin of tolerance	Date by which limit value is to be met
Sulphur dioxide			
One hour	350 μg/m³, not to be exceeded more than 24 times a calendar year	150 μg/m³ (43 %)	–(1)
One day	125 μg/m³, not to be exceeded more than 3 times a calendar year	None	–(1)
Nitrogen dioxide			
One hour	200 μg/m³, not to be exceeded more than 18 times a calendar year	50 % on 19 July 1999, decreasing on 1 January 2001 and every 12 months thereafter by equal annual percentages to reach 0 % by 1 January 2010	1 January 2010
Calendar year	40 μg/m³	50 % on 19 July 1999, decreasing on 1 January 2001 and every 12 months thereafter by equal annual percentages to reach 0 % by 1 January 2010	1 January 2010
Benzene			
Calendar year	5 μg/m³	5 μg/m³ (100 %) on 13 December 2000, decreasing on 1 January 2006 and every 12 months thereafter by 1 μg/m³ to reach 0 % by 1 January 2010	1 January 2010
Carbon monoxide			
maximum daily eight hour mean(2)	10 mg/m³	60 %	–(1)
Lead			
Calendar year	0,5 μg/m³ (3)	100 %	–(3)
PM_{10}			
One day	50 μg/m³, not to be exceeded more than 35 times a calendar year	50 %	–(1)
Calendar year	40 μg/m³	20 %	–(1)

(1) Already in force since 1 January 2005.
(2) The maximum daily eight hour mean concentration will be selected by examining eight hour running averages, calculated from hourly data and updated each hour. Each eight hour average so calculated will be assigned to the day on which it ends i.e. the first calculation period for any one day will be the period from 17:00 on the previous day to 01:00 on that day; the last calculation period for any one day will be the period from 16:00 to 24:00 on that day.
(3) Already in force since 1 January 2005. Limit value to be met only by 1 January 2010 in the immediate vicinity of the specific industrial sources situated on sites contaminated by decades of

industrial activities. In such cases, the limit value until 1 January 2010 will be 1,0 µg/m³. The area in which higher limit values apply must not extend further than 1000 m from such specific sources.

ANNEX XII

Information and alert thresholds

A. Alert thresholds for pollutants other than ozone

To be measured over three consecutive hours at locations representative of air quality over at least 100 km2 or an entire zone or agglomeration, whichever is the smaller.

Pollutant	Alert threshold
Sulphur dioxide	500 µg/m³
Nitrogen dioxide	400 µg/m³

B. Information and alert thresholds for ozone

Purpose	Averaging period	Threshold
Information	1 hour	180 µg/m³
Alert	1 hour(1)	240 µg/m³

(1) For the implementation of Article 24, the exceedance of the threshold is to be measured or predicted for three consecutive hours.

ANNEX XIII

Critical levels for the protection of vegetation

Averaging period	Critical level	Margin of tolerance
Sulphur dioxide		
Calendar year and winter (1 October to 31 March)	20 µg/m³	None
Oxides of nitrogen		
Calendar year	30 µg/m³ NO_x	None

ANNEX XIV

National exposure reduction target, target value and limit value for $PM_{2,5}$

A. Average exposure indicator

The Average Exposure Indicator expressed in µg/m³ (AEI) shall be based upon measurements in urban background locations in zones and agglomerations throughout the territory of a Member State. It should be assessed as a three-calendar year running annual mean concentration averaged over all sampling points established pursuant to Section B of Annex V. The AEI for the reference year 2010 shall be the mean concentration of the years 2008, 2009 and 2010.

However, where data are not available for 2008, Member States may use the mean concentration of the years 2009 and 2010 or the mean concentration of the years 2009, 2010 and 2011. Member States making use of these possibilities shall communicate their decisions to the Commission by 11 September 2008.

The AEI for the year 2020 shall be the three-year running mean concentration averaged over all those sampling points for the years 2018, 2019 and 2020. The AEI is used for the examination whether the national exposure reduction target is met.

The AEI for the year 2015 shall be the three-year running mean concentration averaged over all those sampling points for the years 2013, 2014 and 2015. The AEI is used for the examination whether the exposure concentration obligation is met.

B. National exposure reduction target

Exposure reduction target relative to the AEI in 2010		Year by which the exposure reduction target should be met
Initial concentration in $\mu g/m^3$	Reduction target in percent	
< 8,5 = 8,5	0 %	
> 8,5 – < 13	10 %	
= 13 – < 18	15 %	2020
= 18 – < 22	20 %	
≥ 22	All appropriate measures to achieve 18 $\mu g/m^3$	

Where the AEI in the reference year is 8,5 $\mu g/m^3$ or less the exposure reduction target shall be zero. The reduction target shall be zero also in cases where the AEI reaches the level of 8,5 $\mu g/m^3$ at any point of time during the period from 2010 to 2020 and is maintained at or below that level.

C. Exposure concentration obligation

Exposure concentration obligation	Year by which the obligation value is to be met
20 $\mu g/m^3$	2015

D. Target value

Averaging period	Target value	Date by which target value should be met
Calendar year	25 $\mu g/m^3$	1 January 2010

E. Limit value

Averaging period	Limit value	Margin of tolerance	Date by which limit value is to be met
STAGE 1			
Calendar year	25 $\mu g/m^3$	20 % on 11 June 2008, decreasing on the next 1 January and every 12 months thereafter by equal annual percentages to reach 0 % by 1 January 2015	1 January 2015

STAGE 2[1]			
Calendar year	20 μg/m^3		1 January 2020

(1) Stage 2 – indicative limit value to be reviewed by the Commission in 2013 in the light of further information on health and environmental effects, technical feasibility and experience of the target value in Member States.

ANNEX XV

Information to be included in the local, regional or national air quality plans for improvement in ambient air quality

A. Information to be provided under article 23 (air quality plans)

1. Localisation of excess pollution
(a) region;
(b) city (map);
(c) measuring station (map, geographical coordinates).

2. General information
(a) type of zone (city, industrial or rural area);
(b) estimate of the polluted area (km2) and of the population exposed to the pollution;
(c) useful climatic data;
(d) relevant data on topography;
(e) sufficient information on the type of targets requiring protection in the zone.

3. Responsible authorities
Names and addresses of persons responsible for the development and implementation of improvement plans.

4. Nature and assessment of pollution
(a) concentrations observed over previous years (before the implementation of the improvement measures);
(b) concentrations measured since the beginning of the project;
(c) techniques used for the assessment.

5. Origin of pollution
(a) list of the main emission sources responsible for pollution (map);
(b) total quantity of emissions from these sources (tonnes/year);
(c) information on pollution imported from other regions.

6. Analysis of the situation
(a) details of those factors responsible for the exceedance (e.g. transport, including cross-border transport, formation of secondary pollutants in the atmosphere);
(b) details of possible measures for the improvement of air quality.

7. Details of those measures or projects for improvement which existed prior to 11 June 2008, i.e:
(a) local, regional, national, international measures;
(b) observed effects of these measures.

8. Details of those measures or projects adopted with a view to reducing pollution following the entry into force of this Directive:

(a) listing and description of all the measures set out in the project;
(b) timetable for implementation;
(c) estimate of the improvement of air quality planned and of the expected time required to attain these objectives.

9. Details of the measures or projects planned or being researched for the long term.

10. List of the publications, documents, work, etc., used to supplement information required under this Annex.

B. Information to be provided under article 22(1)

1. All information as laid down in Section A.
2. Information concerning the status of implementation of the following Directives:
   1. Council Directive 70/220/EEC of 20 March 1970 on the approximation of the laws of the Member States on measures to be taken against air pollution by emissions from motor vehicles[1];
   2. Directive 94/63/EC of the European Parliament and of the Council of 20 December 1994 on the control of volatile organic compound (VOC) emissions resulting from the storage of petrol and its distribution from terminals to service stations[2];
   3. Directive 2008/1/EC of the European Parliament and of the Council of 15 January 2008 concerning integrated pollution prevention and control[3];
   4. Directive 97/68/EC of the European Parliament and of the Council of 16 December 1997 on the approximation of the laws of the Member States relating to measures against the emission of gaseous and particulate pollutants from internal combustion engines to be installed in non-road mobile machinery[4];
   5. Directive 98/70/EC of the European Parliament and of the Council of 13 October 1998 relating to the quality of petrol and diesel fuels[5];
   6. Council Directive 1999/13/EC of 11 March 1999 on the limitation of emissions of volatile organic compounds due to the use of organic solvents in certain activities and installations[6];
   7. Council Directive 1999/32/EC of 26 April 1999 relating to a reduction in the sulphur content of certain liquid fuels[7];

[1] OJ L 76, 6.4.1970, p. 1. Directive as last amended by Directive 2006/96/EC (OJ L 363, 20.12.2006, p. 81).

[2] OJ L 365, 31.12.1994, p. 24. Directive as amended by Regulation (EC) No 1882/2003 (OJ L 284, 31.10.2003, p. 1).

[3] OJ L 24, 29.1.2008, p. 8.

[4] OJ L 59, 27.2.1998, p. 1. Directive as last amended by Directive 2006/105/EC.

[5] OJ L 350, 28.12.1998, p. 58. Directive as amended by Regulation (EC) No 1882/2003.

[6] OJ L 85, 29.3.1999, p. 1. Directive as last amended by Directive 2004/42/EC of the European Parliament and of the Council (OJ L 143, 30.4.2004, p. 87).

[7] OJ L 121, 11.5.1999, p. 13. Directive as last amended by Directive 2005/33/EC of the European Parliament and of the Council (OJ L 191, 22.7.2005, p. 59).

8. Directive 2000/76/EC of the European Parliament and of the Council of 4 December 2000 on the incineration of waste[1];
9. Directive 2001/80/EC of the European Parliament and of the Council of 23 October 2001 on the limitation of emissions of certain pollutants into the air from large combustion plants;
10. Directive 2001/81/EC of the European Parliament and of the Council of 23 October 2001 on national emission ceilings for certain atmospheric pollutants;
11. Directive 2004/42/EC of the European Parliament and of the Council of 21 April 2004 on the limitation of emissions of volatile organic compounds due to the use of organic solvents in certain paints and varnishes and vehicle refinishing products[2];
12. Directive 2005/33/EC of the European Parliament and of the Council of 6 July 2005 amending Directive 1999/32/EC as regards the sulphur content of marine fuels[3];
13. Directive 2005/55/EC of the European Parliament and of the Council of 28 September 2005 on the approximation of the laws of the Member States relating to the measures to be taken against the emission of gaseous and particulate pollutants from compression-ignition engines for use in vehicles, and the emission of gaseous pollutants from positive-ignition engines fuelled with natural gas or liquefied petroleum gas for use in vehicles[4];
14. Directive 2006/32/EC of the European Parliament and of the Council of 5 April 2006 on energy end-use efficiency and energy services[5].

3. Information on all air pollution abatement measures that have been considered at appropriate local, regional or national level for implementation in connection with the attainment of air quality objectives, including:
   (a) reduction of emissions from stationary sources by ensuring that polluting small and medium sized stationary combustion sources (including for biomass) are fitted with emission control equipment or replaced;
   (b) reduction of emissions from vehicles through retrofitting with emission control equipment. The use of economic incentives to accelerate take-up should be considered;
   (c) procurement by public authorities, in line with the handbook on environmental public procurement, of road vehicles, fuels and combustion equipment to reduce emissions, including the purchase of:
      – new vehicles, including low emission vehicles,
      – cleaner vehicle transport services,
      – low emission stationary combustion sources,
      – low emission fuels for stationary and mobile sources,
   (d) measures to limit transport emissions through traffic planning and management

[1] OJ L 332, 28.12.2000, p. 91.
[2] OJ L 143, 30.4.2004, p. 87.
[3] OJ L 191, 22.7.2005, p. 59.
[4] OJ L 275, 20.10.2005, p. 1. Directive as last amended by Regulation (EC) No 715/2007 (OJ L 171, 29.6.2007, p. 1).
[5] OJ L 114, 27.4.2006, p. 64.

(including congestion pricing, differentiated parking fees or other economic incentives; establishing low emission zones);

(e) measures to encourage a shift of transport towards less polluting modes;

(f) ensuring that low emission fuels are used in small, medium and large scale stationary sources and in mobile sources;

(g) measures to reduce air pollution through the permit system under Directive 2008/1/EC, the national plans under Directive 2001/80/EC, and through the use of economic instruments such as taxes, charges or emission trading.

(h) where appropriate, measures to protect the health of children or other sensitive groups.

ANNEX XVI

Public information

1. Member States shall ensure that up-to-date information on ambient concentrations of the pollutants covered by this Directive is routinely made available to the public.
2. Ambient concentrations provided shall be presented as average values according to the appropriate averaging period as laid down in Annex VII and Annexes XI to XIV. The information shall at least indicate any levels exceeding air quality objectives including limit values, target values, alert thresholds, information thresholds or long term objectives of the regulated pollutant. It shall also provide a short assessment in relation to the air quality objectives and appropriate information regarding effects on health, or, where appropriate, vegetation.
3. Information on ambient concentrations of sulphur dioxide, nitrogen dioxide, particulate matter (at least PM_{10}), ozone and carbon monoxide shall be updated on at least a daily basis, and, wherever practicable, information shall be updated on an hourly basis. Information on ambient concentrations of lead and benzene, presented as an average value for the last 12 months, shall be updated on a three-monthly basis, and on a monthly basis, wherever practicable.
4. Member States shall ensure that timely information about actual or predicted exceedances of alert thresholds, and any information threshold is provided to the public. Details supplied shall include at least the following information:

   (a) information on observed exceedance(s):
   - location or area of the exceedance,
   - type of threshold exceeded (information or alert),
   - start time and duration of the exceedance,
   - highest one hour concentration and in addition highest eight hour mean concentration in the case of ozone;

   (b) forecast for the following afternoon/day(s):
   - geographical area of expected exceedances of information and/or alert threshold,
   - expected changes in pollution (improvement, stabilisation or deterioration), together with the reasons for those changes;

   (c) information on the type of population concerned, possible health effects and recommended behaviour:
   - information on population groups at risk,

– description of likely symptoms,
– recommended precautions to be taken by the population concerned,
– where to find further information;

(d) information on preventive action to reduce pollution and/or exposure to it: indication of main source sectors; recommendations for action to reduce emissions;

(e) in the case of predicted exceedances, Member State shall take steps to ensure that such details are supplied to the extent practicable.

ANNEX XVII

Correlation table

[not reproduced]

STATEMENT BY THE COMMISSION

The Commission takes note of the text adopted by the Council and the European Parliament for the Directive on ambient air quality and cleaner air for Europe. In particular, the Commission notes the importance attributed by the European Parliament and the Member States in Article 22(4) and recital 16 to Community measures for the abatement of air pollutant emissions at source.

The Commission recognises the need to reduce the emissions of harmful air pollutants if significant progress is to be delivered towards the objectives established in the Sixth Environmental Action Programme. The Commission's communication on a thematic strategy on air pollution sets out a significant number of possible Community measures. Significant progress on these and other measures has been made since the adoption of the strategy:

– the Council and Parliament have already adopted new legislation limiting the exhaust emissions of light duty vehicles,
– the Commission has adopted a proposal for new legislation to improve the effectiveness of Community industrial emissions legislation including intensive agricultural installations and measures to tackle smaller scale industrial combustion sources,
– the Commission has adopted a proposal for new legislation limiting the exhaust emissions of engines installed in heavy duty vehicles,
– in 2008 the Commission foresees new legislative proposals that would:
– further reduce the Member States' permitted national emissions of key pollutants,
– reduce emissions associated with refuelling of petrol cars at service stations,
– address the sulphur content of fuels including marine fuels,
– preparatory work is also underway to investigate the feasibility of:
– improving the eco-design and reducing the emissions of domestic boilers and water heaters,
– reducing the solvent content of paints, varnishes and vehicle refinishing products,
– reducing the exhaust emissions of non-road mobile machinery and thereby maximise the benefit of lower sulphur non-road fuels already proposed by the Commission,
– The Commission also continues to push for substantial emissions reductions from

ships at the International Maritime Organisation and it is committed to bringing forward proposals for Community measures should the IMO fail to deliver sufficiently ambitious proposals as foreseen in 2008.

The Commission is, however, committed to the aims of its Better Regulation initiative and the need for proposals to be underpinned by a comprehensive assessment of the impacts and benefits. In this regard and in accordance with the Treaty establishing the European Community, the Commission will continue to evaluate the need to bring forward new legislative proposals but reserves its right to decide if and when it would be appropriate to present any such proposal.

STATEMENT BY THE NETHERLANDS

The Netherlands has always supported the development of ambitious and effective European policy on air quality and will continue to do so in the future. It is, therefore, happy with the compromise agreed by the Council and the European Parliament and compliments the Parliament, the Commission and the Presidency on the results achieved. The new Directive on ambient air quality marks significant progress for both the environment and public health.

As the Netherlands pointed out when the Common Position was drawn up, the air quality in our country is strongly influenced by transboundary developments and will therefore benefit enormously from an effective European approach. The Netherlands' main concern has been that the Directive should contain a balanced package of European and national measures, as well as realistic time limits to achieve the air quality targets. Only then will Member States be able to achieve the ambitious targets that have been set.

The Netherlands is pleased with the Commission's statement that it will present Community measures in good time. Timely, EU-wide compliance with the air quality standards will depend on sound European policy tackling pollution at the source. The Netherlands would especially point to the lack of data and prevailing uncertainties about emissions and concentrations of fine particulates ($PM_{2,5}$). It will of course make every effort to meet the objectives of the Directive by the target date. On the basis of the knowledge currently at our command, this will largely be feasible. The Dutch government is developing a National Air Quality Cooperation Programme to tackle locations where emission ceilings are persistently exceeded, so that, there too, air quality standards may be met by the target date.

The Netherlands is pleased that the Council and the European Parliament concluded their second reading in time for the Directive to take effect as of early 2008. This is essential for our own national programme, as well as actions in the countries around us. The Netherlands will work hard to ensure that the national cooperation programme and all local and regional measures are sufficient.

Index

Harry H. G. Post (Ed.), The Protection of Ambient Air in International and European Law, 189-192.